Taken
As Red

Taken As Red

How Labour Won Big and the Tories Crashed the Party

Harper
North

HarperNorth
Windmill Green
24 Mount Street
Manchester M2 3NX

A division of
HarperCollins*Publishers*
1 London Bridge Street
London SE1 9GF

www.harpercollins.co.uk

HarperCollins*Publishers*
Macken House, 39/40 Mayor Street Upper
Dublin 1, D01 C9W8, Ireland

First published by HarperNorth in 2024

1 3 5 7 9 10 8 6 4 2

A catalogue record for this book is
available from the British Library

HB ISBN 978-0-00-869790-7

Printed and bound in the UK using 100%
renewable electricity at CPI Group (UK) Ltd

MIX
Paper | Supporting
responsible forestry
FSC
www.fsc.org
FSC™ C007454

This book contains FSC™ certified paper and other controlled
sources to ensure responsible forest management.

For more information visit: www.harpercollins.co.uk/green

For Ethan, Rory and Leo

Contents

PART III

The Tories

PART IV

The Election

PART V

Governing

Preface

The Exit Poll

Polling day, Thursday 4 July 2024. My producer Lili and I had arrived just after 7 p.m. with a strict instruction that the address of this central London location must remain secret – for reasons of security. We were given the number of a man called Duncan who met us at the door, handed us bright pink wristbands and then led us down some stairs and along a corridor to an area flanked by security guards. Duncan ushered us into a side room where we took seats and waited – nervous and excited.

A few minutes later, ITV's election analyst, Professor Colin Rallings, and our head of special events, Emma Hoskyns, came in and sat down opposite us. People would be voting for almost another three hours. But Colin, whose analysis has been central to ITV News's election coverage for decades, already knew what was unfolding.

'This will be a Labour landslide,' he told us, with the Conservative vote-share falling back everywhere, taking the party to its lowest point since 1832. But it was not only Labour who had benefited. All over the country, the Reform UK vote had risen; the Liberal Democrats were on track for their best result ever; and the Greens looked likely to pick up seats. Labour could have a 'big victory built on a relatively small share of the vote,' Colin explained.

'What about Scotland?' we asked.

'It looks as though the SNP have had a disaster,' he said. Emma added that the word 'apocalyptic' had been mooted. And we would have the former Scottish National Party leader and First Minister of Scotland Nicola Sturgeon beside us in our news studio all night.

But for now we were in the nerve centre of the exit poll. Just metres from where we were sitting, some of the brightest and best analysts and psephologists in Britain, including Sir John Curtice and our team's own Chris Prosser, were huddled together poring over responses from 20,000 voters at 133 polling stations across the country, crunching and modelling the raw data on behalf of the three major UK broadcasters: ITV, the BBC and Sky News.

For the first time, journalists like us had been allowed within touching distance. We were not part of the exit poll process, had no influence over its outcome, but we would be able to go on air with a new confidence and a more thorough understanding of the story the data was telling – and therefore better able to use our powerful data tools to explain what we were witnessing from the get-go.

And what a story: if the exit poll was right, Keir Starmer had just reshaped Britain's political landscape. In my twenty years as a political journalist, spanning six general elections and eight prime ministers, I'd never experienced anything quite so thrilling as knowing the likely results of a general election three hours before anyone else – including the man set to lose his job at the top of government and the one about to replace him.

At that same moment, Conservative prime minister Rishi Sunak was at home in his constituency of Richmond, North Yorkshire, surrounded by family, including his parents. The night before, he had embraced them both emotionally ahead of a speech in Romsey on the Hampshire coast, where he had attended primary school.

Elsewhere, Keir Starmer was also with his wife and children. He would soon leave to go to a friend's house to watch the exit poll moment with family and a few advisers. There they ate and drank, but strictly no alcohol. Jill Cuthbertson (then director of the Leader's

Office, now director of government relations in Downing Street) wanted everyone clear-headed and ready for what was to come, not least a speech on the steps of Downing Street in the early hours. 'Not on my watch,' she joked.

But that was all to come. At 9 p.m., after the 8.45 p.m. data drop had been modelled and briefed out, we dashed out of the building and jumped into a waiting cab to make it back to the studio in time for the opening of that night's election show. The wrong cab as it turned out – it was Emma and Chris's – meaning they were left wandering the streets and watching the top of the programme on their phones. Perhaps the least worst thing to go wrong at this stage of the night.

As we sped towards the studio, I was almost shaking with nerves. Colin too. A general election night is to politics what a World Cup final is to football, and time was accelerating. That last half hour you could feel the tension in the air.

Colin leant forward, slipping a hand into his bag, and muttered, 'I might have to let you in on my secret.' And then this eminent political scientist pulled out a miniature bottle of vodka and took a swig. 'Just once every few years, it calms my nerves,' he said. My producer and I burst out laughing. Now we were ready.

Our election night studio is a giant room, painted all in green, the canvas for the virtual set containing live data, including my 'wall' where we can show off our graphics, maps and the all-important 'Battle Board'. In the middle is a huge desk, with host Tom Bradby at its head and to his right, polling gurus, Professor Jane Green and Professor Colin Rallings.

When we entered the room, it was buzzing as camera operators, producers, presenters and analysts prepared for transmission. Less than forty-five minutes to go.

We pre-recorded the top of the show and then, at 9.30 p.m., the producers asked everyone to leave apart from the key small group who had all signed non-disclosure agreements, including Nicola

Sturgeon; former Conservative chancellor George Osborne; and Ed Balls, who had shadowed him from Labour's frontbench before losing his seat in the shock result of the night in 2015. Microphones were switched off, laptops were closed and mobile phones turned face down. Colin began his briefing. Jane gave us the numbers. For the first time, we learned the final seat projections: a Labour majority of 170.

I watched each of the guests to absorb the impact of the news as they processed this moment in history. For Sturgeon, the party she had led for nine years had just been decimated at Westminster; for Osborne it marked the start of bitter soul-searching for a Conservative Party that had come close to wipeout; and Ed Balls was digesting the reality of an immense Labour result, one that would have a political and personal impact as it made his wife Yvette Cooper Britain's new home secretary.

The first and clearest trend was that everywhere, whatever the demographic breakdown, support for the Conservative Party was being dramatically washed away, instead surging towards Labour, but also to the Lib Dems and Reform UK. The night that would make Sir Keir Starmer prime minister would also deliver Reform leader Nigel Farage to Parliament on his eighth attempt. His party may only have won five MPs, but a scattered vote of 4.1 million meant that in dozens of other constituencies the party would finish second. The Lib Dems meanwhile, after an exceptionally targeted campaign, had a stunning night that saw them achieve a result in which their seat total was almost proportional to their vote-share, for the first time in their history. The Greens would also triumph in all four of their main target seats.

Was this the 'fuck you' election for voters my colleague Emma had predicted? It was certainly true that an angry backlash could be seen everywhere. Not just towards the Tories, but towards all the governing parties including the SNP in Scotland and the Democratic Unionist Party in Northern Ireland. Even in Wales – where the Conservatives were wiped off the map – the governing Welsh Labour

Party saw its vote-share drop, while Plaid Cymru's rose. Across English constituencies with Labour-run councils and high Muslim populations, a different form of anger helped five independent candidates to win the day, taking down a big beast for Labour, Jonathan Ashworth, and coming uncomfortably close for others like the future health secretary Wes Streeting and Home Office minister Jess Phillips.

Professor Jane Green described the night as a 'record breaker', with the 'highest ever fragmentation … the lowest two-party share … and the highest disproportionality' between votes and seats gained, ever seen. The UK's trajectory towards greater volatility, she said, had just fifteen years ago resulted in hung parliaments and coalitions, but this time delivered a landslide to Labour. The party won just over a third of votes, but almost two-thirds of seats in Parliament: 'The combination of proportional system type voting in a majoritarian electoral system can deliver really extraordinary outcomes,' she said. How had this unfolded?

My mind raced back through the events of the last two decades, from witnessing the previous Labour government under Tony Blair and then Gordon Brown to the rise and fall of five Conservative prime ministers, from David Cameron to Theresa May, Boris Johnson, Liz Truss, and finally Rishi Sunak.

In recent years, there had seemed to be no end of chaos at the heart of the Tory government, which no doubt had a profound impact on voters' perceptions of this political party once famed for its ruthless election-winning ability. In December 2021, when the worst of the Partygate revelations emerged, I was reporting on a by-election in North Shropshire where residents were already lining up to tell me that their frustration at being unable to secure GP appointments (in a health service warping under the weight of the Covid pandemic) meant they could no longer back Boris Johnson's party. Then that video of Johnson's aides laughing at alleged parties inside 10 Downing Street emerged, and I saw the instant effect. Having all shared in the national trauma of Covid, these revelations from my colleagues at ITV News were simply staggering. I could see the catastrophic loss of trust on people's faces. And when, almost a year later, Liz Truss's mini-budget wrought havoc in the markets, I received calls from Conservative MPs mortified about the impact of the crisis on their constituents' mortgages. Even as other global factors acted to keep interest rates high, time and again voters would point to that moment to explain their financial pain.

On election night, we looked at the 30 seats with the highest proportion of voters holding a mortgage to watch the impact of the exit poll on that dataset. It was an elucidating moment. Every single one of those seats had voted Conservative in 2019, as denoted by the narrow blue strip to the side of the seat. But now with the exit poll data, so many of these high-mortgage seats were predicted to change hands. Labour would win 19 of them; the Lib Dems five. Was this the final electoral reckoning for that calamitous 2022 mini-budget?

The other striking shift was just how far Labour's crimson tide would reach across England, even beyond the seats that made up Tony Blair's 1997 landslide. We had already isolated from our data-set those seats that had always voted Conservative. Immediately we could see the red swathe of Labour wins starting to spread. Keir Starmer's party won the once true-blue Chelsea and Fulham; the seat of former chancellor Ken Clarke, Rushcliffe; the home of the British Army, Aldershot; Hexham, the only north east constituency that remained Tory in the Blair years (by 222 votes in 1997); and West Worthing, the community represented for decades by Peter Bottomley, father of the House of Commons.

So the scale of the change was unprecedented, but not a surprise. I had been closely scrutinising Keir Starmer's election-winning operation for months by this point. I had already spent many hours speaking to dozens of people who had been at the heart of this campaign; from the leading politicians who are now running the country to key political strategists, policy and communications teams and activists on the ground.

Many have called Labour's victory shallow. Starmer's 33.7 per cent vote-share handed Labour an enormous mandate this time, whereas Jeremy Corbyn's 40 per cent in 2017 delivered the party an election loss. Meanwhile, the 60 per cent national turnout was the second lowest in any UK election since 1885 (only 2001 was lower). A clear disillusionment with politics was threaded throughout this result.

And yet the sheer breadth of Starmer's 2024 election win was eye-watering. It should, and must, be seen as a strategic coup. After all, this was the shape of victory that the party's strategists were deliberately aiming for – ruthless targeting of efforts into marginal constituencies in the full knowledge that the consequence would be falling vote-share in safe seats. The outcome was by no means seamless, given those losses to the Greens and Independents, but if nothing else it showed how necessary it is for Labour to reach far and wide across the country if it wants to translate votes into a governable majority.

In what is best described as an astonishingly 'efficient' result, Labour managed to secure the support of a third of voters so perfectly spread out across the country that they got Starmer's party over the line in more than 400 constituencies. Consequently, individual majorities in these seats were much smaller, with the median figure at just over 6,000 compared to over 11,000 in 2019, as was perhaps inevitable given their plan. And while there was a clear fragmentation away from the largest two parties, it seems likely that the people voting Lib Dem, Green or Reform did so knowing that their vote against the Conservative Party would help to deliver Keir Starmer to Downing Street.

That said, the Reform UK surge, in particular, almost certainly served to inflate Labour's majority. It drew its support largely from those who had voted Conservative in 2019 and so helped Starmer to win many more seats than perhaps even he imagined, including some unexpected results during the night. Consider the moment that came as perhaps the biggest shock, when at 6.48 a.m. we watched Liz Truss standing almost motionless as the returning officer revealed that she had lost her South West Norfolk seat. Labour's narrow majority here of just over 600 was dwarfed by almost 10,000 votes secured by Reform UK. Labour would argue that even those Reform voters were only willing to desert the Tories because of the changes Starmer had made to his party; but still, this was not a Labour target seat. The party did not divert any significant resources towards trying to beat Liz Truss in this election.

As Jane Green put it to me: 'The Reform surge matters so much because, by taking votes from Conservatives, it lowered the bar for Labour in so many places. That's not attributable to Labour strategy, but the ruthless vote efficiency is.'

So what might the result have looked like without the Reform surge? At the time of writing there is more analysis to do, but. YouGov's Patrick English tells me Labour would have still won big, but with a much-reduced majority. Around sixty Conservative MPs would have been saved, he reckons, leaving Starmer with a majority of around eighty – closer to Boris Johnson in 2019 than Tony Blair in 1997.

Much has been made of Sunak's decision to spring a July election on the country, in a move that surprised his own MPs as much as anyone. As I delved into that decision, I found a Tory leader desperate to avoid a summer in which he might face further defections; hamstrung by his impossible pledge to 'Stop the Boats' crossing the Channel; and, due to overcrowding in the country's prisons, forced to release dangerous criminals before time. We now know that had he kept his nerve and played the long game for a November election, as his key strategists were suggesting, interest rates would probably have fallen and the August headlines would have heralded stronger than expected economic growth along with a sharp decline in migrant numbers as a result of his decision to restrict visas. And yet one of Sunak's closes aides still thinks the election was not too early but much too late.

Certainly, the way the political pendulum has swung from heady Conservative (and SNP) victory and Labour loss to the exact opposite indicates a new volatility. Keir Starmer is acutely aware things could quickly flip back. As I write, barely weeks after the result, senior Labour figures are talking about what they can do to try to consolidate this shallow victory. But it is worth remembering just how far they have come. In 2019, Labour found itself at the bottom of a political mountain – with its worst election result since 1935. In order to climb it, the party needed to win an eye-watering 125 extra constituencies. A political swing equivalent to the one achieved by Tony Blair in 1997 would have handed Starmer a majority of two. And yet, in July he walked away with a majority of 172.

The shift was mind-blowing. On the Monday right after the election, I walked into Parliament and saw dozens upon dozens of new Labour MPs huddled with their teams in Portcullis House waiting for their keys to a new office, while those Conservative MPs, who had felt part of the Westminster furniture for so many years, were simply gone.

Clearly, Conservative decline was a major part of this story. But how had Starmer navigated Labour to a place from which it could take such massive advantage of this political opportunity? Was his 'Ming vase' strategy the key? Many commentators used that metaphor, summoning up an image of the Labour leader shuffling slowly across a polished marble floor, not daring to take any risks that might dislodge that precious poll-lead lest it smash to smithereens. It is certainly true that deeply restrictive fiscal rules designed to win back economic confidence prevented Labour from offering the radical edge of previous policies, ones that excited the left and may have once lit up the eyes of the younger, idealistic, human rights barrister Starmer himself. Even the former Bank of England chief economist Andy Haldane described these rules as unnecessarily limiting.

But it is also clear that Starmer did what he needed to in order to win. And after so many months closely observing our new prime minister's strategy, I see something very different to Ming-vase caution. What I've discovered is an obsession about winning, a streak of ruthlessness and a willingness to take on significant levels of political risk.

Eyes

PART I

Eyes on the Prize

1

When the Wind Blows

'Are you sure?'

Sir Keir Starmer looked nervously at his campaign director, Morgan McSweeney.

McSweeney, an unassuming man of 5ft 10 with ginger hair and a soft Irish accent, nodded decisively; but in truth he too was anxious.

Outside Labour's conference, politics was moving fast. Two days earlier, on 23 September 2022, the Chancellor, Kwasi Kwarteng, had delivered that infamous mini-budget on behalf of the new Prime Minister, Liz Truss, unveiling £45 billion of tax cuts. Then – in a down-the-line interview that very morning, the following Sunday – Kwarteng had gone still further. On BBC One's *Sunday with Laura Kuenssberg*, coming live from the Museum of Liverpool next door to the conference centre, he had said there was 'more to come'. Outside the basement studio in the BBC's Broadcasting House, Kwarteng's shocked Treasury officials buried their heads in their hands. This was bad, but they could hardly interrupt their boss in the middle of a live television interview.

These three careless words would fire a dart into Britain's financial markets. Their destabilising impact was such that the following morning the country woke up to news of the pound plummeting to a record low, and the cost of borrowing up to a dizzying spike. Panic spread through the Treasury.

The fallout would not only have a profound effect on the country; it would also mark a key turning point for Leader of the Opposition Keir Starmer. Its repercussions would surely turn more and more heads towards the Labour Party, and so it proved.

That Sunday, however, as he paced nervously in the dark corridor that runs behind the stage of Liverpool's Arena and Convention Centre (ACC), watching the audience outside on the big screens, Starmer wasn't thinking about the weeks, months or even years that would follow. His mind was focused on a single minute. If he could achieve just sixty uninterrupted seconds of silence, he believed it would go a long way towards symbolising a changed Labour Party.

Starmer had long believed that one of the most important shifts needed to return Labour to power was to prove to a patriotic nation that his party loved Britain, and Morgan McSweeney shared his obsession. When they later hired former New Labour adviser and political analyst Deborah Mattinson as strategy director, her research into the voters Labour needed to win back told the same story: people needed to see a demonstration of Starmer's love of country. The way the party responded to the death of Queen Elizabeth II just a few weeks earlier was absolutely critical. With the nation thrown into mourning, Starmer and his team had hurriedly changed their conference slogan from 'A Fresh Start' – which now seemed crass – to 'A Fairer, Greener Future' and swiftly made plans to open the event with a fitting tribute. McSweeney told friends that he wanted Labour to put on the most patriotic show possible.

A few days before the conference opened, McSweeney met Gary Smith, the general secretary of the GMB (a key Labour-backing union) at the Victorian Horseshoe Bar in Glasgow, to discuss how things might pan out. The conference hall itself, they hoped, would be a sea of Union Jacks: that familiar red, white and blue making up the entire backdrop of the stage. Smith commented that the hall would look like Ibrox – the nearby stadium where loyalist Glasgow Rangers fans had turned the stands into a huge Union Jack in honour of the late Queen. Some fellow drinkers, GMB gas workers, joked that they would happily join them to hammer out 'God Save the King' at the top of their voices. One tipped back his head and began belting out the words.

But the National Anthem had never before been sung at a Labour conference and only a year earlier Starmer's speech to conference had been disrupted by heckling. The minute's silence was seen as a real gamble. On the one hand, this simple gesture could demonstrate the scale of the change in Labour; on the other, shouts or heckles would instead paint a picture of disunity or, worse, a lack of control. In other words, more of the same.

Starmer's team took every step they could think of to avoid that outcome. All delegates were searched comprehensively on arrival at the Liverpool ACC and given a warning that any shouting would result in their passes being shredded. The Unite union – which had been most unconvinced about Starmer's leadership and most supportive of his predecessor, Jeremy Corbyn – had seen its seating area moved further back in the hall, and in the end not many of its delegates turned up. Everyone recognised how critical the moment was. 'It was so tense,' said one attendee.

As Starmer took to the stage with Labour's deputy leader, Angela Rayner, shadow chancellor, Rachel Reeves, and party chair, Anneliese Dodds, Morgan McSweeney moved to stand behind Prentice Hazell, the leader's diary manager.

'The late Queen Elizabeth II was this great country's greatest monarch [...] Even now, after the mourning period has passed, it still feels impossible to imagine a Britain without her. She created a special, personal relationship with all of us. A relationship based on service and devotion to our country,' said Starmer, reminding the crowd that almost no one could remember a time before her reign.

Dressed in a black suit, with dark-red tie, tipping his head from side to side to follow the autocue rolling up over small, almost invisible screens, he said, 'For us, the late Queen has always been simply The Queen, the only Queen.

'Above all else, our Queen, and I'm proud to lead our party's tribute to her …' He paused, as applause bubbled up across the room.

And then the moment arrived. Almost wincing with nerves, McSweeney gripped Hazell's arm, as one by one Starmer, Rayner, Reeves and the whole shadow cabinet dipped their heads and waited. As the seconds ticked by, the apprehension was palpable. One of those present described the atmosphere as 'charged'; another called it 'the longest minute of my life'.

A 'three-line whip' (like those sent to MPs demanding they vote with the party or face sanction) had been issued to Starmer's full team to be inside the hall, according to one person present. The room was packed, leaving many watching on screens across the ACC.

Behind the stage was Carol Linforth, with her legendary calm control of conference operations. Out in front were the rest of the shadow cabinet, including the shadow chief secretary to the Treasury Pat McFadden, who would go on to become Labour's campaign director for the general election. Ellie Reeves, who would be his deputy and, later, party chair was there too. Dotted around, were other figures who would play a key role in propelling Starmer to Downing Street. Among them Deborah Mattinson, Vidhya Alakeson, Claire Ainsley and Stuart Ingham, directors respectively of strategy, external affairs and policy; Jill Cuthbertson, gatekeeper to Starmer as she once was to Gordon Brown and Ed Miliband; and David Evans, Labour's general secretary.

Elsewhere were Starmer's attack chief, Paul Ovenden, whose role in outing Conservative deceit including through the Partygate scandal would be a significant factor in the downfall of Boris Johnson; Katie Martin, who as chief of staff to the shadow chancellor would, with Alakeson, help overhaul the party's reputation with business; and the 'three Matts' – Doyle, Faulding and Pound – who spanned communications, candidate selections and party management.

To the side of the stage, the leader's press secretary Steph Driver scanned the room nervously, panicking at one point because of a rustling she feared was a sign of protesters. In fact, it was just a man finishing a packet of crisps. In the days before, when even McSweeney said he was unsure that they would pull this off, Driver had been steadfast. Close by was her colleague Sophie Nazemi, who would go on to become Starmer's press secretary in Downing Street.

One figure, sometimes described as 'the most powerful woman in the Labour Party', also stood in the shadows at the front. Hollie Ridley, whose later leadership of the entire field operation would lead one colleague to describe her as 'Field Marshal Ridley', was secretary of the conference arrangement committee. She scanned the audience nervously for the full sixty seconds.

And then it was over – with a collective outtake of breath. There had been no disruption whatsoever. Ridley, whose team was responsible for building the audience, smiled and told friends she was proud of the party.

In the press room, where staff members who couldn't fit into the hall had watched on televisions, there was a celebratory mood. This felt like a turning point.

And then, 'God Save the King' began to ring out across the hall as delegates began to sing, some with the aid of the printed lyrics placed on every seat. Sam White, then Starmer's chief of staff, described the moment as 'heart-stopping'. He would later pass the chief of staff baton to Sue Gray who stepped out of government as its most well-known civil servant and returned in 2024 as the woman who would run Starmer's Downing Street operation.

Jeremy Corbyn would later describe the decision to sing the anthem as 'very, very odd': a comment that would only delight this new set of Labour advisers, who had come to relish disagreeing with their most recent former leader.

Labour peer Tom Watson remembered being struck by the significance of the moment as he watched the scene from home. Back in September 2015, soon after Watson had been elected deputy leader of the party, he attended a commemoration service marking the 75th anniversary of the Battle of Britain. As the National Anthem began to ring out in St Paul's Cathedral, Watson noticed that Corbyn was standing silently, his hands clasped together. As Watson scanned the pews his eyes landed on the Conservative defence secretary, Michael Fallon, who was in turn, staring at the silent Labour leader.

Walking out of the service together, Watson leant over to Corbyn and whispered, 'I noticed you didn't sing the National Anthem.'

'I couldn't remember the words,' came the reply. Watson was taken aback and now says: 'I don't know to this day whether it was a quip or not.'

Back in Liverpool, the conference quickly moved on to celebrate a very different predecessor. Shabana Mahmood, then the campaign's coordinator inside the shadow cabinet, delivered a speech during which she played a video of Tony Blair. Unlike in 2011, when a mention of Blair's name resulted in boos ringing out from parts of the hall, this time it was met with a resounding cheer.

These were not the only decisions over those four days in Liverpool designed to demonstrate change. According to sources, organisers fought 'tooth and nail' to keep a motion that would allow MPs to join picket lines off the agenda, even as public sector strikes rumbled on. Starmer and his team feared the imagery of Labour siding with its union 'stakeholders' over voters.

Then came a last-minute crisis. Ahead of Starmer's keynote speech on the Tuesday, it was reported that Rupa Huq, Labour MP for Ealing Central and Acton, had made a comment at a fringe event, describing Chancellor Kwasi Kwarteng, as only 'superficially' Black, leading to accusations of racism. The Guido Fawkes website, which broke the story, called for her head, and the party quickly obliged. Huq immediately had Labour's Westminster whip taken away from her (although it was later restored after she apologised and carried out anti-racism training). Huq was mortified by the interpretation of her words and reached out personally to Kwarteng, who accepted her apology.

But to those within Starmer's team, nothing was quite as symbolic as that minute's silence. In some ways, it felt as if the Labour leader had been reaching for a moment like this for two years: for a spectacle that he could point to as an indication that things were now very different.

The ability to demonstrate change was something the Labour Party had hoped for ever since April 2020, when Starmer first entered the labyrinth of offices on the second floor of a parliamentary building, just beyond Westminster's Portcullis House, assigned to the leader of the opposition – an office known as LOTO. It was just weeks after the full scale of the Covid pandemic had been realised and the country placed into lockdown. Many of Starmer's parliamentary advisers were having to work remotely, struggling to get any attention, as all eyes turned to Boris Johnson's daily press conferences, designed to reassure a nation still in shock.

Once they were able to meet in person, a small group gathered in LOTO's boardroom, a large room lit through windows looking out across the bank of the river Thames. Sitting spaced out around the long, thin table that stretches through the centre, the team discussed the scale of the challenge ahead: namely, how to reconnect with a group of voters they all knew would be key to any electoral success. They believed that the Labour Party they had inherited was utterly broken.

At the time, Starmer's director of policy was Claire Ainsley, who had come from the Joseph Rowntree Foundation, and was the author of a book called *The New Working Class*, which warned that Labour had lost touch with the very voters it was founded to represent. She said that the Labour Party was like a boat ravaged by storms. To those colleagues who wondered aloud if Labour had any hope of winning the next election, she reasoned that while they could not control the political weather, they had to fix the boat so that if the wind ever caught the sails, they would be ready to go.

The metaphor chimed with Starmer's plan to focus the first stage of his leadership on fixing the party. And what was happening that

Sunday morning in Liverpool in September 2022 was exactly the type of thing Ainsley had been talking about.

What they may not have quite realised was just how furiously the wind was starting to pick up. The implosion of Truss's mini-budget would soon turn into a political gale, blowing in the exact direction that Starmer wanted to head.

There was 'more to come' Kwarteng had said before pulling off his microphone and walking out of the BBC Broadcasting House studio on 23 September.

Dressed in a dark suit, with a relaxed demeanour, there was nothing in the chancellor's face that morning to indicate he had any serious concerns about the interview, although his words had produced a surprised response from Laura Kuenssberg, asking: 'This is just the start?'

'You doubled down,' the shocked Treasury officials told him as he emerged from the basement studio, warning that the reaction to his pledge to keep cutting taxes would be bad. But those familiar with the scene say Kwarteng shrugged off their concerns with his usual easy style. His view, and that of Prime Minister Liz Truss, had been that the markets did not react with fright to the much bigger £100 billion plus intervention in the energy market, and so could handle these £45 billion worth of tax cuts. After all, the vast majority of measures had been promised explicitly in her leadership campaign, they insisted.

A week later, it was the Conservative Party's chance to host their annual conference, this one in Birmingham. On Sunday 2 October, Kwarteng took a seat in the restaurant of the city's Malmaison hotel. The large, modern room, with red-and-black leather seats, was packed and felt chaotic. In front of him were the most senior figures from the *Sun* newspaper including the editor, Vic Newton, and political editor, Harry Cole. Those present said Kwarteng seemed laid-back, as he reiterated things would be fine. Cole argued that a U-turn on the policy to abolish the 45p top rate of tax, as some were demanding, would be such a huge step it could bring down the government. Surely that would not happen? Kwarteng agreed.

But further down the table, the chancellor's adviser, Cameron Brown, was not so relaxed. Sitting beside the *Sun on Sunday*'s political editor Kate Ferguson, his phone kept buzzing. The calls were from Truss's deputy chief of staff, Ruth Porter, and eventually Brown stepped aside to take a call.

'The prime minister wants to see the chancellor now,' Porter said. Brown warned that his rushing out of dinner with the *Sun*'s political editor would alert the media to a problem. Moreover, Kwarteng was insisting he stay until his main course – a curry – arrived.

But soon Brown became too edgy, and Harry Cole suddenly noticed him holding up four and then five fingers, in a sign to Kwarteng. 'What was that?' he asked sharply, wondering if the government was indeed about to U-turn on the 45p policy. Brown, quick on his feet, insisted that his gesture was meant to indicate an urgent meeting at 9.45 p.m. The pair left and made their way to Truss's suite on the 24th floor of the Birmingham Hyatt hotel.

Earlier, the prime minister had met with Sir Graham Brady, the Conservative MP who represented backbenchers as chair of the 1922 Committee, who warned that things were starting to feel extremely 'choppy' within her party. When Brady had walked into her suite, he crossed the Kent MP, Damian Green, coming out. As chair of the One Nation group of more liberal Tories, Green had urged Truss to take a more emollient tone in the conference speech she was due to give that Wednesday, arguing she urgently needed to reach out across the party. Both symbolically – a massive tax cut for the super-rich in the middle of a cost-of-living crisis – and practically, in terms of driving up borrowing costs, the 45p policy was seen as the key problem.

At the time, one Conservative MP rang me, freaking out about the impact the whole fiasco was having on his constituents' mortgages. 'Mortgages!' he bellowed. 'How could we do this to our own voters' mortgages!?'

Up on the 24th floor, Truss was clear that the policy had to go. 'Kwasi, it's dead as a dodo,' she said. A plan was made to ditch it, and 'rip off the plaster', the next morning at 7 a.m.

But back in the Malmaison, the *Sun*'s political editor Harry Cole was already suspicious. Just minutes after Kwarteng and his adviser left, out came the food, with the table filled up with plates of steak and the chancellor's curry. Cole ate quickly and then headed over to the conference's main hotel, to join a drinks party for journalists hosted by Conservative chairman at the time, Jake Berry. On the way up he saw Truss's director of communications, Adam Jones, looking agitated, and then as the drinks continued to flow, he noticed that key members of Truss's inner circle had suddenly disappeared.

Cole followed Jones down the corridor, and then the pair could be heard arguing by the lifts as the Downing Street adviser refused to confirm the policy had been ditched. Jamming his foot in the lift door, Cole shouted, 'We're running the story unless you deny it!'

With no response, the *Sun*'s most senior political journalist made his way out to the hotel's smoking area, which was heaving with people drinking and smoking, and quickly typed up the story on his phone.

At just after midnight, the *Sun*'s declaration that the 45p policy was dead appeared on the newspaper's website, followed by a tweet from Cole that set off a chaotic reaction across the vast conference centre, where the faith of the gathered MPs and party activists, many tipsy from an evening of dinner and drinks, was shattered.

Cole was nervous when he went to bed, but at 6 a.m. he woke up to the pips of BBC Radio 4's *Today* programme, and the headline that a U-turn was about to land. His story was right.

Soon after, Kwarteng flew to Washington, DC to attend the Annual Meetings of the International Monetary Fund, held between 10 and 16 October. Broadcasters asked the chancellor if he was going to be in his job a month from then. 'Absolutely, 100 per cent. I am not going anywhere,' he replied.

In fact, he was soon headed straight back to the airport, summoned home to Westminster for a sacking that would stretch the definition of humiliation. Kwarteng had been sure this would not happen because he told aides, 'If I go, surely she goes too?'

That much was true. It was just thirty-eight days into Truss's chaotic reign as prime minister, and six days before the entire project imploded.

It seemed unthinkable that in less than a fortnight the Conservative government had not just lost another leader and prime minister but trashed its own reputation for economic competence. According to a poll in the *Observer* at the height of the controversy, 71 per cent said they felt Truss and Kwarteng had 'lost control' of the economy.

If Starmer had realised how pivotal that mini-budget would be, it wasn't obvious from his face as it was being delivered, three weeks earlier, in the House of Commons. Dressed in a smart, dark-blue suit with a lilac tie, as the newish chancellor hit the crescendo of his offer in bombastic style, leaning forward, his hands planted on either side of the dispatch box. He was flanked on one side by Truss, whose face flickered with a slight smile as each idea was announced, and a beaming Simon Clarke, the new levelling-up secretary, on the other.

When Kwarteng finally got to it – booming, 'I have another measure Mr Speaker' – behind him on the green benches Tory MPs 'oohed' excitedly.

'The higher the tax, the more people seek to avoid them. Take the additional rate of Income Tax – at 45p … I'm not going to cut the top rate. I'm going to abolish it altogether!' he exclaimed.

'YEAH, YEAH, YEAH,' the Tory benches chanted as Kwarteng poked the table, also promising to cut the basic rate of Income Tax earlier than planned, before sitting back onto the front bench, a relieved and satisfied look in his eyes.

My phone buzzed with a text message from a backbench Conservative MP who would go on to become a cabinet minister under Rishi Sunak. 'It is either brilliant – or bonkers,' he wrote.

In the House of Commons, Labour's shadow chancellor, Rachel Reeves, took the floor. 'It is a budget without figures. A menu without prices,' she hollered, hitting out at the chaos and confusion of the Conservative government, as she argued that the mini-budget was an admission of economic failure over twelve years in power. Her critique, that the PM and chancellor were like 'two desperate gamblers in a casino chasing a losing run', would turn out to be prophetic.

Truss and Kwarteng's policy choices that October would badly backfire, sending the Conservative Party's polling position plummeting to a twenty-plus point deficit, from which it would never recover. The howl of fury from voters over the economic impact of the mini-budget was swept together with the winds of anger already swirling around the Conservatives as a result of the Partygate scandal. Rarely have I witnessed something as raw and intense as voters' reaction to the images of Boris Johnson's inner circle boozing while the entire nation was reeling from the grief of the Covid pandemic.

Some argue that the sheer strength of that wind blowing against the Conservatives was enough to sweep Starmer up and fly him all the way to the threshold of 10 Downing Street. Others say that Labour would never have been able to take full advantage of that Conservative downfall without the boat-fixing exercise that Starmer embarked upon the minute he began as leader. An exercise that saw him immediately replace the party's general secretary, purge members from Labour's left flank and ditch policy promises from his leadership campaign.

Faced with questions about whether such a sharp shift in position would damage trust in Labour and in himself as a politician, Starmer would go on to argue that it was simply a decision to put the country's interests ahead of those of the Labour Party.

Over the past year, I've spoken to over 100 people who have worked closely with Keir Starmer throughout his political career, and it is notable that most seem to describe him in two, very distinct ways.

Firstly, they call him incredibly caring. This is the Starmer who was among the first to turn up in person on Neil Kinnock's doorstep after the former leader lost his beloved wife Glenys (despite being told by Kinnock himself, 'You don't have time for this; you've got a party to lead.') Ask Kinnock now and he'll tell you that Starmer is truly 'authentic'. 'He's the real thing – he can't be bothered pretending.'

One former employee broke down in tears as, over a cup of coffee, she recounted his kindness when she lost a loved one. Another described his final day working with Starmer and arriving home to find that the Labour leader had called his partner in advance to check he was okay.

But most of the same people point to a very different side to this politician – our new prime minister. They say Keir Starmer is also ruthless.

Take the phone call he made just twenty minutes after becoming Labour leader. Jennie Formby, who had run the party machine for the previous two years as Labour general secretary, had wanted to discuss how they would work together in the coming weeks. His response to her? 'We won't.'

One ally, in whom Formby confided after the phone call, said there had been a warning that Starmer would quickly move against her, but still she was shocked. This friend claimed Formby, who had cancer and had been pretty unwell from weekly chemotherapy sessions, did not want to remain in the role but had hoped to hand over the reins and stand down with 'dignity'.

They described Formby's re-telling of the phone call. She had felt like Starmer was reading from a script when he told her she should publicly resign the next morning. Fearing that this would imply she had been sacked for gross misconduct, Formby entered talks with the party that ended weeks later with rumours of a substantial payout.

On 26 May, the deal was done and Starmer appointed his first-choice candidate, David Evans, to the role of general secretary.

'There is no precedent for sacking the general secretary on your first day as leader,' an ally of Starmer's predecessor, Jeremy Corbyn, told me. 'Blair didn't do it. Miliband didn't do it.' The source seemed taken aback by this swift execution.

'It took us three years to take control of Labour's National Executive Committee,' they said of the efforts by the left of the party to wrestle influence during Corbyn's leadership. 'Keir Starmer did it in a month.' Corbyn, who faced significant hostility to his leadership within the party, took almost three years to remove the general secretary he inherited – Iain McNicol, who was handed a golden ticket to the House of Lords, as is customary. A few weeks after her ousting, when Formby left the Labour Party, it was made clear that there would be no peerage offered, though she had already said she would not have wanted one.

To Labour centrists, this was a sign that Starmer was ready to take the helm of the Labour ship and turn it sharply away from the party's members, and towards voters. They were convinced that for Labour to have any chance of winning an election, it needed to drastically reform, from the bottom up.

But to the left, it was the moment that Starmer's leadership pledge regarding 'unity' crumbled. They saw it as the first act of a 'ruthlessly factional' purge. To one source close to Corbyn, this showed that when it came to party management, Starmer was ready to pursue a 'Year zero … scorched earth' strategy, in which Labour would rebuild from scratch.

To be deemed ruthless is something most of us would probably prefer to avoid. It's literal meaning might be defined as a willingness to be *very* harsh, cruel even; as being prepared to do anything to achieve what you want.

For Starmer's close friend of almost thirty years, Parvais Jabbar, with whom he worked closely in opposing the death penalty around the world, however, this picture of a hard-hearted and unbending leader doesn't even slightly fit the man he knows behind the scenes. 'On a personal level, Keir is the opposite of ruthless,' he told me.

But on a political and professional level, this is a critique that not even Starmer himself shies away from. In fact, when I put the notion to him once, he embraced it. It was a Tuesday in October 2023, and I was standing with colleagues in a Liverpool carpark. We were waiting, right by the bins and in the glare of bright sunshine, for Starmer to emerge from what was perhaps his most important speech up to that point. Exactly a year after the minute's silence, this was the final Labour Party conference before a general election and I was due to interview the frontrunner to be the next prime minister.

The Labour leader burst out of the backdoor of the ACC in a shirt still flecked with the glitter thrown on him by a protester inside, and gripping the hand of his wife, Vic.

I pointed out how during his keynote speech Labour members had repeatedly risen to their feet in a stream of standing ovations, perhaps a sign that the most critical, left flank of his party had now been silenced.

'Some say that you've been quite ruthless in getting that change,' I said.

Without even a beat of hesitation, Starmer replied, 'Yes … and for a purpose.'

He argued that the Labour Party needed to serve working people, and that it couldn't do that from opposition. 'The [electoral] position we are in vindicates the change,' he added.

My colleague Robert Peston, who has seen British politics cycle round and round for more than thirty years, says Starmer is the most ruthless Labour leader he has known.

'More ruthless than Tony Blair?' I asked him.

'Much more ruthless than Tony Blair,' he said.

2

Sir Keir

On 8 May 2015, I tweeted: 'Keir Starmer – possible future Labour leader? #GE2015'

The time stamp on the message was 5.08 a.m.; the place, Witney, the Oxfordshire constituency of Prime Minister David Cameron.

I was almost nine months pregnant, exhausted after a gruelling general election campaign in which I had criss-crossed the country on the Conservative leader's trail. As the sun rose, I watched Cameron take in the news that his Conservative Party had just defied expectations to retain power by a slim majority. Even the exit poll, although pointing to a strong Conservative lead, had suggested the party would fall just short and leave the country with a hung parliament.

Some 66 miles away in north London, a new Labour MP had just been elected in the safe seat of Holborn and St Pancras with an enormous majority of almost 28,000.

If power was on Keir Starmer's mind back then, friends say it would have been limited to a hope, or perhaps even expectation, that Labour leader Ed Miliband might make him attorney general. But the Labour government they had assumed was imminent did not materialise. Instead, Starmer watched an exhausted and resigned-looking Miliband tell the country: 'I take absolute and total responsibility for the result and our defeat in this election.'

Miliband apologised to his colleagues who had lost seats, including Shadow Chancellor Ed Balls along with almost every Labour candidate in Scotland. He joked about the 'most unlikely cult of the twenty-first century – "Milifandom"', that had seen him followed by clamouring groupies desperate for selfies, before tendering his resignation. It was time for Labour to have an 'open and honest' debate about the way forward under a new leader, he added.

I cannot claim any great foresight when I tweeted about Starmer's possible rise, but simply a hunch because of his impressive legal CV. As a celebrated human rights lawyer at the renowned Doughty Street Chambers who had later switched sides to become director of public prosecutions, he stood out among this new crop of MPs.

Of course, he was far too new to be included in the following day's reported speculation about who might next lead Labour. The *Guardian* listed frontbenchers like Chuka Umunna, Andy Burnham, Liz Kendall and perhaps, it mused, Yvette Cooper. It reported that Tom Watson would likely run for deputy leader. One name missing from much of the coverage was that of the left-wing firebrand Jeremy Corbyn who had first entered Parliament in 1983 and had just been re-elected as the MP for Islington North for the eighth time.

Allies say that if Starmer was wondering if he might one day be a contender for Labour leader, it was no more than a 'dot' in his mind. Urged by some to stand for the leadership in 2015, requests that were said to embarrass him, he knew he was far too politically inexperienced. Instead, he backed Andy Burnham in the leadership race, perhaps expecting him to win. However, a change to the rules pushed through in the Miliband years, paired with a backlash against austerity that had left many wanting more radicalism from Labour, helped forge the way to the eventual result. A new 'one member, one vote' system had reduced the influence of trade unions and MPs, while increasing the voice of individual members who were able to join the party for just £3. And they did. The Labour Party gained more than 100,000 new members ahead of the 2015 leadership contest, with the membership surging from 190,000 in May that year to 325,000 in September, and to 515,000 by the following summer.

Within Labour, Jeremy Corbyn's victory felt like an earthquake, pushing many 'moderate' MPs to the edges of the party. Some would later be seen as pariahs by this enormous new membership. One senior cabinet minister in Starmer's new government texted me to say they felt like they were going to attend the Labour Party's 'wake' as they made their way to Corbyn's coronation in 2015.

But while some MPs were clear from the start that they could not serve on Corbyn's frontbench, others felt it was right to give this newly elected leadership a go. Many of Corbyn's critics squealed at the idea that he would appoint his political fellow traveller John McDonnell to the role of shadow chancellor, but as one of the pair's allies pointed out, he was one of only three 'Corbyn loyalists' in that first shadow cabinet, along with Diane Abbott and Jon Trickett.

Around the table was the new deputy leader, Tom Watson, Hilary Benn, Angela Eagle, Lucy Powell and Charlie Falconer, who had been Tony Blair's justice secretary.

Starmer's more junior position, shadowing the immigration minister, found him working for shadow home secretary Andy Burnham. It was there that he first met Carolyn Harris, the Swansea MP who often brightens up Parliament's Portcullis House as she sweeps through with her bubbly demeanour, thick Welsh accent and shock of pink – or sometimes purple – hair. One of those present in the team at the time described Harris as the 'original Starmerite'. She doesn't deny that she liked what she saw.

'Did I like him? I loved him! He was wonderful!' she told me, describing how she'd Googled 'Keir Starmer' in advance and been impressed by his legal background. One day Harris, finding herself sitting behind Starmer in the House of Commons chamber, poked him hard in the back and said, 'Oi, are you Keir Starmer?'

When he nodded, she replied, 'One day I'm going to make you leader of the Labour Party.'

Harris said that Starmer stood out as 'head and shoulders' above anyone else, with constructive and sensible advice on legislation, or what she joked was the 'big boy politics'. The pair became instantly close, with Starmer and his family visiting Harris for annual holidays in Swansea. The group would eat fish and chips on Mumbles Pier and she describes Starmer as always taking the time to chat to anyone who recognised him.

'I've never seen him get annoyed or anxious,' she added, saying his one rule was to always walk away from his family for a chat, to keep them out of any limelight. 'He could be in the middle of his fish and chips but he would still go, even though the food would be cold when he came back. He's brilliant at listening to people.'

And, indeed, within weeks of his entering Parliament, there were signs that he was already doing what might be needed to one day position himself to challenge for the top spot. Those efforts would build over the years so that finally when the time came, in terms of preparation for a leadership race, Starmer was streets ahead of his opponents.

Perhaps that was because his new adviser, Chris Ward, was so much clearer about the potential destination. Having spent years inside the Labour machine, he wasn't interested in going to work as a researcher for a perennial backbencher. Ward was looking for a star; and in Starmer, he felt he'd found one. Although the 52-year-old Starmer, older than many newcomers to Parliament, had long been a Labour member, Ward knew that he was not steeped in the party or in the internal mechanisms of how it worked.

So in his new role, the first thing Starmer did in summer 2015 was to travel across the country to places like Dover to hear views on immigration, something that would heavily influence his own thoughts on an increasingly thorny policy area for Labour. Corbyn's allies said that, even years later as shadow Brexit secretary, Starmer often referenced that tour as having cemented his opinion that the party could never return to a policy of free movement.

In some ways this was the first sign of the start of a future Starmer leadership campaign beginning to build momentum, as his team used the opportunity to get their man to as many constituency Labour parties as possible, making sure to place him in front of plenty of party members.

And there were other moves that appeared to betray that as-yet unspoken ambition. After watching Corbyn's response to Chancellor George Osborne's budget in March 2016, Starmer returned to his corner office in Parliament and told colleagues, including Ward, and new parliamentary assistant Yasmeen Sebbana, that what he had witnessed in the Commons that day was terrible.

'Well, how would you do it?' Ward asked. From then on, the pair began to develop Starmer's ideas on how they felt Labour should rebuild and get to a place where it could win elections. As well as thinking up budget responses, they would spend each Thursday tackling a different policy area, like social care or education or health. When later that year, Stuart Ingham, now head of the Policy Unit in Downing Street, joined the team, he would also attend these sessions.

Unsurprisingly, when it came to European Union membership this north London human rights lawyer was a committed Remainer. But as the Referendum drew closer, Starmer would tell colleagues about the sheer public anger he had heard first-hand and the need to deal with free movement after the Brexit result, which he still expected to be a vote to Remain. Despite what he had heard on the streets, when Starmer attended weekly meetings of Burnham's shadow ministerial team he argued that in urban areas the Remain votes would pile up. Burnham disagreed, telling colleagues that he was sure the UK would vote to leave the EU. 'No one in Leigh [Burnham's then Greater Manchester constituency] is voting Remain,' he would say. Carolyn Harris's conversations in Swansea made her tilt the same way.

Still, when the news came, it was a shock. Sitting in the back garden at home on the morning of 24 June 2016, Starmer told Ward that the result was a 'catastrophe'. He was more upset than any of his team had seen him, asking what kind of world his children would grow up in. But there was no talk of Labour trying to fight the result. Starmer argued that any conversation about rejoining the EU would not be countenanced for many years.

Some of those close to Starmer say that he generally responds to a kick in the teeth with a period of introspection before searching for a practical solution. In the weeks that followed, Starmer would sketch out where he thought the UK needed to land in future Brexit negotiations, drawing concentric circles on scraps of paper, with the Eurozone in the middle, and then the wider EU. Finally, he drew a circle in which he added a series of 'X's, to represent countries like Turkey or Ukraine. 'That is where we need to be,' he would argue. 'Just outside the institutions but as close as possible.'

These were thoughts that would become central to his role in the future. But on that day of the Referendum decision, something else was unfolding inside the Labour Party.

There were several things that led MPs to launch the mis-timed coup against Jeremy Corbyn. With hindsight, it was always destined to fail. One factor was the raw grief of the loss of Jo Cox who had been so cruelly murdered in the run-up to the Referendum. I had known Cox before she came into Parliament and she was a force of nature: vivacious, sassy, talented and incredibly kind. That sense of loss was felt acutely by so many MPs, with some observing that the Labour leadership had failed to respond empathetically enough to her death.

The other was the feeling of collective bewilderment at the result of the Referendum. That day, Portcullis House felt like a ghost town, with just a few researchers milling around. But sitting at one table were a group of Labour advisers who each worked for a shadow cabinet member. They looked distressed, some close to tears. And they were all furious with Corbyn, who they felt had not fought hard enough for the cause.

Although the Labour leader had attended plenty of events for the Remain campaign, there was a sense that he had done so half-heartedly, even claiming on national television that his support for the EU was around 'seven, seven-and-a-half' out of ten. Corbyn's team believed that was the right message for Labour voters who were divided on this issue. They felt that a promise to Remain but also reform the institution was the best way to appeal to the large number of traditionally Labour supporters who were sceptical about the EU and were wavering in their votes. But many in the shadow cabinet disagreed, believing that lukewarm support would damage the Remain cause.

In the week before the Referendum, the Labour leadership team had met and agreed that if there was a Leave vote, it was critical that the party respected the democratic outcome. Corbyn's allies insist that was what he was trying to indicate when, on the morning of the result, he said on television that Article 50, the process that would start a two-year clock ticking on the Brexit process, should be invoked 'now'. His advisers quickly tried to clarify that he did not mean literally 'now', but by then it was too late. Labour MPs, who seemed almost grief-stricken by the result, simply could not believe that their leader had raised the prospect of beginning a legal and time-limited process without any debate.

At the long shadow cabinet meeting led by Corbyn that day, key members of his frontbench team took turns to describe how the vote to leave the EU was a disaster – for Britain and for Labour. The mood was sour – and the plotting was already underway. But the problem for the rebel MPs was that the Labour membership did not blame Corbyn and were simply not ready to oust this radical, anti-austerity leader whom they had only elected nine months earlier.

Corbyn's team took a more cynical view about the motives for the attempted coup. Key figures had been so convinced that one was coming, with or without Brexit, that they had organised their holidays to avoid the two days they considered most likely – Friday 6

May 2016, when the country woke up to local council election results, or Friday 24 June, following the Referendum result.

And so it was that the ill-fated challenge began on that Friday in June, as Labour MPs Margaret Hodge and Ann Coffey asked for a confidence vote in Corbyn, to take place on the Monday. Then, on the Saturday night, the shadow foreign secretary Hilary Benn began asking colleagues if they would call on Corbyn to resign. A story from *Observer* journalist Daniel Boffey declared: 'Hilary Benn seeks shadow cabinet backing to oust Corbyn.'[1]

At the time, some of the leader's team were underground without mobile reception and when they emerged their phones 'exploded'. In a phone call with Corbyn and his advisers – including Seumas Milne, Karie Murphy, Simon Fletcher and Andrew Fisher – a decision was taken to sack Hilary Benn.

The call to Benn was made just after midnight. What followed was a long and painful Sunday in which dozens of shadow cabinet ministers and then large parts of the frontbench behind them stepped down one by one, first from the right of the party, then the centre, and eventually the centre-left.

But there were exceptions. Andy Burnham, who would later fight to become mayor of Greater Manchester, did not step down. At first, neither did Keir Starmer. Some of those working with the key rebels were furious that Starmer did not resign earlier. 'What's he doing?' muttered one colleague to a friend, as Sunday evening drew in. With hindsight, that same person now wonders if this was the first move of Starmer's leadership long-game. Was he already thinking about how his every action would be interpreted by the Labour members who would be so critical to any future leadership election?

His allies insist the hesitation was more to do with his shock at just how disorganised the coup appeared to be, and his belief that it would fail. 'The time hasn't come,' he told one colleague.

In the end, Starmer was one of the last to jump ship, waiting until there was virtually no frontbench to speak of, and refusing to give any broadcast interviews or to criticise the party leader publicly.

Corbyn's team also noticed that the resignation letter which Starmer tweeted at 3.26 p.m. on Monday afternoon was kinder than others, stating that he recognised the leader's mandate from party members and adding: 'I have never spoken out publicly against you and I do not intend to now.' When the party leader rebuilt his shadow cabinet after the ensuing leadership challenge concluded, the tone of this letter would be remembered.

Starmer reasoned that the EU Referendum result was 'catastrophic for the UK', arguing he had deliberately maintained his support for Corbyn through the weekend, but that the scale of resignations had made it 'simply untenable' to offer effective opposition.

In spite of the mass defection, however, Corbyn refused to resign. As an interesting aside, Starmer's father, Rodney, proposed a motion in support of Corbyn and against the coup at his East Surrey constituency Labour Party. One person present at the meeting described the older Starmer's 'rousing speech', and how he also told others there that his son got on with almost everyone but claimed he 'could not stand Diane Abbott'.

Some were urging deputy leader Tom Watson to run against Corbyn, but he declined. He was convinced Corbyn would win because of the dramatic change to the party's membership. Polling that had been commissioned by others in the party found that in 2016 around 40 per cent of Labour members agreed with the statement: 'I would rather lose an election than compromise my principles.' 'Mother Teresa would have lost to Corbyn,' one MP joked at the time. After some party wrangling in which Angela Eagle first tried to stand, another MP Owen Smith went forward as the candidate.

Corbyn's second overwhelming victory was announced at the Labour Party conference in Liverpool in September 2016. In some ways it is astonishing that Corbyn survived losing most of his shadow cabinet and dozens more frontbenchers, but he was able to do so because the system of accountability within Labour had been so heavily shifted towards the party's membership.

Within the parliamentary Labour Party are a number of different groupings based on political affiliation. Furthest to the left is the pro-Corbyn Socialist Campaign Group; most right-wing are Progress and Labour First. But dozens of MPs opt for neither wing, joining instead the so-called Tribune Group, chaired by Clive Efford, MP for Eltham and Chislehurst since 1997, and claiming the politics of the 'soft left'. It was there that Starmer decided to place himself politically when he first entered Parliament.

At a Tribune dinner in Liverpool just after Corbyn's re-election had been announced, the mood was described as 'grim'. Starmer found himself sitting beside his friend, the Darlington MP Jenny Chapman, who would go on to play a key role in his future leadership race.

Chapman had a very 'normal' upbringing. Her grandparents on both sides had a military background and both her parents were nurses; she attended state schools and lived in council houses until her family bought a house in Darlington when she was ten. Her Labour politics were really to the right of the Tribune group but with so many of her friends in Parliament on the soft left, this is where she had found her tribe, including her husband, Nick Smith, MP for Blaenau Gwent.

In Liverpool that night, Chapman was flanked by Starmer on one side, and on the other Dan Jarvis, MP for Barnsley Central – another politician being pushed as a possible future Labour leader. 'You both might need to go back and serve,' she told them. 'But don't do it for free. Do it on your own terms.'

Later, in the bar of the Pullman hotel, heaving with Labour MPs, advisers, journalists and members, Starmer bumped into Ben Nunn, former chair of the constituency Labour Party in Camden, whom he had first met over a coffee in 2014. Starmer told Nunn he now wanted to be part of Corbyn's new shadow cabinet, but only in a sufficiently serious job to justify the decision. He wanted to be shadow home secretary, a role to which he could bring his expertise as former director of public prosecutions and highlight an issue that has always been a priority for him – violence against women and girls. Andy Burnham would help by recommending him. Alternatively, he would accept shadow Brexit secretary, a position he saw as being critical to the public interest and which he must have realised would bring with it an enormous public profile.

Starmer argued that whatever was to come the country needed a Labour Party, and that he needed Nunn to join his team. Bruised after running the communications for Owen Smith's failed leadership campaign, Nunn responded, 'You should serve, but I'm done for now.'

Was this latest decision a more overt indication of Starmer's leadership hopes? One MP claimed overhearing Starmer tell colleagues in the Commons tea room: 'The next leader of the Labour Party will come from within the shadow cabinet.' They described feeling both 'awe-struck' and 'appalled' all at once.

Those close to Starmer admit that, by then, what had been a distant 'dot' of leadership ambition was starting to swell. They argue that this was not all about self-interest but a desire for Labour to eventually shift back at least some way from the left flank where Corbyn had placed a flag in the ground.

One thing is certain, Starmer and his team had taken a key lesson from the failed coup: they believed that if he was to fulfil this ambition, he would have to be loyal to Corbyn, whether he believed in the Labour leader's political project or not.

The decision to appoint Starmer to the new shadow cabinet was taken at the Novotel on Lambeth Road, just south of the river from Parliament. It was 10 October 2016 and, having just been re-elected as party leader with an enormous mandate, Corbyn had gathered his inner circle for a strategy away-day. The team knew they had to reach out to some of the rebel MPs, but Corbyn was adamant that no one who had stayed loyal during the coup should be sacked and so the openings were limited.

They had been told that Starmer would take only one of two positions and only one was available. Corbyn's strategist Seumas Milne had argued that Diane Abbott should be appointed shadow foreign secretary. Given both his and Corbyn's interest in foreign policy, he was keen to have an ally in that position who shared their politics. He suspected Labour MPs would prefer Abbott in this role than with a domestic brief and reasoned that it would send a powerful message to appoint a Black woman to such a critical position. But Abbott wanted to be shadow home secretary.

When Starmer's name was raised for the shadow Brexit role, John McDonnell argued that a former barrister could be a good fit because he would be across the detail. Not everyone was fully convinced. Some present that day say that Milne raised concerns. He was nervous about giving such a politically sensitive role to someone outside Corbyn's close circle of supporters, but ultimately accepted that they needed to reach out. McDonnell did not disagree that there was political risk in bringing someone in who clearly 'wasn't our politics'. He suggested that Shadow Business Secretary Rebecca Long-Bailey be present at all meetings with Starmer, almost as a 'minder'.

When Starmer received a call from Karie Murphy offering him the job as shadow secretary of state for exiting the European Union, he was abroad in Taiwan, campaigning to change its law on the death penalty. He quickly rang his adviser Chris Ward to discuss the opportunity. Ward had reservations about how tricky the Brexit negotiations could become, but also about the wider reshuffle, warning that Starmer looked like the 'odd man out'.

But Ward's concerns were moot: Starmer had already said yes.

As Big Ben struck its first note at 10 p.m. on 8 June 2017, another general election exit poll shocked the country. Theresa May's Conservatives would have 314 seats to Labour's 266. The Tories would be the largest party, but only just. Far from the 100-seat majority that some had predicted, the prime minister's gamble on an early election had swept away her majority and plunged her party into hung parliament territory.

'This is a simply stunning result,' my colleague Tom Bradby said, before adding, 'Theresa May's authority, if this poll is correct, looks to be shredded.'

Former Conservative chancellor George Osborne was sitting to his left. If the poll was correct, said Osborne, it was 'completely catastrophic for the Conservatives and for Theresa May'.

Journalist Sam Coates, then at *The Times*, described a 'stony silence' at Conservative Party headquarters, where they were expecting a majority of seventy or more. He wrote that one aide had a copy of a news report on the YouGov MRP poll, which had suggested a hung parliament. Convinced it would be wrong, they had it ready to frame and hang on the wall the next day.

At Corbyn's Islington home, where he was watching the news with his wife Laura Alvarez and two key advisers, Karie Murphy and Seumas Milne, the mood was buoyant. Murphy wrapped the party leader in a hug as the team cracked open bottles of Peroni, picked up at the local corner shop.

Milne was cautious about whether the results predicted by the exit poll would play out through the night, telling colleagues 'it's too early'. But this felt like vindication. Earlier in the campaign, when Labour had trailed the Conservatives in the polls by 24 points, Corbyn's team had been summoned to a meeting at the party's headquarters in Southside where they were told that manifestos make no real difference; election campaigns can never shift votes by more than 2 per cent; and that they should run an entirely defensive campaign, accepting from the start that thirty MPs could not be saved.

Corbyn's team, for their part, would argue that a radical Labour manifesto promising to re-nationalise energy, water and the railways, scrap tuition fees, expand free childcare, end zero-hour contracts and ramp up Income Tax for the richest, had closed the gap by inspiring hope and excitement. Corbyn's critics nevertheless would claim the campaign had been lost by Theresa May and her decision to include in the Conservative manifesto a disastrously unpopular policy on social care, and not won by Labour. May's team would point out that their vote-share actually increased, but that was little consolation.

Many Labour MPs were shocked. Corbyn had not won, but by securing 40 per cent of the vote he had certainly challenged the notion that his left-wing politics would always be unpalatable to swathes of middle England.

But the person for whom the result perhaps represented the biggest game-changing moment, was Keir Starmer. He had watched the exit poll at home along with Chris Ward (now Starmer's parliamentary private secretary and the new MP for Brighton Kemptown) and had been surprised by how close the margin was. 'How wrong can an exit poll be?' he asked.

A number of Labour MPs, expecting a terrible performance, were preparing to launch leadership bids. One had even asked me to go and see them ahead of the exit poll so they could set out their plans for the next few days. I'm told that Corbyn's team had sketched out different scenarios and had decided that even with a more convincing election loss he would do everything he could to stay in place, including standing in any ensuing leadership contest.

Starmer's team had also started to gather the names of potentially supportive MPs in case there was an opportunity to challenge for the party leadership. But those there at the time say he wasn't really ready and it was far from the top of his mind.

Corbyn's team had so far found Starmer to be a reliable colleague who had impressed them by how he navigated the vote in February 2017 in support of the government triggering Article 50 and starting the Brexit process. For many on the Labour side, including the forty-seven MPs who rebelled, it had been a heartbreaking moment. One colleague described Corbyn having to shepherd a distraught Diane Abbott through the lobby.

Labour had gone into the 2017 General Election accepting the Brexit result and promising to build a close new relationship with Europe: one focused on workers' rights, as well as protections for consumers and the environment. The party said it wanted to retain the benefits of the single market and customs union, but did not suggest rejoining these institutions, clear that for millions of Labour voters that would be a step too far.

The 2017 result would not shift the team from that red line on free movement, but it would open the door to the possibility of a softer Brexit, and Starmer knew it. By then he had built a shadow ministerial team with key allies including Jenny Chapman and Matthew Pennycook. Representing Darlington in the North of England and the London seat of Greenwich and Woolwich respectively, between them the pair brought the perspectives of a wide span of Labour voters.

Starmer then approached Ben Nunn once more, persuading him that things were different now; that a hung parliament would give Labour huge influence over the Brexit process. And so, Nunn became Starmer's communications chief.

Although their minds were focused on Brexit, Starmer's team knew that this period would provide the ideal platform to perfect his candidacy should he ever choose to stand. One source, who had been sceptical about the shadow role, admitted it was a 'terrific pathway' to the three key groups that Starmer would need if he were ever to challenge for the top job: Labour members, affiliated trade unions and fellow MPs.

Two factors, it was argued, would help any future leadership hopeful take the Labour mantle: first, a demonstration of loyalty to Corbyn and second, a pro-Remain stance in the Brexit debate.

After the 2017 Election, Starmer could lay claim to the former but not yet the latter. But a slow shift towards a softer Brexit did follow, with Starmer eventually supporting the idea of putting a deal with the EU to a further vote, and finally arguing that Remain should be an option in a second referendum. Whether this was an inevitable shift in position because Parliament was blocked, clever strategic planning by someone with an eye on the leadership, or something Starmer was forced into by the restless right-wing of his party, can be debated. Perhaps it was all three.

There are plenty who see Starmer as a 'lucky general' whose positioning in the leadership race happened to land with members and whose timing coincided with the Tories' implosion. But those close to Starmer argue that while clearly there was a good dose of luck along the way, he – and they – identified early on the path he had to travel to place himself in contention, and then made sure he did not step away from it. They also insist that he was not the only one who recognised this, pointing out that then shadow foreign secretary Emily Thornberry had her eyes on the same prize and was ready to follow a similar course.

Regardless, some members of Corbyn's team now look back with cynicism, arguing that after the 2017 Election Starmer began to shift the party's Brexit position towards a second referendum. The move certainly increased his popularity with party members but, they assert, it divided Labour voters and made it harder to win an election.

'It was like salami-slicing it,' said one, suggesting it was designed to push the party step-by-step towards a Remain position. They now contend that a second referendum Brexit position, pushed by Starmer, played a crucial role in Labour's disastrous 2019 Election defeat. They believe that Starmer placed his political ambitions ahead of the party's electoral interests, pointing out that for all his support for a second referendum, he later decided that Labour would back Boris Johnson's Brexit deal.

At the end of 2023, I asked Starmer: 'Do you regret pushing for a second referendum?' By this time we'd heard him repeat a number of times that there would be no prospect of rejoining the EU. 'No,' he said, without hesitation. 'Because we had reached a stage where there was a complete impasse in Parliament. I didn't push for a second referendum in the early days after the Brexit vote.'

Starmer's allies would argue that Corbyn was the author of his own downfall, pointing to the leader's handling of the anti-Semitism crisis, his response to the poisoning of Sergei and Yulia Skripal by the Russian state, and an 'ill-disciplined' manifesto with a long list of spending pledges.

Whether or not Starmer's team were explicitly discussing a leadership challenge in 2017, they clearly were trying to shift public perception of their boss. His close team of Chris Ward, Stuart Ingham, Ben Nunn and Yasmeen Sebbana – in charge of strategy, policy, communications and logistics respectively – ensured that Starmer used his role as shadow Brexit secretary to reach out to as many trade unions and constituency parties as possible. These visits were both a core part of his job and also provided a platform from which to build relationships with union general secretaries as well as their political officers and regional secretaries.

Meanwhile, Nunn laid out three clear priorities to improve Starmer's standing with the media. One was to add 'depth' to who he was, with the team throwing particular effort into two longer-form podcasts with the BBC's Nick Robinson and comedian Matt Forde.

Next was a plan to boost Starmer's visibility; to present him as what the team called a 'ten-to-eight or ten-past-eight' politician – in other words, they would offer him only for the most prestigious slots on Radio 4's *Today* programme. Starmer would also no longer appear on panels with other MPs, as Nunn said that he shouldn't be seen as a commentator but a political leader.

Finally, Starmer must demonstrate that he was good in opposition; that he could land blows to humiliate the Conservative government. And that meant being opportunistic. In November 2018, for example, Starmer's team leapt on reports that the environment secretary Michael Gove had argued for the cabinet to be shown the government's full legal advice on the contentious Irish backstop (designed to ensure no hard border between Northern Ireland and the Republic of Ireland following Brexit). Nunn quickly bashed out a press release arguing that if the cabinet could see the legal advice, so should Parliament. Starmer then used a fairly archaic parliamentary procedure known as a 'humble address' that would force the government to release the papers.

The team also decided to court favour with the Democratic Unionist Party, who had propped up Theresa May after her 2017 electoral disaster but hated the backstop, which they saw as weakening Northern Ireland's place in the UK by placing it into a customs union with the EU. Nunn texted the DUP's Westminster leader, Nigel Dodds, with the message: 'Keir wants to see you'. The parties agreed to sign a joint letter, along with the Lib Dems and the SNP, to force a motion to find ministers in contempt of Parliament for the government's failure to publish the legal advice. And indeed, the government lost the ensuing vote, generating front page headlines.

For the first time in history, government ministers were found to be in contempt of Parliament, and the case had been prosecuted by Starmer.

In a long read for *GQ* magazine, political journalist John Crace called it 'complete humiliation' for May and argued that Starmer had 'played a blinder'.[2] But he also noted that there was a 'twist in all of this'.

'Starmer's rising star – both with the Labour benches and Parliament in general – has not been altogether well received by Corbyn's team,' Crace wrote.

With a day job as the *Guardian*'s parliamentary sketch writer, Crace spent hours on end leaning forward in the seats that wrap round the balcony in the Commons chamber, watching closely as MPs clashed across the green benches. And in their shifting body language, Crace could literally see the growing tensions between Starmer and Corbyn.

'There's a feeling that he may be lining himself up as a potential rival to take over as leader,' he noted.

Some of Corbyn's inner circle thought Starmer had gone 'rogue'. They were increasingly distrustful of his politics for several reasons. One was his attitude towards so-called 'state aid rules' and market liberalisation. In the EU Referendum, Corbyn had stood on a platform of 'Remain and reform' and one thing he wanted to reform were the rules that limited a country's ability to subsidise (or even nationalise) key industries and also rules that forced competition into public services. But aides say that Starmer could not understand what was wrong with this system, a position that they felt placed him to the right of former leader Ed Miliband. Moreover, they feared Starmer was more factional than he appeared, citing the occasion when he and his wife turned up at a ward-level branch meeting in his constituency, to vote against Laura Murray – the daughter of a left-wing trade unionist.

But Starmer had also been fighting Brexit battles on the opposite front. Just three weeks after the June 2017 election result, a group of anti-Brexit rebels led by Chris Leslie and Chuka Umunna laid down an amendment to the Queen's speech calling for the UK to have 'full access' to the single market. Starmer knew that far too many MPs (including Chapman in his own team) thought that remaining in the European Economic Area was totally unacceptable. They warned that a Norway-style deal, in which a country is inside the single market but outside the customs union, would require free movement, which would be anathema to Red Wall Labour voters.

Starmer was also not convinced by the Norway-model and not only because of free movement. On a visit to the country, Starmer asked Chris Ward to meet him for breakfast at 5 a.m. so the pair could travel to a checkpoint into Sweden. Watching Norwegian trucks being stopped at the border, Starmer became convinced that the customs union was the bit of the jigsaw that Labour should be fighting for.

His first collision with Corbyn's team over Brexit was about that issue, when at a meeting on 10 January 2018, he furiously accused LOTO of trying to water down Labour's customs union pledge ahead of a speech the leader was due to deliver in Coventry.

A much bigger clash came later that year over the question of a second referendum. Labour's decision to eventually back a fresh vote on the Brexit deal was strongly opposed by shadow Brexit minister Jenny Chapman. When Starmer told her about it, the Darlington MP who was acutely aware of just how many of her constituents had voted for Brexit, replied: 'I can't do this, I have to resign.' But he persuaded her not to.

At the start of the party's annual conference that autumn 2018, at a so-called 'compositing' meeting on Sunday 23 September, delegates hammered out a position on a second referendum. The group agreed to the sentence: 'If we cannot get a general election, Labour must support all options remaining on the table, including campaigning for a public vote.'

But Starmer was then irritated to see Shadow Chancellor John McDonnell suggest in a broadcast interview that any vote would only be on the Brexit deal itself, suggesting it would not leave the door open for remaining in the EU. Starmer's conference speech had by then already been signed off by Corbyn's communications chief, Seumas Milne. Starmer told strategist Chris Ward that he wanted to add a line about keeping the option to Remain on the table, insisting that the wording was in line with the sentiment of the agreed motion.

Ward paced at the back of the hall as he watched the speech get underway. After Starmer talked of the option of a public vote on the deal, he lifted his head and spoke off the cuff. 'Nobody is ruling out Remain as an option,' he said.

Later, Starmer would be collared by one of Corbyn's aides, furious at his decision to go off script. But in the hall delegates rose to their feet in delight, including Chapman who jumped up to immediately join in the applause. Even though the Darlington MP was against a second vote, she wanted Starmer to have this moment; and to win over the room. After all, by then she had already told him that she wanted him to run for the leadership, and they had agreed that to do so he had to remain in the shadow cabinet.

Through all of this, Corbyn's Labour was mired in a growing controversy around anti-Semitism. Some say that Starmer, whose wife Vic is Jewish, was ready to quit more than once, telling aides that he could not stand it anymore. However, he never threatened to resign during shadow cabinet meetings, although he did push for Labour's general secretary to deliver regular reports about the handling of anti-Semitism cases.

Jenny Chapman's turning point had come in March 2018, after the Salisbury poisonings. When Corbyn responded to Theresa May to ask whether samples of the nerve agent deployed in Salisbury had been sent to Moscow for testing, Chapman could not believe her ears. She quickly left the Commons chamber to find colleagues in the tea room, telling them she found the statement offensive and naive.

The following Saturday, she rang Starmer from her home in Darlington and said: 'I do not know if you have thought about it but I think you should consider standing, and if you do we will work together to do what is necessary.'

Almost a year later, Starmer asked Ward and Nunn to accompany him for a drink at The Admiralty on Trafalgar Square. Sitting in a booth by the window, Starmer told them that he had spoken to his wife, Vic, and had decided that if Corbyn lost the next election he would stand for leader. The die was cast.

And by then, Starmer had already met Morgan McSweeney, the man who would help run his leadership campaign and later the 2024 General Election, and who is now Starmer's chief political adviser inside Downing Street.

3

The Morganiser

It was a total fluke.

The reason Morgan McSweeney first began working for the Labour Party, a week before the 2001 Election, was because of a bizarre injury.

The recent graduate in marketing and politics from Middlesex University was getting work experience at the party's headquarters when a receptionist dropped a flowerpot on her foot. It was bad enough to take her out of work at a critical time and the party, urgently looking around for a replacement, landed on their 25-year-old intern. McSweeney was more than happy to stand in. He would remain in or around the party for the next twenty-three years and counting.

In 2002, Cork-born McSweeney joined the Greater London Labour Party team as an administrator. It was there that he got his first taste of the job that would go on to dominate his working life. McSweeney was in awe of Hilary Perrin, who as Labour's Greater London organiser was charged with running campaigns to try to win elections. He kept asking her if he could have a go at doing it himself. 'No,' she repeatedly told him. 'You're not ready.'

When Perrin sent him to help out in a Welsh Assembly election in Clwyd West, it was with the strict instruction not to try to organise himself. But in the chaos of the campaign, McSweeney managed – in the words of one friend – to 'blag it'.

His first go at election organising was not exactly a roaring success. At one point the team thought they had lost the seat but then, at the end of a tense count, someone arrived with an extra box of votes. Labour edged it by a mere 1 per cent – and McSweeney was hooked.

Moving back to organise in London seats, things hardly improved for McSweeney. First, in 2003, Labour lost a by-election in Brent East to a future Lib Dem Coalition minister, Sarah Teather, and then in the 2005 Election, lost Hammersmith and Fulham to a man who would later become a Conservative minister and party chair, Greg Hands.

After these bruising defeats, McSweeney spent the summer rethinking what it meant to be an election organiser, formulating new ideas around using personalised direct mails to tell stories, and engaging community figures to build trust. He felt Labour was listening too hard to what he called 'party stakeholders', and not listening hard enough to the voters themselves. Moreover, the messaging too often appeared as though the party expected residents to be grateful for much-needed new schools and hospitals.

When McSweeney turned his attention to the Lambeth Council elections in early May 2006, it was with these new ideas in mind. Lambeth is a long, thin borough stretching from the London Eye and Waterloo Station, through Vauxhall and Clapham, and ending at Streatham Common. And it was here that this twenty-something Irishman would develop the techniques he would go on to deploy in 2024, in Labour's first general election victory for two decades.

It was Steve Reed, later also a key figure in Starmer's 2020 leadership election campaign, who gave McSweeney the Lambeth job. Four years earlier, Labour had lost control of the south London council to a Lib Dem/Conservative coalition. Reed, then leader of the Labour group in opposition at the council, was desperate to turn the situation around when he spotted this talented organiser working on a campaign for the London Assembly.

In McSweeney, Reed had found someone just as obsessed as he was about winning. The pair had two fairly simple principles they believed this local Labour Party had let slip. The first was to ask voters (as opposed to 'stakeholders', like trade unions) what their priorities were and then focus on them, relentlessly. The second was to bring in a system of almost street-level targeting of a smaller group of voters who – if persuaded – could swing the overall result. The aim was to improve the 'efficiency' of the vote, making it easier to succeed.

Reed and McSweeney also became convinced that Labour's failures in Lambeth were linked to the historic dominance of the party's most militant leftists on the council. The former leader, 'Red' Ted Knight, had been a controversial figure once expelled from Labour in the 1950s for supporting the Trotskyist Socialist Labour League.

Reed had grown up on the Watford edge of St Albans, close to the sprawling Odhams printing works where his dad, uncles, aunts and grandparents had all worked. His politics was shaped by what happened in the 1980s, when Margaret Thatcher was prime minister. Reed's dad was one of hundreds of print workers to receive a letter from media baron Robert Maxwell in 1983 warning them the factory that printed his newspapers would be closing down, leaving what felt like half the local community redundant. Reed's mother subsequently took on four jobs, including as a cleaner and receptionist, telling him: 'Thatcher can take your dad's job, but she isn't taking our house.'

Perhaps in a nod to Reed's politics, his lodger back in the noughties was Richard Angell who would go on to become director of Progress, a Labour pressure group representing the centrist wing of the party. The Labour MP for Vauxhall and Camberwell Green, Florence Eshalomi, also came up this way, cutting her teeth as a council candidate.

Based in an office on Rosendale Road, Herne Hill, the team worked and played hard. One of those present during that 2006 campaign described it as like being 'in the trenches' together, claiming that when 'soldiers fight a common cause' they become incredibly close. Others remember drinking in the Trinity pub in Brixton and sometimes moving on to karaoke at the Cavendish Arms in nearby Stockwell.

'Morgan loved karaoke,' said one friend from the time, claiming he would sometimes opt for the Irish folk song, 'The Irish Rover', or belt out U2's 'With or Without You'. Reed would sing whatever was asked of him, while another colleague, council candidate Pete Robbins enjoyed performing 'Wuthering Heights' by Kate Bush (sung in a falsetto, no less).

Some have described McSweeney's approach to campaigning as somewhat eccentric. In his job interview, he told Reed that he would only accept the role if he had access to two Risograph printers, from which he could churn out leaflets even in the middle of the night, and a folding and stuffing machine to get them ready to be sent out. He didn't take a day off between 1 January and polling day on 4 May 2006, sometimes setting up a camp bed to sleep in the office – a move that some say lost this workaholic his then girlfriend. 'The room was disgusting,' said one friend. 'Always full of Mars Bar wrappers and cigarette packets.'

Council candidates were given numbers, not names, and when McSweeney carried a box of direct mail round to the home of 'Stockwell 3', he had no idea who he was going to meet. He turned up at the house of Imogen Walker (now Labour MP for Hamilton and Clyde Valley) with a box of leaflets about traffic calming measures in south London.

Walker had heard all about McSweeney's reputation as a fierce political organiser and about some of his eccentricities – apparently, he wore a waterproof poncho in the office because the Risograph constantly splashed out ink. Friends say she was surprised by McSweeney who she found softly spoken, mild mannered and charming.

Soon Walker was part of the karaoke set, opting for Tina Turner's 'The Best', although it was another three years before she and

McSweeney became a couple, later marrying and returning to her home of Scotland.

The crux of the Lambeth campaign strategy was outlined on a single piece of A4 paper, with a list of descending numbers. Under the title 'We're On Your Side', were the words: 'Lambeth targeting strategy'. Underneath read:

Population: 265,000
Electoral register: 200,000
Vote in elections: 100,000
Live in key wards: 33,000
40 per cent Labour target: 13,000

The campaign was almost entirely designed around this last line – the votes required to get over the 40 per cent victory line in just the key wards. They believed that if they could persuade only 13,000 voters to vote Labour, a mere 6 per cent of the total, it would be enough to win the entire borough. And they were right.

Over the following months, Reed, McSweeney and others targeted these key voters relentlessly, with conversations and leaflets. As I understand it, each doorstep visit was carefully orchestrated with clear messaging, tailored to the individual.

How this worked was set out in a table on that same piece of A4 paper. Across the top was the single issue they had identified as persuasive to every voter in the borough: the claim that the council coalition leadership had hiked up Council Tax then squandered the money. Then for each of the 13,000 voters a second-order issue was identified from a list of five: housing fraud; borough traffic wardens being incentivised to hand out parking tickets; a lack of school places; the threat to local swimming pools; and anti-social behaviour and crime. Finally, below that, was a message linked specifically to the road where the voter lived. For example, an activist would say, 'I just saw a burnt-out vehicle up the street and I've reported it to the council.'

For council candidate Pete Robbins, this strategy addressed a problem that had emerged in 2002. By then, while the memory of Ted Knight and the hard-left's influence in Lambeth still loomed large, Labour was run by a more moderate team and Robbins believed the election failure was actually organisational rather than ideological – and it was that problem that McSweeney and Reed had seemingly fixed.

In 2006, Labour won back Lambeth, propelling Steve Reed to leader of the council. And it was a victory that felt so at odds with the national result that later regional organisers would invite him to visit party offices across the country to share tips on strategy.

Across London, and even in those Lambeth wards that had not been targeted, there had been a 9 per cent swing away from Labour. But where the team had pounded voters with this bespoke political messaging, deliberately crafted around those key issues of Council Tax, crime, parking and swimming pools, there was a big enough swing towards Labour in those wards for the party to take control of the council.

Years later, Reed and his team, including Lambeth Council Chief Executive Derrick Anderson, would focus on turning their ideas into a strategy to run local government. Reed came up with 'cooperative councils' in which residents would be more involved in designing public services. By then, Robbins was the Lambeth cabinet member for children and young people. He sensed a disconnect between what middle-class parents wanted from youth services (centres with activities like table tennis) and what young people wanted (skills and access to work). So, he instigated the 'Lambeth Youth Council' as an attempt to put young people in charge of the commissioning process. These ideas would go on to influence the politics of Labour Together, the group that Reed and McSweeney were later involved with and which heavily influenced Starmer's leadership campaign.

McSweeney stayed on in Lambeth as Reed's chief of staff for eighteen months, but with his heart in campaigning, he then moved on to new challenges. First, in 2008, he was tasked with trying to understand why Ken Livingstone had lost the London mayoralty, concluding that in his campaign the Labour grandee (who back then was not seen as quite so tribally 'leftist') should have focused more on crime than the congestion charge extension.

Next, he went to work at a behavioural insight consultancy, the Campaign Company, with now Labour Party general secretary David Evans. The pair first met when McSweeney worked as a receptionist at Labour HQ and Evans was the party's assistant general secretary helping to devise the organisational strategy for the 2001 Election. Evans had become fascinated by voter motivation as he sought to understand how, without the engine of a deeply unpopular Conservative government, Labour could persuade people to stick with it after the landslide of 1997.

In this new role, McSweeney turned away from party politics to work on campaigns such as promoting breastfeeding in Brighton and smoking cessation for teenagers in Barnsley. But then came news of a surge in popularity for the British National Party in east London led by Nick Griffin.

In 2006, this far-right, anti-immigration organisation had stood 13 council candidates in Barking and Dagenham, historically a solid Labour constituency, and won 12 of the 51 seats, while Labour won 38 and the Conservatives one. Two years later, the BNP had won a London Assembly seat. Fearing for their growing appeal in the 2010 elections, McSweeney and Evans headed to Barking and Dagenham to join the fightback. It was there that McSweeney met Jon Cruddas, then Labour MP for Dagenham and Rainham.

It was a political battle that I remember well. Covering what I believed was one of the most significant votes in the country, I walked through the streets of Goresbrook in Dagenham, past identical terraced houses, with largely well-kept gardens and a solitary Union Jack, where I talked to locals about why so many were considering backing Griffin's far-right party. There I started to see the reality of what would later come to be described as 'left-behind' communities: voters who had loyally backed Labour for years, decades even, but had come to feel let down by the government.

At a bingo session in a local community hall I met 67-year-old Iris Elliot, who told me the problem was immigration. 'There are too many foreigners,' she said, complaining of 'Africans' letting rubbish pile up in their front gardens and sub-letting room by room. Iris had the impression that these residents had been given £45,000 to move to the borough.

As the caller screeched out the numbers 'Five and eight, fifty-eight … all the threes, thirty-three …', the locals explained that their families felt priced out of London's East End – places like Bethnal Green, Bow, Canning Town – and now felt out of place once again. Marion Buthlay, a pensioner with a shock of white curly hair, told me, 'Children born here can't get the houses or places for their children in school. We don't feel it is our country anymore. But I'll vote Labour – always have.'

The problem for Labour was that so many others were no longer minded to. Nick Griffin was taking on Labour's Margaret Hodge, the MP for Barking and the heart of Dagenham since 1994, as he tried to gain a seat in Parliament, but that wasn't his party's main target. 'The council,' said Griffin. 'That's the real prize.'

The BNP had successfully identified just how anxious residents were feeling and responded to them by pointing the finger of blame firmly in one direction – at 'the Africans'. McSweeney and Evans knew they had to focus on voters' genuine concerns about immigration and its impact on their own access to public services. That meant taking on the BNP's 'rumour mill', but also offering solutions to issues such as untidy gardens and anti-social behaviour.

Labour's 'war-room' occupied a vast space in a derelict building on the site of the old Ford factory in Dagenham and was shared with the anti-fascist campaign group, Searchlight. Cruddas remembers 'Billy Bragg singing in one corner and vats of delicious curry' being ladled out in the other. I saw political activists, councillors and researchers hunched over computer screens or huddled in meetings. On one wall hung a giant banner with the words 'Hope Not Hate'.

Part of Evans' and McSweeney's plan was to recruit 'community communicators' – a network of people working in places like bookies and hairdressers – as trusted local voices who could help drive the conversation. He also put local concerns such as knife crime and a campaign to tackle fly-tipping at the top of the agenda. The council also launched Eyesore Gardens, a project that would see officials enter homes with front yards piled high with rubbish – abandoned car tyres or even wizened brown Christmas trees lurking still in spring – and give landlords and residents a choice: clean it up, with help from the council, or face a fine.

The campaign attracted a solid stream of supporters, including 21-year-old student, Hollie Ridley, now high up in the Labour hierarchy, who had grown up on a local estate with her mum Lorraine, a family support worker, and lorry-driver dad, Dave. Labour's new party chair, Ellie Reeves, was also on the doors back then as a local trade union lawyer.

As a young activist Ridley knew that the people she had grown up around would never vote Conservative, but were feeling the pain of the financial crash and increasingly felt that growing immigration was affecting them negatively. So she spent her weekends and holidays at home from the University of Brighton knocking on doors for the party.

To Cruddas, what was happening in Barking and Dagenham should have been the 'canary down the coalmine'. Here was a community of disaffected working-class voters, who had always backed Labour but who no longer felt that their concerns were being addressed. This was east London, not the East Midlands, but those on the ground understood that it might be the first domino to fall. 'We were all on the ground, seeing what was happening, long before the Red Wall came tumbling down,' said Cruddas.

But in 2010, there was one big difference with the Red Wall defeats in 2019: here, the campaign worked. In Barking, Hodge 'smashed' the

BNP, winning almost 25,000 votes, while Griffin secured less than 7,000. And Labour triumphed in the council elections too, winning all 51 council seats while the BNP lost each of the 12 they had previously held.

If McSweeney's experience in Lambeth with Steve Reed best reveals the organising techniques he would carry forward into 2024's general election, then arguably the 2010 battle for Barking and Dagenham offers the best insight to the politics that drive him – and Keir Starmer.

As the Labour government now gears up to take on a new potential threat to their political coalition in Reform UK, it is telling that McSweeney, Evans, Ridley and Ellie Reeves, all key figures in Starmer's 2024 election machine, cut their teeth in a political contest that was about regaining the trust of working-class voters, long before large swathes of the party realised it had been lost. Evans's argument was that these voters were experiencing change in their communities and believed they had lost out as a result. But instead of trying to make them feel safe and address the underlying causes of their anxiety, many Labour councillors had 'abandoned the pitch' and didn't even dare walk down their streets. 'So we devised a neighbourhood walk that would help get activists back onto the doorsteps to ask people, "What are your concerns?"'

Over the years, political splits have emerged. Jon Cruddas has been critical of the Starmer/McSweeney project and another figure from that campaign, Sam Tarry, has been effectively pushed out of the Labour Party in what many see as a result of factional tussles. But that experience of pounding the streets of Barking and Dagenham does help to place McSweeney's politics certainly on the right of the Labour movement but with a different grounding to that offered by former leader, Tony Blair. McSweeney was a huge fan of Blair's but his solutions to the post-2010 disaffection were different.

As the journalist Tom McTague has put it, 'Not only does McSweeney reject Tony Blair's central analysis of politics and what Labour should do as a result, but for much of his time trying to retake the Labour Party, McSweeney was not just battling the Corbynite Left, who were determined to maintain control of the party, but the Blairite Right, many of whom had concluded it was already dead and were determined to create something new in its place.'[1]

But in the leadership contest after Ed Miliband's resignation in 2015, McSweeney decided to back the candidate who was painted as the most 'Blairite' of those available, running Liz Kendall's campaign, which also included Matthew Doyle, a former press adviser to Blair who would also end up working with Starmer.

While Kendall's campaign failed to get off the ground, and she finished fourth of four, those involved believed that she embraced the same communitarian politics that had shaped McSweeney and others. Indeed, the platform she adopted, which included trying to lean further towards Conservative voters – rebuilding trust on the economy, being passionate about wealth creation and 'putting the country first' – is remarkably similar to that which Starmer put to the country in 2024. But Andy Burnham and Yvette Cooper were also defeated in that leadership contest by an anti-establishment and anti-politics mood. A bubbling anger that had risen up through the Iraq War, and exploded during austerity, resulted in Jeremy Corbyn winning the overwhelming backing of the party's members.

McSweeney, bruised and battered after the leadership battle and convinced no one would hire him again, felt it was the right time to step away from organising. He had, he realised, let slip the most important rule of this political game – listen to the voters and focus on their priorities. In the race to be Labour leader, the electorate was not the general public but the party's increasingly idealistic members.

He would remember that, if ever he was involved in a Labour leadership race again.

4

Labour Together

'Ooooooohhh Jer-emy Cor-byn!'

The chant rang out across the huge crowd, tens of thousands of people in the shadow of Glastonbury's iconic Pyramid stage.

Pacing slightly, dressed in a blue linen shirt and loose beige trousers, Jeremy Corbyn hollered into the microphone.

'The commentariat got it wrong!' he declared, to a deafening rolling cheer. 'The elites got it wrooong!' A camera swung across the crowd and the image of a child sitting on his father's shoulders clapping his hands above his head flashed up on the giant screens flanking the stage.

Corbyn finished by quoting Shelley's 'The Masque of Anarchy':

Rise like lions after slumber, in unvanquishable number
Shake your chains to earth like dew
Which in sleep had fallen on you –
Ye are many – they are few.

The chant from the crowd bubbled up again, spreading across the elated throng, as Corbyn, who had just turned 68, waved out at the almost indistinguishable sea of bodies, and Glastonbury founder, Michael Eavis, joined him on stage and wrapped an arm around him.

It was 24 June 2017 and the Labour leader had never been stronger. Some in Labour make fun of the idea that Corbyn supporters treat the May 2017 General Election like a victory when, in fact, it was a loss. But in reality, the Labour leader had defied his detractors who were expecting a repeat of Michael Foot's 1983 election drubbing and instead watched Corbyn strip Theresa May of her parliamentary majority.

Moreover, Corbyn had won 40 per cent of the national vote, more than the 35 per cent that handed Tony Blair a significant majority in 2005 (though where those votes came from is something we will return to later). In the short term at least, this unexpected result muzzled Corbyn's most vocal internal critics, who had claimed that voters would always reject his brand of left-wing politics.

Meanwhile, some 130 miles away in a Brixton park, Morgan McSweeney was sitting on a bench, thinking about what the scene at Glastonbury meant for his new job. The day after the 8 June General Election, he had left the Local Government Association to run a new parliamentary group funded by two donors: Jewish businessman and philanthropist Trevor Chinn and hedge fund owner Martin Taylor.

Labour Together, as the operation became known, was explicitly not about trying to defeat Corbyn through any internal coup – they now considered that to be impossible. But it would try to defeat Corbynism – and the Corbynite who would inevitably run in any future contest to lead the party.

Sitting on that Brixton bench, McSweeney was among those who took the 2017 result very seriously and believed that Corbyn, whose politics he despised, could win the next election. Counterintuitively, he found the Glastonbury scene reassuring.

McSweeney later told a friend that he saw this as Corbyn's 'Icarus moment', in which he imagined the Labour leader standing backstage at Glastonbury with a choice: take that election result and turn to the country to cement the deal; or walk into the warm embrace of festival goers, who (McSweeney believed) were unrepresentative of the wider electorate. To him, Corbyn had just flown too close to the sun.

Regardless, he knew Corbyn was riding high, enjoying the overwhelming support of 80 per cent of party members, and for the first time since he had been leader, Labour were ahead in the polls. Corbyn's empathetic response to the survivors of the tragic fire that engulfed London's Grenfell Tower in the days after the election was in stark contrast to Prime Minister Theresa May's refusal to meet victims – a decision that some believed could thwart her premiership within days or weeks.

Today, Labour Together is an influential Starmerite think-tank. Its former director Josh Simons now sits in Parliament as a new MP, switching roles with Jonathan Ashworth who has become the group's CEO after losing his Leicester seat. To some critics, it emerged from a secretive cabal with a 'chilling nature' (according to the author Paul Holden) that has forced Labour to the authoritarian right of the party.[1] To its supporters, it is the vehicle that saved the party with a strategically brilliant plan to win it back from the radical left.

The organisation emerged from an earlier grouping of MPs and strategists named Common Good Labour which drew on the ideas of intellectuals like Labour peer Maurice Glasman (considered the godfather of the 'Blue Labour' movement) and others like the then Dagenham MP Jon Cruddas who, with Jonathan Rutherford, had run a policy review for the former Labour leader, Ed Miliband. Founded in late 2015 by activists trying to understand why Labour had lost, the group was associated with the politics that Rutherford later described in the *New Statesman* of giving people 'the power and responsibility to take control of their lives'.

By then Cruddas, Steve Reed (now MP for Streatham and Croydon North) and Lisa Nandy (MP for Wigan) were involved in the same group of MPs and took the reins of the renamed Labour Together. Rutherford wrote that an early report to dozens of MPs argued that Labour needed to be 'economically radical and fiscally conservative, stop patronising socially conservative voters, and recognise that it was becoming a culturally exclusive party of progressive social liberals.'[2] They all believed that Blairism had ultimately 'hollowed' Labour out and were searching for a new answer.

In a way, the aim was unity of ideas: they wanted to persuade almost everyone in Labour who was not central to the Corbyn project that the party could be rebuilt in his political wake, which some of those involved felt sure would eventually come.

Those who developed Labour Together brought a wide span of political credibility: Steve Reed was more associated with the 'moderate' wing of the party, while Lisa Nandy was widely seen as on the 'soft left' but with arguments about the politics of towns that rooted her in a communitarian politics. Reed's Lambeth work on how councils could engage communities through a cooperative model meant he was pushing for similar solutions.

They knew that some restless colleagues were itching to leave Labour and set up a new entity, and so they pitched Labour Together as a vehicle for anyone who wanted to 'stay and fight'. Some described it to me as trying to 'build a bridge' between those in Labour seen as on the right of the party and the 'soft left' – those MPs more likely to define themselves as socialist and in favour of tax-and-spend policies, but who had also now rejected the Corbyn wing of the party.

With some funding, the founders had enough money to hire one member of staff who could help them to organise and to win support within Labour. Steve Reed knew just the person in Morgan McSweeney.

But why was it that Reed and McSweeney were already so determined to take on Corbynism? Simply because to them this was the politics of the 'hard left'. Reed's experience in Lambeth had greatly influenced his views on this wing of the Labour Party; he would later speak of conspiracy-led politics including anti-Semitic tropes about Jewish people 'controlling the Middle East for capitalist imperialism'.

Reed also told colleagues of the soaring taxes and public service collapse in south London that had convinced him and McSweeney of the need for public sector reform. Sharing reports that outlined a series of failures in Lambeth Council when its leadership was 'hard left', he would warn of corruption and child abuse in the borough's children's homes. He was convinced that a blinkered ideology with negative attitudes towards the police and a refusal to believe what young people were warning of had resulted in the scandal. And for McSweeney, he was not only convinced that anti-Semitism was baked into the world view of the hard left on this wing of politics, but he also opposed its take on international matters as too black and white, including on issues such as Russia and NATO.

When I put some of these complaints to figures who would consider themselves to be on the Corbynite left of Labour, they refuted this description of their politics. They said they would call themselves radical rather than 'hard left', with a span of views on foreign policy, and argued that while the political left is not immune to anti-Semitism, it is not part of their politics and they strongly oppose it. One source also argued that Lambeth had been under the influence of one small part of the left, which wasn't representative of the larger popular movement that backed Corbyn.

For McSweeney, the Labour Together job was a risk, especially in light of Corbyn's bold response to the election defeat, but he decided to give it a go. His first presentation to the group's MPs – who soon would swell to include figures like Shabana Mahmood (Birmingham Ladywood), Jim McMahon (Labour and Co-operative MP for Oldham West), Lucy Powell (Manchester Central), Bridget Phillipson (Houghton and Sunderland South) and Wes Streeting (Ilford North) – was typically eccentric.

McSweeney made clear his mission to those gathered in Reed's parliamentary office: 'to move the Labour Party from the hard left when JC steps down as leader and to reconnect the Labour Party with the country [and] build a sustainable winning electoral coalition ...' He then pointed to a slide of soldiers holding up huge shields, completely covering their bodies. 'Operation Red Shield,' he said. The first job, he argued, was to protect supportive MPs from accusations of disloyalty. The next slide zoomed in on a Greenpeace logo. This would be their model, McSweeney told the gathered MPs: soft branding that made them seem warm and cuddly.

Cruddas and McSweeney even arranged a meeting with Corbyn himself to present the project as consensual. Sitting in the boardroom of the LOTO offices, they told him about Labour Together, saying they were planning a 'renewal' project. Reportedly, one of Corbyn's aides leaned back in his chair, scrolling through social media and not paying much attention to what they were saying.

Early plans focused on building a relationship with at least one trade union, positioning themselves on the left, and thus able to reach out to Corbyn supporters.

So, how much funding did this small parliamentary group attract, and why? Sources tell me that Reed met Trevor Chinn and Martin Taylor through Cruddas and Maurice Glasman, who were already receiving financial support for their 'Blue Labour' ideas. Before 2017, when Labour for the Common Good was set up, Chinn and Taylor decided to 'take a punt' and offered £75,000 to cover the cost of some early research and the first member of staff. When McSweeney took over the director role after the election, the group bid for more backing, winning around £150,000 over three years, with perhaps half a million by the time the Labour leadership campaign got underway. It was also helped with the implicit backing of deputy leader Tom Watson, who told funders he was keen that a number of groups focused on Labour renewal should flourish. Watson's association lent the group credibility with donors and attracted some of its early MPs into the fold.

But there were mistakes. Early on, Labour Together failed to declare £730,000 in donations from millionaire venture capitalists and businessmen, resulting in an Electoral Commission investigation and a fine, though the group blamed 'human error' and said they themselves had self-reported.

All involved were always clear that they would 'need a candidate to win a future leadership election on the political platform we are developing', but they each put a different level of emphasis on that motivation. For McSweeney and Reed, choosing the best person to try to win Labour back from the left was absolutely central. Reed wanted to draw in reams of data and apply rigorous analysis to decide who they should put forward; McSweeney wanted to find the character most likely to win a general election.

But to Cruddas, who had led policy reviews for the former leader Ed Miliband, Labour Together was far more of an intellectual pursuit, to build a policy platform that could unite the party in the future.

Interestingly, in a SWOT (strengths, weaknesses, opportunities, threats) analysis, McSweeney claimed that one of the key problems the group might encounter was 'a Labour government' – making explicit that his concern was not whether Corbyn could win, but that if he were to become prime minister it would prevent the renewal they were focused on.

One of McSweeney's obsessions was the Canary, an alt-left website that had seemed to appear from nowhere and grow to a peak of 8.5 million hits a month. In 2017, the Canary was the UK's 288th most read website, above *The Times*, *Reuters* and the *Daily Star*. Moreover, Corbyn supporters trusted the site equally to the *Guardian*, their other favourite source of information. And so McSweeney had an aim – to schmooze the *Guardian* and kill the Canary.

'Destroy the Canary or the Canary destroys us,' he told the Labour Together MPs.

After a few months working from a park bench, the group funded a small office in Vauxhall, and soon it reached out to former Labour advisers to work alongside them with a focus on online anti-Semitism. In an early review, they identified problem posts in hundreds of Facebook groups with links to either the party or left-wing politics. Some of these were aimed at Labour's female Jewish MPs.

They then farmed out the posts they uncovered to journalists who were themselves reporting on rising evidence of anti-Semitism on the left. Together with a row over whether the party would adopt all the examples linked to the International Holocaust Remembrance Alliance (IHRA) definition of anti-Semitism, the scandal was becoming increasingly destabilising for Corbyn.

One source said the aim was to 'shame' people out of being part of Facebook groups with unacceptable content but argued that it wasn't really working. So, next they took aim at news websites they considered to be either alt-left or alt-right, including Evolve Politics, TR News, Rebel News, Dorset Eye and perhaps not surprisingly, the Canary.

As part of a 'Stop Funding Fake News' campaign, they took screenshots of articles they felt had either racist or fake content, then posted messages on Twitter aimed at brands that were advertising on the websites' pages.

Unquestionably, the readership of the Canary took a hit. In an editorial, the website noted that 'people who don't like our politics have encouraged our advertisers to blacklist us. That's come at a cost.' Its contributors' coverage, it argued, had been targeted at Israel and not Jewish people and said they'd been 'smeared with accusations of anti-Semitism'. However, the result would be a 'much leaner' Canary newsroom with a dedicated team of seven staff members, rather than a network of freelance writers.

As for the *Guardian* schmoozing, I witnessed that first-hand. At the time I was the joint political editor at the newspaper and found myself invited with colleagues to a dinner in a private dining room in the basement of Browns in Covent Garden. We sat on red chairs with gold trimming, set around a long, thin table covered with a white tablecloth, listening to McSweeney, Cruddas, Reed, Nandy and Mahmood tell us about Labour Together's plans for renewal. They had brought with them another MP who was just starting to do more with the group – Keir Starmer. The project was pitched, as planned, with the soft, cuddly Greenpeace framing. They neatly side-stepped our more cynical questions about their plans for a future leadership.

Alongside me that night was *Guardian* news editor Dan Sabbagh, who has since told me he immediately wondered if Starmer was their candidate. Even if McSweeney was wondering about Starmer as a possible leader as early as 2017, it was not spoken about and another hopeful also later emerged from the same group. Back then, the mere prospect of an opportunity to either take control of Labour's leadership or win a general election still felt very distant.

But McSweeney was clear about the type of coalition he would need to build within Labour to support a future leadership bid and was already reaching out to figures on the left of the party. In November 2017, sources describe a quiet and unassuming McSweeney turning up at Dartington Hall in Totnes for an away-day organised by the soft left group, Compass, run by Neal Lawson. There were people there linked to the socialist magazine *Red Pepper*, and others closely allied to Corbyn.

Laura Parker had worked for the Labour leader. The former civil servant, in her mid-40s with the smart look of a CEO, stood out somewhat in contrast with his army of younger and much more casually dressed aides. But Parker was a committed socialist who had recently moved over to become national coordinator of the Corbyn-supporting grassroots movement, Momentum. The event was full of people who might be classified as at the softer end of the radical left, or the radical end of the soft left – the exact type of people that Labour Together wanted to unite with those in the centre and to the right of the party.

With two major challenges brewing – the party's restless MPs on one hand, and members still uber-loyal to Corbyn on the other – Labour Together MPs would meet regularly in Reed's parliamentary office to discuss their next steps.

The growing desire of some Labour backbenchers to break away from Corbyn's control and set up alone was seen as a major problem. Chris Leslie, Chuka Umunna, Gavin Shuker and others were also meeting regularly to discuss the possibility of a breakaway party – an idea that was an anathema to Labour Together, whose entire raison d'être was to try to win back and rebuild this century-old political institution. They did not believe that the core Labour membership had become 'cult-like' and were convinced it could be persuaded to back a more moderate candidate. But, if sixty or seventy Labour MPs walked away, they knew their efforts would be in vain.

McSweeney had visited Chris Leslie in his constituency of Nottingham East, armed with data he hoped might persuade him to stay on board. The argument Labour Together wanted to make was that while Labour members were loyal to Corbyn now, their real loyalty was to their own idealistic politics. McSweeney set out part of his argument on slides in presentations, under the letter heading, 'V.U.C.A.' Politics, he said, was 'Volatile, Uncertain, Chaotic and Ambiguous', so there was no point trying to predict anything.

Key centrists in the Labour Party were also unconvinced by the breakaway plan, including the MP who chaired the Progress group, Alison McGovern. She and Progress director Richard Angell wrote to Shuker (then MP for Luton South) to warn that the group would not support any breakaway. The deputy leader Tom Watson was also working harder to keep people inside the Labour movement. And on a different wing of the party, Shadow Chancellor John McDonnell shared the same fears about MPs walking away, claiming that a desire to avoid that outcome was one of the main reasons he backed the party edging towards a softer Brexit and second referendum, even though he knew that would also be electorally risky.

In the end, the various counter arguments clearly landed with a number of the MPs who were wobbling. Around twenty politicians led by Shuker had been meeting at a Sussex farmhouse, but when it came to it, on 18 February, only seven MPs walked through the room full of journalists and onto a stage at the launch of The Independent Group, as they were then known.

Luciana Berger, whose decision to defect was best understood by colleagues after she faced an onslaught of anti-Semitic abuse online, began her speech: 'I am the Labour and …' pausing as the room laughed and she started again.

'I am the Member of Parliament for Liverpool Wavertree,' she said, dropping the name of the party she had first stood for in 2010, and explaining her decision to resign. Another Labour MP would join the new grouping – which along with Umunna, Leslie and Shuker, now included three Tories – before it would relaunch as 'Change UK', hoping to mirror Emmanuel Macron's *En Marche* revolution across the Channel.

At that moment, the implications of this split felt huge. Looking back at political news stories with so-called 'cut-through' in 2019, few matched the emergence of Change UK. But the incipient revolution turned out to be a damp squib, and years later when Starmer welcomed Luciana Berger back into his party, he would see it as a huge coup, and a sign that his zero-tolerance approach to anti-Semitism was working.

Soon after the Change UK MPs left the Labour Party, Labour Together sent a document to prospective donors, which has since been leaked to me. It warned that the Labour Party was 'politically and morally in a crisis' claiming the 'Hard left […] will divide our party, condemn us to electoral defeat, attempt to drive out democratic socialists and corrupt our moral purpose in the interest of ideological aims.'

Whether it was written by McSweeney or not, I'm unsure. But the document set out three potential options for Labour's 'moderates'. The first, to set up a new party, was rejected because the paper argued that every option to keep Labour together should be exhausted first. 'Once it is attempted there is no way back,' it warned, arguing there was insufficient evidence that a new party could flourish in the UK's first-past-the-post system.

The second, to try to attract 220,000 new members to Labour and to challenge Corbyn, was also ruled out because by then Corbyn's 68 per cent support among members, while slightly down, was still too high to be challenged. 'Logistically this looks nearly impossible,' the document added.

And so, to the final option: to 'win a majority position from within the current Labour Party when Jeremy Corbyn leaves his position and/or is defeated in a General Election. [...] The route we are travelling is the third one,' the paper declared, before setting out why Labour Together believed it could find a winning candidate.

The document made clear what these moderates saw as their problem: a 'hard left' in control of the party machinery, including Labour's National Executive Committee (NEC) and most regional boards. To achieve their aims, they would need to dominate the communication channels that party members most trusted; capture the political territory that the 'soft left' cared about most, for example social justice; and avoid the looming threat of sympathetic politicians facing deselection by a membership that had lost trust in MPs.

This was not the only Labour renewal document being circulated among potential donors, and there were still many significant figures opposed to Corbyn's leadership who were said to be unsure about this direction of travel. While Tony Blair was publicly insisting that he would not 'advocate' for a new party, sources have suggested the former prime minister was among those who believed Labour was finished.

One group, 'United for Change', backed by donor Simon Franks, believed it could seize an anti-politics sentiment with a new movement. Another funding document shared with donors was called 'Political Movement, Planning Document'. It's still not clear who was behind it but it argued that 'Britain is stuck' and the 'old left/right binary divide can no longer provide a platform that meets the challenges of today'. It called for a new movement to take on traditional parties.

Labour Together was building the opposite strategy. Part of the effort was to reach out to groups across Labour like the Fabian Society, Blue Labour and Red Shift while also winning the trust of more party-focused media outlets like LabourList (McSweeney even tried to get onto its board).

Meanwhile, Bridget Phillipson, now education secretary, was sent to Scotland, where money from donors was being used to run focus groups that would help them understand if Labour could start winning back seats north of the border. A few surprise wins in 2017 had boosted their hopes. One notable piece of feedback was that Scottish voters wanted a stronger Scottish voice in Labour ranks, highlighting the historic strength of leading parliamentarians from Gordon Brown to Robin Cook and Alistair Darling.

In a report, Phillipson and her aide Scott Dickson argued that Scottish voters would take their time to forgive Labour for perceived complacency during the 2014 Scottish Referendum and warned that the way in which Brexit had played out added another layer of complexity. They said that Labour/Conservative switchers seemed more winnable than those who had switched to the SNP and concluded that there was a 'substantial mountain to climb'.

But there were more pressing concerns for Labour Together as Corbyn finally began to take control of a series of levers within the Labour Party, such as the NEC. McSweeney and co's first obsession had to be the membership.

At one meeting, McSweeney gathered MPs together to scour their data. Their polling suggested Labour members could be split into three groups. On the left were 25 per cent who the group labelled 'ideologues' – true believers in the Corbyn project. To the right were another 25 per cent of 'instrumentalists' – those on the Blairite wing of Labour, who would always be opposed to Corbyn. The members of both of these groups were more likely to be men. But in the middle lay a bigger group representing 50 per cent of the Labour membership that they labelled 'idealists'. The idealists were more likely to be female, younger, liberal, university-educated, Remain-supporting and – most critical for Labour Together – persuadable.

In a way, MPs were able to quickly test out McSweeney's theories as many of them had to go through what was known as a 'trigger-ballot process', in which party members would be given the chance to boot out sitting politicians and choose fresh candidates. There was a fear that hostility from Corbynite members towards certain MPs could result in some being ousted from the party.

Progress' Alison McGovern MP was one of the first to face the selection vote. She and the organisers she worked with wanted a 'wedge issue' that would demonstrate unity between their politics and that of members. One issue stood out beyond others: a joint passion for the EU and despair at Britain's choice to exit the political union. With this insight, along with the information from McSweeney's data, McGovern was able to win the ballot in her own seat and then help colleagues to do the same.

Labour Together's strategy seemed to be working – but could they agree on the perfect candidate?

The 'Corbyn factor' was a powerful and very real phenomenon. I saw it in play for myself when I was covering the 2017 election campaign. I trailed the Labour leader around the country and witnessed what felt like an almost cult-like response to his presence. In a heaving carpark in Reading, packed full of acolytes despite just two days' notice of the event, a woman breathlessly set out why she loved the Labour leader so much. 'Honesty, integrity, authenticity,' she said, her words punctuated by the shouts of 'Corbyn! Corbyn! Corbyn!' from the crowd.

'In thirty years we haven't seen something like this,' said another man, as I squeezed through the crush.

In Middlesborough I watched people wait four hours to glimpse him, in the pouring rain, some swooning with excitement when he finally arrived. One woman was desperate for him to pose for a selfie with her dog.

And at Prenton Park, the ground of Tranmere Rovers in Birkenhead, that familiar chant: 'Oooooohhh Jer-emy Cor-byn!'

Most of the people at these rallies did not strike me as being on the extreme left of politics. Instead, I met teachers, doctors, nurses, who had voted for Tony Blair's Labour and then had become disillusioned, first due to the Iraq War, then the years of austerity. For them, politics felt broken and they just yearned for change.

What I was seeing was very similar to what that Labour Together polling had set out. They knew what these people cared most about: issues like housing, poverty and Britain's membership of the EU. Corbyn had built a bridge between these idealistic supporters and the more hardcore political grouping to their left. Labour Together's mission was to sever that tie and bring together a new coalition between the centre and the right of the party.

To test out how to reach out to these Labour members, the group got involved in internal campaigns including the selection for Labour's mayoral candidate in Lewisham. One hopeful, Damian Egan, grew up on a council estate with his mother and sister, in a family that twice experienced homelessness. Stressing his belief that everyone had a right to a secure home, Egan won the contest on the first ballot. Shabana Mahmood also helped Labour MP Liam Byrne to beat two Corbynites to become Labour's candidate for the mayoralty in the West Midlands, although he was eventually defeated by the Conservative Andy Street.

According to sources, initially Labour Together's polling suggested three candidates who looked most likely to do well in the overall party leadership contest – Shadow Chancellor, John McDonnell; Shadow Foreign Secretary Emily Thornberry; and Shadow Brexit Secretary Sir Keir Starmer. Some of the group were convinced that Starmer had the best chance of success on the grounds that he was liked and respected by 'idealistic' Labour members; he had shown the loyalty they demanded; he had a brief that allowed him to reach out to members' Remainer instincts; and his background as former director of public prosecutions ensured prime ministerial authority.

Not everyone agreed. At the final meeting before the general election, Lisa Nandy suggested that she had a different idea before promptly leaving the room. The next McSweeney and Reed heard from her was an announcement that she too would be running, warning the party that, 'Unless we change course, we will become irrelevant.' Nandy attracted Cruddas's support while Wes Streeting headed in a different direction to run Jess Phillips's campaign.

Starmer's core team believed that neither Nandy nor Phillips were positioned well enough to reach out to that 50 per cent of Labour members in the centre. In Nandy's case, some argued that she had not served Corbyn since 2016 and, with her Wigan voters in mind, had pursued a more pro-Brexit position which would not appeal to enough members. Polling also suggested a lack of name recognition. The one candidate who they knew was well placed was Emily Thornberry, but they felt she would lack sufficient support among MPs to get onto the ballot.

Throughout this period, those working with Starmer urged him to remain in the shadow cabinet, even if he wobbled. They claim that when he once said he did want to quit – over anti-Semitism – MP colleagues told him he must stay put.

The opponent they all feared the most was the one who would be carrying the Corbynite flag, Rebecca Long-Bailey, although they were relieved it was not John McDonnell, who had made clear he had no intention of running.

But could key figures in Labour Together really not find a single female candidate who fit their brief and could beat Long-Bailey to the final prize? What exactly is the Labour Party's problem with women leaders? Some of those involved loved Nandy's politics, and yet judged her to be unable to win. They would argue, perhaps, that they saw the outcome of the leadership race as a matter of life or death for the Labour Party, so they simply had to embrace the candidate most likely to succeed. And, no doubt, Starmer has plenty of leadership qualities. Moreover, key figures like McSweeney and Reed had both backed Liz Kendall for the leadership back in 2015, so ostensibly had no issue with female leadership.

And yet I can't help but feel that the idea that members and voters might consider Starmer (who was up against four women) the most 'prime ministerial' cannot be completely unwound from the glaring fact that he is a man. Long-Bailey's friends were struck by how often people commented that she seemed young and inexperienced, despite being in her 40s – and older than Rishi Sunak. One female

Labour MP argued that left-wing politicians tend to be more disruptive than those on the right, and furthermore that 'women who challenge the status quo are seen as threatening', making it harder for them to reach the very top. Meanwhile, the Conservative Party had already crowned three female prime ministers.

For his part, McSweeney was persuaded by Starmer's politics, telling his wife, Imogen Walker, that he believed the former DPP had a visceral understanding of voters' concerns about crime. If he had any misgiving it was that Starmer's history at the Crown Prosecution Service might pose a problem for Labour members. Friends say Walker encouraged him to back the candidate who he believed would make the best prime minister.

In the summer of 2019, McSweeney became much more heavily involved in preparing Starmer for an ultimate campaign. By then Jenny Chapman and her husband, Nick Smith – along with Chris Ward, Ben Nunn and Starmer himself – had been meeting regularly at Chapman and Smith's London home. Named after the street the couple lived on, this would become known as the Arlington Group.

It was there that Chapman first met McSweeney. With shared politics, the two instantly hit it off, talking not only about politics but psychology, with a shared interest in the author Jonathan Haidt and what they could learn about how to win an argument. One thing was very clear: the message to the hundreds of thousands of members who had backed Corbyn must not be that they were wrong.

Another obsession was the so-called 'efficiency' of the vote, which had been key back in the noughties in Lambeth, where McSweeney and Reed had calculated which 13,000 voters would help them to win over the entire borough. Chapman could see how inefficient Labour's vote had become and would sometimes spar about it with her shadow ministerial colleague, Matthew Pennycook. If Pennycook ever complained about losing voters to the Liberal Democrats, Chapman would argue that with a 20,000-plus majority in Greenwich and Woolwich, he could afford to. Friends described her declaring, 'Good!' to his losses, warning that she had a majority of just over 3,000 in the northern town of Darlington and that Labour's offer was too skewed towards the large cities.

McSweeney presented the data to the team, and Nunn wrote on a Post-it note the three words he wanted to dominate the campaign: 'Unity. Radical. Win.' To persuade the party membership to back Starmer they believed they needed to unify the centre and right of its coalition; offer a radical agenda focused on issues like housing and poverty; and argue that Starmer was best placed to win a general election.

But first they needed to wait for Corbyn to have his turn with the electorate.

PART II

Leader of the Opposition

5

Leaning Left

Dozens of men and a scattering of women were gathered in a large, open-plan room lined with white pillars and bright strip-lights. Most were standing in silence, staring at the television screens dotted all around. And then suddenly, they erupted. 'Yeeeeesssss!' they screamed, bouncing up and down and flinging their arms into the air as if England had just scored the winning goal in the World Cup final.

It was 10 p.m. on election night, Thursday 12 December 2019; the venue, Conservative Party headquarters. In a video, shot from the back of the room, to the right of the throng, a man with dark hair and a beard wrapped his arms around his partner with a smile on his face. 'Ooooooh Isaac Levido', began to echo out to the tune of 'Seven Nation Army' by the White Stripes, a copy of the 2017 'Jeremy Corbyn' chant but dedicated here to the Australian-born campaign director who had just made Boris Johnson's night. The exit poll had placed the Tories on track for a hefty victory.

Johnson himself was inside Downing Street's Thatcher Room watching the result with family and his closest aides, including key strategist Dominic Cummings and communications chief Lee Cain. The pair had worked closely with Johnson ever since their time together on the 2016 Vote Leave Brexit campaign, and they'd brought some of their controversial and aggressive campaigning techniques to the Number 10 operation. For a start, since becoming PM – less than five months earlier – Johnson had prorogued Parliament and booted twenty-one Conservative MPs out of the party, including two former chancellors and Winston Churchill's grandson Nicholas Soames, for rebelling with the aim of blocking a no-deal Brexit. The conflict resulted in the PM's own brother Jo Johnson resigning from government.

A source suggested this style of leadership was a 'madman' strategy, a term originally associated with US president Richard Nixon who was said to portray himself as unpredictable and volatile in order to scare communist countries into thinking that he might just be crazy enough to press the nuclear button. Would Johnson's volatility persuade Brussels that he was prepared to crash out of the EU without a deal? Some close to Johnson say he had no choice, because, from day one of his premiership, if he failed to reach an answer on Brexit his 'head was on the chopping board'.

Cain told Cummings the size of the Tory win that December was vindication of their forthright strategy. Cummings wasn't so sure. Not convinced that Johnson really believed in Cummings's project to shake things up in government, and concerned that his wife Carrie would now want to bring her own people in, he replied, 'We've won too big, they won't need us now.'

In the months ahead those tensions would explode, but at that moment the Conservative Party was simply delighted. In Conservative Campaign Headquarters (CCHQ), Levido climbed onto a table and told the crowded room that those who wanted to continue to drink and celebrate should do so downstairs, because there was still plenty of work to do. For many in the room, the result was not a total surprise. Just days ahead of the election, the company responsible for all the Conservatives' data modelling – Stack Data Strategy – started to predict unexpected wins in seats like Redcar and Burnley, telling Johnson that he looked to be on track for a majority of around eighty.

Labour's Shadow Chancellor John McDonnell had prepared for a grim result but, hoping against hope, had dragged himself exhausted to the BBC studios where he met the exit poll with a moment of resigned silence. As the numbers flashed up on the screen, presenter Andrew Neil, who himself had been frustrated by Boris Johnson's point-blank refusal to be interviewed by him during the campaign, was said to lean towards McDonnell and whisper, 'Johnson didn't deserve that.' Then they were on air and Neil turned to camera and with a booming voice announced: 'If this exit poll is anywhere near right this result is a catastrophe for you, Jeremy Corbyn, and the Labour Party.' A weary looking McDonnell agreed as he reached for an explanation.

Later that night, the Labour leadership set out its reasoning for such a poor showing in a press release. It suggested that the result was 'overwhelmingly down to one issue – the divisions in the country over Brexit; and the Tory campaign, echoed by most of the media, to persuade people that only Boris Johnson can "get Brexit done".'[1] It insisted that Labour had changed the terms of the debate during the campaign, placing public ownership, a green industrial revolution, and an end to austerity centre stage. But it also admitted that the party would need to learn the lessons of this defeat, 'above all by listening to those lifelong voters who we lost in working-class communities.'

Others in the party were turning in a different direction, pointing the finger of blame firmly towards Corbyn himself and the anti-Semitism crisis that had long engulfed the party. Although Corbyn had planned to stay and fight whatever the 2017 result, this time he announced that same night that he would not contest another general election as Labour leader.

For Starmer, who was at his home in north London watching the results with his wife and close aides, including Chris Ward and Ben Nunn, the result marked the beginning of a new campaign. But it was one, into which he knew he had to be cautious about stepping. Friends say Starmer was taken aback by the scale of the defeat and worried about friends who were about to lose their seats. He rang Jenny Chapman in Darlington. She was at her friend Veronica's house, where food was laid out on the kitchen table – the fuel they would need to get them through a difficult night. The moment she saw the exit poll, she knew she was gone. As Chapman headed to the count, the advice of a former colleague was ringing in her ears – whatever else happens, try not to embarrass your children. Chapman was determined not to cry on live television that night.

At least she knew that she had a new job to go to. After getting her team through the next few days, Chapman would head to London to chair Starmer's party leadership campaign: a further reason why she was deliberately careful with her language and demeanour that night.

Elsewhere, though, Labour colleagues were letting rip. 'Has Jeremy Corbyn cost you your job tonight?' a reporter asked outgoing MP Gareth Snell in Stoke-on-Trent Central.

'Erm … probably,' he said.

'Absolutely, completely,' added Ruth Smeeth, who had lost in Stoke-on-Trent North.

On ITV that night Jon Lansman, founder of the left-wing activist group Momentum, clashed furiously with former Labour home secretary, Alan Johnson. As Lansman argued that the problem was that voters were not persuaded by Labour's Brexit position, but that the anti-austerity policies the party had set out were popular, Johnson spat back. 'Corbyn was a disaster on the doorstep. Everyone knew he couldn't lead the working class out of a paper bag,' he said, calling the movement a 'cult' and describing this as Labour's worst result since 1935. 'Go back to your student politics,' he quipped.

But in Darlington Chapman offered only muted criticism of Corbyn, acutely aware that many Labour members still admired their party leader; members she now needed to back her man.

Morgan McSweeney, meanwhile, had been helping his old ally Jon Cruddas in Dagenham, but after the exit poll he drove to north London to see Starmer. According to some of those close to the ensuing leadership campaign, the first job for Team Starmer was 'to roll the pitch'. In particular, they wanted to neutralise two likely attacks: did Labour really need another man? And how could a politician representing north London truly understand the collapse of dozens of Red Wall seats across the Midlands and North of England?

Chapman was chosen for this job; a week later she published a piece in the *Mirror* arguing that if a leader's gender or location had been key, then the people of Darlington would not have picked 'an old Etonian [man] from Islington who speaks Latin' to be their prime minister. Voters, she contended, wanted someone to protect their 'national security, their children's future, their mortgages, their pensions', and they had made clear at this election that they did not trust Corbyn and Labour to do that.

Continuing the argument on Radio 4's *Today* programme the next morning, she suggested it would be patronising to suggest voters simply needed a leader with ovaries and a northern accent. They wanted someone they could see as prime minister. Chapman hinted that she was so convinced that Keir Starmer was the right choice and that she would sit in his office until he agreed to stand. But, of course, she knew he needed no persuading: his leadership campaign was already up and running.

On the left of the party, as out-going shadow chancellor John McDonnell grappled with how to save Corbynism, even though Corbyn himself was on his way out, he understood that Starmer posed the biggest threat. Membership polling suggested the left's best hope was McDonnell himself, but there was no chance of that. He had suffered a heart attack in 2014 and felt physically unable to do it, particularly after years of (in his view) fighting off attempted coups within Labour, including from the likes of Peter Mandelson who once said he worked every day to try to undermine Corbyn. McDonnell wanted a woman to run, and personally backed Rebecca Long-Bailey. But why not Angela Rayner who had also remained loyal to Corbyn? Sources tell me that McDonnell saw Rayner as further to the right, having clashed with her over scrapping tuition fees, which she didn't believe was the right spending priority.

Some on the left of the party admit themselves that they had failed to do any serious succession planning in advance and so the launch of Long-Bailey's campaign was chaotic. Emotions were still raw from the election defeat and there were claims that Long-Bailey's heart wasn't really in it. But she told friends that she had a 'moral duty to carry on'; to try to fight to save the policy agenda Corbyn had carried into the 2019 election.

The timetable for the election was set by the party's National Executive Committee (NEC) on 6 January 2020. After securing enough MP nominations (Clive Lewis dropped out after falling short), on 13 January 2020 Starmer, Rebecca Long-Bailey, Lisa Nandy, Jess Phillips and Emily Thornberry proceeded to the next stage of the contest. And then, with union and constituency Labour Party support totted up, the competition narrowed to the top three candidates, with Starmer by then the favourite to win.[2] He had been nominated by 88 MPs and Unison; Long-Bailey by 33 and Unite; Nandy by 31 and the GMB. Angela Rayner would later emerge as favourite to be elected deputy leader.

As planned, Starmer's campaign was framed around those three words scrawled on Nunn's old Post-it note: 'Unity. Radical. Win'. On the first point, he reached across the Labour Party for support. The new ally who was perhaps most critical in building Starmer's credibility on the left was Simon Fletcher, who began his career working for the veteran socialist Tony Benn, later becoming chief of staff to Ken Livingstone as London mayor and then one of Corbyn's key aides. Fletcher not only backed Starmer but went to work for him (a decision he would later say he regretted), writing in the *Huffington Post* that what had persuaded him was a 'refusal to over-steer away from Labour's radical policy framework [and] a commitment to seek to unify the party'. And Fletcher was not alone.

McSweeney had met Momentum's national coordinator Laura Parker at that away-day in Totnes in 2017 and had stayed in touch with her ever since. Their discussions had not been about a future leadership campaign or Starmer, though, but Labour's position on the EU. Parker, a Remainer who had strongly advocated for a second referendum, ultimately wanted a return of free movement. When Starmer told the Labour Party conference in 2018 that 'Remain' would be on the ballot in a fresh vote, Parker was one of those who had jumped to her feet and applauded passionately. Distrust of Brexit was such a dominant sentiment on the left and right of the Labour Party, that it allowed Starmer to reach out in both directions.

Parker was not totally sold on Starmer, preferring the politics of the Labour MP Clive Lewis. But when the latter failed to get onto the ballot, she backed Starmer because she preferred his position on the EU to that of either Long-Bailey or Nandy. With her own background running children's rights charities, she was also wooed by his legal past as a human rights barrister. And then there was his other promise – the second word on Nunn's Post-it note: 'Radical' – to pursue a left-wing agenda. This matched her priorities.

'Jeremy Corbyn made our party the party of anti-austerity and he was right to do so!' declared an animated looking Starmer, standing on a stage in a dark suit and white shirt. 'We must retain that. We build on that. We don't trash it,' he boomed.

Gesticulating passionately, he added: 'We should treat, if you like, the 2017 manifesto as our foundational document. The radicalism and the hope that inspired across the country was real – anyone who knocked on a door in that election knows it was real. We have to hang on to that.'

At moments like this, some of those close to Long-Bailey's team concluded that she and Starmer were running similar campaigns – 'two socialists in a suit'. Lisa Nandy, although previously always seen to be on the centre left within Labour, was the one who ended up positioned to their right politically. She wowed the media with her impressive performances and tough messaging to a party she claimed had abandoned its traditional strongholds. But her previous argument, that a second referendum would be a 'final breach of trust' with working-class voters, was perhaps not what Labour members wanted to hear.

Parker was sold enough on Starmer to allow his team to include a quote from her saying she trusted him on 'social justice' in his campaign material. One pamphlet folded out into a giant poster of the candidate, with the words, 'Integrity, authority, unity'.

When Starmer went further than some expected and laid out ten pledges that had been drawn up by Simon Fletcher and Chris Ward, his radical credentials were almost certainly cemented with the left. Part of the idea was to neutralise attacks from Long-Bailey's team about tax policy and nationalisation. Each pledge actually carried multiple policies, and within a long list were promises to: increase tax for the top 5 per cent of earners; end the Tories 'cruel' welfare sanctions; abolish tuition fees; oppose 'illegal wars'; support common ownership of rail, mail, energy and water; offer full voting rights for EU nationals; defend free movement as we left the EU; abolish the House of Lords; introduce a green new deal; and a move to radical devolution. Also during the campaign Starmer insisted that he was in favour of changing Britain's voting system.

Certain key figures in Starmer's team have since tried to distance themselves from those ten pledges, although as far as I can tell they had been agreed internally at the time. Some today think that through them he leaned further to the left than was necessary to win over Labour's membership. Others argue that Starmer truly believed in what he was saying, but that the world has since changed, with the reality of the financial impact of Covid and then the mini-budget making it harder now to fulfil some of those promises. Starmer would later argue that the financial situation forced political choices like opting for extra NHS appointments over that promise to scrap tuition fees. He would also point out that a green prosperity plan, radical devolution, and state ownership in rail and renewable energy, if not the Royal Mail and water, would go ahead.

Nevertheless, Starmer's shift from a Corbyn-friendly radical candidate, to a fiscally cautious leader of the opposition and now prime minister, continues to raise questions around trust. When I spent three months following him for ITV's *Tonight* programme, it was an issue I pressed him on. At one point, we travelled to the University of Leeds where he was a student and I pulled out a copy of the radical Trotskyist magazine *Socialist Alternatives*, which he had been involved in in the early 1980s. Inside he had argued that collective bargaining wasn't left-wing enough and opined about the damage that Margaret Thatcher had wreaked as prime minister. Did Starmer still agree with what he had written aged 22? Not all of it, he suggested, and who would? But he did believe that Thatcher was guilty of an 'authoritarian onslaught'.

And what about Corbyn, I went on. 'Hand on heart, did you want him to be prime minister?'

'I didn't think the Labour Party was in a position to win the last election,' said Starmer, in response.

'But you travelled across the country to campaign for him,' I continued.

Starmer reasoned that he believed it was his responsibility to provide political opposition over the question of Brexit after the 2016 EU Referendum. However, his warmth towards Corbyn's radical domestic policy ideas seemed long gone, and he even attacked Rishi Sunak in the 2024 campaign for producing a 'Jeremy Corbyn-style manifesto' full of unfunded commitments.

And what of his belief in the redistribution of wealth, which Laura Parker had so welcomed when she backed him? 'If you are prime minister, would you want to take more money from the super-rich and redistribute it to the poorest?' I asked him.

'No,' he replied. 'That isn't how I want to grow the economy. Of course, I believe in redistribution, but I don't think redistribution is the sort of one-word answer for millions of people across the country.' Instead, Starmer spoke of 'ambition' and a desire that people would find secure, skilled jobs, arguing that redistribution on its own 'fundamentally disrespects individuals'. And when I pressed him on inequality, he would talk about regional inequality rather than income inequality.

But there was another theme that he kept coming back to during the time I spent with him. Standing outside the Emirates Stadium, where Starmer was about to head in to watch his beloved Arsenal, I asked him about the similarities between football and politics. 'It's all about winning,' he said, adding that he did not agree with those people who claim it is the 'taking part that counts'.

Back in 2020, of course, 'win' was the third word on Nunn's scribbled note. As the contest drew on, this was the one he would underline. Starmer's communications adviser became increasingly convinced that, while in 2016 a large number of Labour members claimed they would rather Labour was defeated in a general election than compromise its principles, something had shifted. By 2020 they had become sick of losing and simply wanted to pick a winner.

Starmer and his team travelled the country for one hustings event after another. The campaign was gruelling but those accompanying him said he always tried to make them laugh. On one rail journey, Starmer joked with the catering manager that he could see himself doing his job, and so he was encouraged to do so, pushing the trolley down the train and serving customers.

There were also the inevitable attacks on his personality. Fairly late in the contest I hosted a hustings in Manchester. I asked Starmer about an interview he had done the day before with LBC's Nick Ferrari, who quoted a *Financial Times* piece stating that Starmer was a bit 'boring', and then asked him to name the most exciting thing he'd ever done.

'Is it really taking your children to the football?' I asked. I saw a flash of anger, then Starmer snapped back, 'These questions are somehow supposed to be the measure of us, and they are so, so pathetic.'

That day the crowd roared with delight, but the 'boring' question would follow Starmer at least some of the way to Downing Street; when asked to describe him, voters so often repeated the word to pollsters. When I put it to him again a few years later, Starmer quoted the late former chancellor Alistair Darling. 'He used to say – if they are calling you boring, you're winning,' he said, with a smile. When voters came up to him in the street, he argued, they didn't say: 'Can you entertain me? Tell me a joke.'

'They say, "Do you understand what it's like for me? Do you know what choices I'm having to make, and have you got a plan to do something about it?"'

There was also abuse. His aide Yasmeen Sebbana once answered the phone to a man who screamed that he would come to Parliament to kill Starmer, a threat taken seriously enough to result in court proceedings. Starmer's biggest concern was always for his family's safety and wellbeing, and he hated it when journalists turned up on the doorstep.

But the most difficult thing during the campaign was a terrible tragedy in the middle of it all. One day a colleague passed Starmer a message telling him to call his wife, Vic, urgently. Her mother Barbara had been in an accident and was being moved to intensive care. Two weeks later, she died.

What motivated Starmer to enter the leadership campaign in the first place? His old friend Parvais Jabbar tells me one thing that doesn't drive Starmer is 'money'. 'Not because he was wealthy, but because it wasn't a motivating factor over and above needing it for a purpose. That purpose was usually to look after his parents and siblings. He was like a substitute father in his family – he always made sure he could support [them] financially for the basic stuff – nothing extravagant.'

And it was his family he turned to when, at one point in the campaign, Starmer was asked on a Zoom call with members of his closest team: 'Why do you want to do this?' He told the group about his brother, Nick, who according to Starmer's biographer Tom Baldwin suffered complications during birth and had fairly severe learning difficulties. In the book Starmer is quoted as saying his brother was 'dealt a very different set of cards to me and he's had problems all his life – problems I've never had to face.' But Rodney Starmer would tell his son: 'Nick has achieved as much as you, Keir.'

And so it was his parents' equal treatment of their children that he pointed to as a key motivating factor for his politics.

In the final weeks of the campaign, following London Mayor Sadiq Khan's endorsement on 26 February and former PM Gordon Brown's on 5 March, support for Starmer mounted. A week later the party decided to cancel the special conference at which the leadership result was due to be announced in light of the news that ten people had died in the UK after contracting a new virus that had first been detected in China. By then, there were 596 cases of Coronavirus (Covid) in Britain, the start of a devastating global pandemic that would have a traumatic impact on the nation and dominate our politics for years to come.

On 16 March 2020, Prime Minister Boris Johnson addressed the country, calling for everyone to cease non-essential contact with others, to stop all unnecessary travel and to work from home where they possibly could. So, when Starmer was elected leader of the Labour Party there was none of the usual fanfare. Instead, he delivered his response in a pre-recorded video from home. Ben Nunn, dressed in his running gear, had carried a lectern around to Starmer's house and left it on the doorstep, texting his boss to let him know it was there, not realising that he had just been snapped by a passer-by who sent the photograph to the *Daily Mail*. Two days later, Nunn and his wife Florence Wilkinson returned to film Starmer, standing alone in front of the white shutters of his north London home, as he spoke of Covid bringing normal life to a halt. He also acknowledged that he recognised the scale of Labour's task; and paid tribute to his 'friend' and colleague, Jeremy Corbyn.

Most Labour staff were working remotely from home, but a small group went to collect the material the team needed from the leader of the opposition's offices in the sprawl of rooms just off Portcullis House. In one area the new team found a whiteboard, and on it was scrawled what looked like a rudimentary plan to prepare for the 2019 election. It simply read: 'Day 1: GE called; Day 2: Brexit position speech; Day 3: Landmark Policy; Day 4: –'. Blank.

Afterwards the team logged on to a video call to discuss the next steps. As the new chief of staff, Morgan McSweeney would lead the discussion. In a tone described by others on the call as calm and 'cool', without excitement, he said: 'We've just been given the key to the leader of the opposition's office. Our job is to hand that key to the Conservatives at the next election.'

In April 2020, it seemed almost impossible to imagine that happening within the span of a single parliament.

6

Covid

Some say that Boris Johnson's victory in December 2019 made the Conservative Party feel invincible – and that led to mistakes. One source close to the Downing Street operation during the Johnson years believes that the assumption the party would be in power for ten or even fifteen years embedded an unhealthy complacency in government; a sense that they had plenty of time and so could afford to 'go slow'.

Johnson himself went on holiday that first Christmas and while there was urgency around Brexit, they thought they need not necessarily rush to deliver on the Tory's other big election promise to 'level up' the country. Meanwhile, the prime minister's Vote Leave advisers were urging him to shake things up with sweeping deregulation, planning reform and tax changes. But according to one insider these changes would have been very 'noisy' and Johnson did not want to rock the boat. Instead, there was an idea to bring in 'big thinkers' and draw up longer-term plans; a mindset that had set in when Covid hit.

Everyone knows how utterly discombobulating that period was, as we hurtled into the worst health crisis to hit the planet in more than a century. We now know that during those long months of the lockdowns some shocking failures of government were taking place behind the scenes. In July 2024, I went to the 'lock in' for the first report of Baroness Hallett's public inquiry into the handling of the pandemic. After handing over my phone, I sat down and started to read her 83,000-word conclusion outlining just how ill-prepared we were as a country. By preparing for the wrong pandemic (flu and not Covid) and allowing our health service to be stretched to breaking point, the Westminster government and every devolved administration had 'failed its citizens', she found.

Inside Number 10 there were growing tensions between Johnson and his chief strategist Dominic Cummings. A Downing Street source tells me that when the pair were aligned on the issue of Brexit they were a 'formidable political team', but their instincts divided over how to handle the pandemic. One major problem, as Baroness Hallett noted, was that they had been preparing for the 'wrong war' with that outdated 2011 plan on how to handle an influenza pandemic. The speed at which flu spreads makes containment difficult, so the strategy focused on closing pubs and clubs but only locking down the most vulnerable, while for others the illness would spread and herd immunity would build.

Introducing a full lockdown was rightly seen as a very big deal. As the scientist John Edmunds, a member of the government's Scientific Advisory Group for Emergencies (SAGE) committee, recently told me – no one was thinking about a lockdown from the outset because keeping people in their homes is an extreme step, the 'nuclear option', and one that cannot be chosen easily. Sources say Johnson had been keen to allow Covid to 'sweep through' but that policy was shut down on 14 March when Downing Street's data experts gathered together the most important government figures and laid out the risks of inaction. Some of those who attended describe this meeting as akin to a scene in a 'Jeff Goldblum disaster movie', with one warning that it might become necessary to requisition ice-rinks to store bodies.

The pandemic pitted government departments against each other. Health Secretary Matt Hancock and Chancellor of the Duchy of

Lancaster Michael Gove urged maximum restrictions, while chancellor Rishi Sunak tried to resist, warning of the economic consequences. During one heated session, as one side argued that pubs and clubs must close because they were vectors for the virus, and the other insisted they stay open to avoid the dire economic fallout, one of the government's most senior figures suggested that they allow them to operate but tell the public not to go to them.

Later, when there were fears about a second wave and a circuit-breaker or further lockdown was being debated, another source told me about a presentation by Gove in which he suggested that soldiers may need to be stationed outside hospitals that had reached capacity to prevent other patients getting in; and that people would be dying on corridor floors. Johnson's allies point out that it was an unprecedented situation. Almost all decisions had to be elevated above secretary of state level because of the seriousness and the speed at which the situation and scientific advice was evolving, with departments inevitably fighting to protect the areas they represented. Chaos was inevitable, they argue, but when structures were put in place under an assigned minister, for instance Nadhim Zahawi taking on vaccines, rapid results were delivered.

But what was visible from the outside world in the earlier part of the pandemic was quite different. To a nervous country, the sight of the prime minister flanked by senior scientists in daily Downing Street press conferences was reassuring, as was clear from the polls. On 2 April, eleven days after the country was placed under lockdown, Boris Johnson's Conservative Party was at 52 points on YouGov's voting intention tracker – 24 points ahead of Labour, on 28.

Back then the most popular politician of all was Chancellor Rishi Sunak. Aides who worked with him say he 'loved being in the Treasury' and the civil servants loved him. 'When we were considering an issue he would ask for six reports and a niche book for the weekend, and would have read them all by Monday,' said one.

Sunak would stay up late with Treasury officials and his closest political aides – Liam Booth-Smith, Rupert Yorke, Nerissa Chesterfield and Cass Horowitz – discussing how to respond to the economic challenges presented by Covid. They would sit around whiteboards on which they scrawled different iterations of the plan that eventually became the Coronavirus Job Retention Scheme, or furlough, paying up to £2,500 a month of the wages of people whose jobs did not have a work-from-home option or could not otherwise be retained during the crisis. Sunak did not instinctively like the idea of the government paying salaries (and took a more hawkish line on lockdowns in cross-governmental meetings), but he argued that if lockdowns were going to happen it demanded a huge financial injection from the government. Some close to the then chancellor say they think this Treasury experience may have slightly 'unmoored' him ideologically, as by intervening heavily in people's lives, this traditionally quite right-wing Conservative MP, who had risked career progression by backing Brexit in the 2016 Referendum, became overwhelmingly popular.

For Leader of the Opposition Keir Starmer, in spring 2020 one of the first things he had to do was build a new team. Among his core staff were a new policy director, Claire Ainsley, and deputy Stuart Ingham; Ben Nunn in communications; and Yasmeen Sebbana became head of his private office. McSweeney was appointed chief of staff but immediately turned to internal party matters, while his deputy Chris Ward and political director Jenny Chapman started to draw up lists for a shadow cabinet.

Starmer would later be criticised for the make-up of this first shadow ministerial team, but it was designed to fit with the 'unity' ticket that had just helped him secure the leadership. Starmer's close allies, seen as 'soft left' in the Labour Party (which is where many also placed his politics) got senior positions – with Anneliese Dodds appointed shadow chancellor, and Nick Thomas-Symonds, shadow home secretary. Two of Starmer's leadership opponents were also rewarded: Lisa Nandy became shadow foreign secretary and Rebecca

Long-Bailey got the shadow education gig. Starmer also made his friend and former Labour leader Ed Miliband shadow business secretary, and Jonathan Reynolds became shadow secretary of state for work and pensions. However, the Corbynite left of the Labour Party did not see this as a unified team; their contingent was reduced to just three while the leader filled more than 50 per cent of significant positions with MPs who had backed him.

As for the centrist 'Blairites' – figures like Wes Streeting, Liz Kendall and Jess Phillips who had been less likely to back Starmer from the off – they were given shadow ministerial roles one rung down. But there was an exception. One MP associated with the right of the party really stood out.

Rachel Reeves, MP for Leeds West, had initially supported Jess Phillips in the leadership election and Starmer had only got to know her better a couple of weeks before the end of the campaign, when the pair met for breakfast. 'She's excellent, really excellent, she needs to be high up,' Starmer told his team on his return. Some believed that given Reeves's politics (she was one of those who never chose to serve in Corbyn's administration) and Starmer's leadership campaign, she could not be made shadow chancellor in the first round. But she was appointed to another critical position. As shadow chancellor of the Duchy of Lancaster, Reeves would play a leading role on the two biggest issues of the day: Covid and Brexit.

McSweeney also brought in Sam White – who had worked for Labour chancellor Alistair Darling during the 2008 financial crash – on a temporary basis to help focus on Covid. The team would build contacts with scientists, epidemiologists, economists, hospital doctors, GPs, and their counterparts overseas, discussing their findings each morning in online meetings attended by Starmer, Dodds, Rayner and Reeves. With the newly flexibility of Zoom working, the team spent one session with New Zealand's prime minister Jacinda Ardern to find out about her zero-Covid strategy.

But before any of that could get going Starmer needed to speak to the man he had been elected to oppose. Days before the Labour leadership result, Boris Johnson had tested positive for the virus and was isolating in Downing Street. In a courtesy call, Starmer explained that he wanted his Labour Party to offer 'constructive opposition'. But when he put down the phone, the Labour leader told members of his team: 'He sounds really ill.'

On Sunday 5 April, Johnson called Lee Cain to explain how poorly he was feeling and that he was moving to St Thomas' Hospital. He wanted to discuss who would replace him if he became incapacitated. Sources tell me that Cain asked if it should be Gove or Sunak, but the PM was insistent that it must be his deputy, Dominic Raab. 'Make sure that happens,' he told Cain.

The next morning his aides tried to allay concerns by insisting it was simply a precautionary measure and that Johnson was even still working on his Red Box from his hospital bed. In fact, his condition was worsening and at 7 p.m. he was moved to intensive care in case he needed ventilation. Some of Johnson's aides have told me that they believed that he was likely to die that night. That was the impression shared through the WhatsApp groups of Downing Street's special advisers. People have described the mood in Downing Street that day in various terms, from 'general shock' to 'existential chaos'.

Many of the senior figures in government, including Cabinet Secretary Mark Sedwill and Dominic Cummings, were isolating themselves, but Lee Cain had recovered and rushed to Downing Street. He joined a meeting with the PM's principal private secretary, Martin Reynolds, the deputy cabinet secretary, Helen MacNamara, and the PM's official spokesman, James Slack. Cain had been told that if Johnson was placed on a ventilator, as was being considered, his chance of survival would be 50/50. The group discussed what to do if the worst happened, and quickly realised there was no plan. MacNamara began to work up the options at speed. Meanwhile, the first person Cain rang was the BBC's political editor, Laura Kuenssberg, to let her know that things had escalated. Everyone was in shock.

One source argued that because of the unprecedented nature of the situation and the fact that the fundamentals were changing so fast, it was inevitable that the onset of the pandemic would result in the government looking like it was lurching from one thing to another. So the situation already appeared chaotic. But with Johnson fighting for his life, it felt to some as if the 'system had collapsed'.

'Our assumption around midnight was that he could quite possibly die that day. It was pretty awful. I don't think anyone was ready to deal with it, at any level,' said one insider.

After leaving hospital, Johnson spent time at Chequers, the prime minister's official country residence, where he told a close aide that he had genuinely thought he was done for, adding, 'It was a bloody close call.' He remained unwell for some time, which led some to question whether the deputy prime minister Dominic Raab should have stayed on as an interim. But Johnson was having none of that. 'I can't look weak,' he told aides. Back in charge, he soon had to contend with another problem, though.

On 22 May, the *Guardian*'s Matthew Weaver and the *Mirror*'s Pippa Crerar, jointly broke a story revealing that the police had spoken to Dominic Cummings after he drove across the country to his parents' home in Durham while suffering with Covid symptoms earlier that March. It later emerged he had also driven his wife and son 30 miles to Barnard Castle, claiming the journey had been to test whether his eyesight was good enough to complete the full journey back to London.

Privately, after his aide had explained the sequence of events, Johnson had promised to stand 'shoulder to shoulder' with Cummings. There had already been discussions about whether Cummings should move from his London home after protesters outside threatened him and his family. But Johnson was soon frustrated with having to deal with the sheer scale of anger and suggested that Cummings should hold a press conference himself. He agreed and it was arranged in the Rose Garden of Downing Street. It is my understanding that both Cain and Johnson's chief of staff, Eddie

Lister, advised against the idea, suggesting it could set a precedent and, indeed, Cummings's subsequent attempt to explain what had happened fell on deaf ears. The scandal blew up and caused a public fury that seemed to impact on the popularity of the government, which had already been falling. Five days after the press conference, the Tory lead was down to 10 points. A few months later, Labour went ahead in the polls.

But then, in January 2021, came a dramatic turnaround, thanks to the government's successful bid to secure millions of newly-developed Covid vaccines. As jabs started to go into arms, the polit-ical fortunes of the two biggest Westminster parties began to reverse as the Conservatives surged ahead in the polls. This was the back-drop for Starmer's first major political test as Labour leader: a by-election in Hartlepool on 6 May. Not that the vaccine bounce can fully explain what came next.

This by-election did not have to be held when it did. The town's Labour MP, Mike Hill, had been facing accusations of sexual assault and harassment and had been told by the party leadership to step down in advance of an employment tribunal.[1] Some argued that rather than going to the polls on the same day as local elections, when the region would be also voting for a popular Conservative mayor, it might be electorally sensible to delay the contest.

Labour had held on in Hartlepool in 2019 because the seat was the Brexit Party's number one target and its candidate, Richard Tice, ate into the Tories' slice, winning 10,000 votes. Without the same threat in 2021, Starmer knew there was a risk of a different dynamic playing out. I spent a lot of time in Hartlepool ahead of the 2019 Election, and again for this 2021 by-election. The town felt like a wonderful place, genuinely kind and open, with incredible commu-nity organisers who appeared to be trying their best to improve things. But it quickly became clear that people here didn't just feel 'left behind' but virtually abandoned.

An amazing community organiser, Sacha Bedding, told us the term 'left behind' assumed an equal starting point. For Hartlepool residents like him, however, the last four decades had been like they 'weren't even in the same race.' Post-industrial coastal towns in the North East felt as if they had been 'irrelevant' to politicians, he declared, adding that Hartlepool had voted Labour nationally and locally for many years, but things had not improved.

'What makes a place? We don't have a magistrates' court, we don't have a custody suite at the police station,' said Bedding. He explained that the local hospital had been run down, leaving many women unable to give birth locally, while a promise to build a 'super-hospital' to replace it had not been realised. And then there was the tired high street, with local groups trying to use abandoned space to support entrepreneurs, but without enough input from the government. The result was 'palpable anger'.

Why wasn't that aimed at the national Conservative government? It's hard to say, but Teesside's Conservative mayor, Ben Houchen, was hugely popular and had been turning heads for some years, and he was up for re-election on the same day. And in a place that voted heavily to leave the EU, they quite liked Boris Johnson too. Keir Starmer's name, on the other hand, was greeted with a bit of a 'meh' and Labour's candidate, Dr Paul Williams, ran into difficulties because of his status as the former MP for nearby Stockton South (which he had won in 2017 but then lost in 2019). People described him as 'Stockton's reject'.

During a campaign visit to Hartlepool on 30 April 2021 Starmer and his team travelled up to Durham to the office of MP Mary Foy. There, seventeen people, including Labour deputy Angela Rayner, gathered for a dinner break, eating curry ordered from a nearby takeaway. Starmer also drank a bottle of beer. Outside, a Durham student Ivo Delingpole, son of the well-known right-wing journalist James Delingpole, spotted the Labour leader and filmed him through the window. The clip eventually landed with anti-lockdown activist Laurence Fox who posted it on Twitter, resulting in a story in the *Sun* newspaper the next day. It did not seem problematic at the time.

Six days later it was polling day in Hartlepool but also for councils across the country and some regional mayors. Members of Starmer's team including McSweeney, his deputy Helene Reardon-Bond and the rest of the core team travelled to the by-election constituency to help the 'get out the vote' operation. Sources claimed that some in the party had told Starmer that Labour could win, though it was on a 'knife-edge'. But it did not feel like that on the doors, as voters either refused to tell them how they were voting or made it very clear: 'No, we can't vote for you!'

At 3 p.m. Starmer called Chris Ward to ask how things were going. 'We've lost by a mile,' came the reply. The Labour leader was taken aback. The campaign team had given him a different take.

In the evening, as the party prepared for a long night, McSweeney and Ainsley logged into a group video call from a car. Shadow ministers were on the call as well as Paul Ovenden, then deputy director of communications, who was preparing to do the overnight media shift. McSweeney and Ainsley knew the news was likely to be bad and told colleagues that a loss would simply 'reinforce the message the Labour Party has to change'.

That night, Boris Johnson's party secured a stunning victory, not just taking control of a seat that the Conservatives had never won before but taking it with more than 50 per cent of the vote and a majority close to 7,000. Aides tell me Starmer's reaction was one of shock, 'like he'd been punched in the face'. One described a photograph of him, taken through the windows of the LOTO office, looking as 'white as a sheet', his face scrunched up in irritation.[2] Biographer Tom Baldwin wrote that Starmer came close to quitting that Friday. One person described how the Labour leader ranted that he was less popular than Corbyn; the party was going backwards; and he did not know what to do.

Meanwhile, attacks were coming in from the left of Labour. Veteran MP Diane Abbott said it was 'not possible to blame Jeremy Corbyn' for the crushing defeat, pointing out that he had won there, twice. The former Unite boss Len McCluskey said people didn't know what Starmer's 'vision' was or what Labour stood for. And Corbyn called it a 'loss of hope'.

One idea had been for Starmer to go to Hartlepool and make a bold statement that while his party had lost there, it was going to win in the future. Instead, there was a hastily arranged clip that would be shared by all the main broadcasters in the LOTO offices. But by the time Starmer was able to say, 'I will take full responsibility for fixing things', rumours that he was 'hiding' had started to swirl.

In the days that followed, the full set of local election results would have a few high points for Labour. Although they had lost councils, they had gained some metro and city mayors. McSweeney, typically, was only interested in the places where Labour had just lost.

One person present that day described his mood as hyper: 'Morgan was in one of these moments, where he just speaks at 400 or 500 miles per hour.' The chief of staff pulled out a whiteboard and started writing fast: 'Change Labour', he began, before adding the words: 'signature policy; reshuffle; staff restructure; rule changes'.

In fact, McSweeney had predicted that the May 2021 local election results were likely to be bad enough to at least show that Labour was 'not on course to win a general election' and suggested the party should 'come out of the traps quickly to seize the initiative'.

In a document entitled 'Labour for the Country', produced in March that year (and agreed by Starmer in April), he argued that Labour had become too inward-looking, preoccupied by the whims of its members rather than the demands of its potential voters.

'We cannot build a new relationship of trust with the electorate while we are overly focused on ourselves,' he wrote. 'At the moment the perception is that we talk at them, not to them, about the issues we – not they – care about.'

The 2019 defeat had been about Brexit and Corbyn he argued, but to McSweeney both were symptoms of the same problem – a Labour Party that had turned away from the electorate. He said voters in 2019 had feared Labour would leave the country 'defense-less [sic] and plunge the economy into debt-fuelled chaos'. He claimed that they considered Corbyn to be 'dangerous and unpatri-otic' and felt insulted being asked to vote for his party. He also underlined the electoral nightmare that Labour faced: it would need a 10.5 per cent swing for a majority of just two, with Croydon South the 326th seat that would take them across the line (although, inter-estingly, that particular constituency bucked the trend on election night and remained Conservative).

McSweeney also argued the country was suffering 'collective PTSD' in the wake of the pandemic, which had shaken people's sense of security. Labour needed to focus on the issues consuming the minds of voters. 'People care far more about their jobs, liveli-hoods, crime and public services than the preservation of statues in Bristol, Meghan Markle's struggles with the Royal Family or the number of union flags in our Zoom interviews,' he wrote.

There was individual talent in the shadow cabinet but too many seemed 'lost in a Twitter-driven comfort zone of its own, not push-ing the boundaries and barely competitive.' To win, he argued, Labour needed to keep its 2019 vote as high as possible, win over Lib Dem and Green Party voters, and take back former Labour supporters from the Tories and the Brexit Party. McSweeney's conclusion: 'An election strategy must set out an offer for the whole country, for everyone.'

Phase One of McSweeney's plan was to start on Friday 7 May, the day after the local election results, and the Hartlepool debacle. To his call for a clear offer, McSweeney had added a 'green industrial revolution'; bringing the public into policy development; a shadow cabinet reshuffle; radical structural change (with staff ready to 'walk over hot coals' for Labour to win); town hall events for Starmer; getting off Twitter; and taking control of the party itself, even if internal change led to 'conflict'.

Phase Two would take place at party conference, where he would push for rule changes and a leader's speech that made the case for a different country post-Covid, including an unequivocal celebration of the 'patriotic' achievements of the last Labour government.

And so, straight out of the traps, Starmer began a reshuffle of the shadow cabinet.

His first attempted move was aimed at the party chair and national campaign coordinator, Angela Rayner. She had been explicitly told there was no reshuffle, but by the time she turned up at Labour HQ a journalist had already revealed to her that she was about to be moved on and sent her Starmer's entire reshuffle plan. Rayner was furious and felt that she was being made to carry the can for the Hartlepool result when she believed that key decisions had been shared with senior figures in Starmer's team. The stand-off between the two elected leadership figures went on for hours, with Rayner locked in talks with Starmer's team. And in the end, she emerged stronger – replacing Rachel Reeves as the shadow chancellor of the Duchy of Lancaster, shadowing Michael Gove, along with a new role, on the future of work.

After the disaster of the Hartlepool result, the reshuffle looked shambolic, but Starmer did succeed in pushing through two key changes: Shabana Mahmood became the national campaign coordinator, and his close ally Anneliese Dodds was replaced as shadow chancellor by Rachel Reeves, with the former becoming party chair and heading Labour's policy review.

Reeves was in the dark about the shake-up and had almost given up all hope of promotion when the invite came to become shadow chancellor. A former economist who had joined the party at 17 and had a framed photograph of Gordon Brown on the wall of her university room, Reeves was delighted.

Reeves and her chief of staff Katie Martin came up with four key objectives: they wanted people to trust her with their money; to believe she was on the side of ordinary working people; to see that Labour believed in wealth creation and not just redistribution; and to put forward a plan that would excite and inspire voters.

Reeves also helped Starmer to recruit a new strategy director.

Deborah Mattinson, who had worked for both Tony Blair and Gordon Brown, had met Starmer socially a few times including when he was shadow immigration minister. She had subsequently founded Britain Thinks, a strategy consultancy where she had used polling and focus groups to build an in-depth picture of Britain's different communities, what they cared about, and how they felt about politicians.

I talked to Mattinson quite a lot in the run-up to the Brexit Referendum in 2016 and she told me then that Labour could face a backlash as a result of the Leave campaign: 'When you hear Labour politicians talking about the Leave campaign, they use language that doesn't just denigrate the campaign, it denigrates people who feel concerned about immigration.' Later Mattinson would write *Beyond the Red Wall*, a book in which she attempted to explain why Labour lost so many working-class votes in 2019.

When, in the middle of the tumultuous weekend that followed the Hartlepool result, the announcement of Mattinson's appointment went out, one friend messaged her: 'You must be a saint'. Another, less polite, asked: 'Are you f-ing crazy?' Mattinson was only too aware of the challenges ahead but had come round to the view that if she could help improve things a little, she had a duty to do so.

In the summer of 1988 Andy Mochan was one of 226 men living and working on the Piper Alpha oil-rig 120 miles from Aberdeen in the middle of the North Sea. On the evening of 6 July, an electrical fault with one of the pumps caused a series of explosions which ripped through the rig, setting the entire platform alight. In the worst offshore tragedy the world had ever seen, 167 people were killed, including all those caught inside the accommodation block.

Mochan survived. Speaking to reporters afterwards, he described how colleagues had desperately tried to reach the exits but were beaten back by the thick smoke caused by the inferno. Asked about his decision to leap 150 feet (the equivalent of fifteen storeys) into the water, he turned his head to face the journalist and in a thick Scottish accent said: 'It was fry or jump, so it was jump.'

Many point to the story of Mochan's harrowing escape as the origin of the phrase a 'burning platform' to describe any 'do or die' shift in strategy when facing an existential problem.

Senior figures in Labour saw the Hartlepool defeat as just such a 'burning platform' moment. In their eyes, it spurred on the change needed for Starmer to survive.

Certainly, Starmer emerged with a more steely and ruthless approach to his leadership. But in truth there was already plenty of effort being piled into attempts to change the party before May 2021. And Starmer's willingness to be ruthless had been apparent from day one.

7

Ruthless

Ousting Jennie Formby in the immediate aftermath of his election as party leader would be just one of several ruthless steps for Starmer. He was determined to take control of all three main levers of power inside Labour, and fast.

After securing the leadership and the general secretary post, his team turned its attention to the National Executive Committee (NEC). In many ways, it seems odd Starmer would move so fast on party organisation. Many stress how he keeps the divide strictly between the political and the personal; his friends come largely from his school and university life, legal career and five-a-side. According to long-time friend Parvais Jabbar, Starmer's other friendships 'have remained constant and the longevity of those relationships quite remarkable. He is loyal to them and he receives loyalty in return.' Starmer is not a politician who has grown up within the Labour movement.

His new chief of staff Morgan McSweeney, on the other hand, had long been steeped in internal party matters and knew exactly how to make sure that his boss could wrest control of the organisation's steering wheel. His key lieutenant in this task was Matt Pound, who had joined Starmer's leadership bid as deputy field director. In the 'unity team' Starmer put together, Pound's boss was Kat Fletcher who had been a key figure in Corbyn's leadership bid four years earlier.

Pound's background was in Labour First, one of two high-profile groups on the right of the Labour Party. The other, Progress, has been historically seen as a Blairite, liberal organisation that tends to drive policy ideas. Labour First emerged from the 'old trade union right' and was always more about political organisation, running slates of centrist Labour candidates to be selected as MPs, councillors and on to decision-making committees like the NEC.

Latterly, the battle against Corbynism had united these two centrist groups and on 5 April 2020 (the day after Starmer was elected party leader) they came together under one umbrella: Labour To Win, with the contention that ultimately their more pragmatic (and thus less radical) politics was the way to secure power.

Pound told Starmer that certain figures in the Labour Party were deeply opposed to his election and could make his life difficult. One way to solve that, he suggested, was to quickly orient the NEC towards members more loyal to his leadership, the very thing Corbyn had failed to do in reverse when he first got the top job. With a nod, Starmer told Pound to go for it.

The NEC is the power centre of the Labour Party; a sprawling committee with over forty members spanning different parts of the movement from the leader himself, his deputy and selected front-benchers, along with representatives from affiliated trade unions, constituency Labour parties (CLPs), councillors and backbench MPs. This body decides how Labour elects its leader, selects its candidates, signs off general secretary appointments, and is the arbiter of the party's powerful Rule Book. If he was to lead effectively, Pound argued, Starmer needed an overall NEC majority. And, by changing the people sitting in the three seats normally reserved for shadow cabinet members, he immediately secured it.

Corbyn allies Diane Abbott, Rebecca Long-Bailey and Jon Trickett were out, making way for Starmer loyalists Jim McMahon, Jo Stevens and Jonathan Reynolds. Sounds easy, but it was a move that took Corbyn more than a year. In fact, it was not until his second overwhelming leadership election, and following the failed coup, that Corbyn felt the political strength to replace Jonathan Ashworth on the NEC – and even then, it caused a backlash.

Now Starmer had a thin majority, but that did not feel quite secure enough to his team. Pound had another idea. That summer, when the nine CLP seats around the NEC table came up for re-election, he pushed for a change to the voting system. He argued that if the first-past-the-post (FPTP) system was replaced by the more proportional single transferable vote (STV) it would help the right of the party secure victory in at least three of the contests, more than was otherwise expected. This suggestion caused fury among the most left-wing figures but gained the support of 'soft left' groups who tended to prefer more plural voting systems. Pound managed to secure the change and, although five candidates were elected on a left-wing Momentum slate, three vacancies were won by 'moderates', edging up Starmer's majority.

Finally came the make-up of the NEC officers group – comprised of the Labour leader, his deputy, the NEC chair and those leading various sub-committees. In this small but powerful grouping, the left had more members. Pound argued that the precedent had always been to select the NEC's longest serving member as the next chair, but recently they had started to opt for the vice chair instead. By switching back to the old way of doing things, and now with a Starmer-friendly majority, the NEC could pave the way for Tony Blair's final foreign secretary, Margaret Beckett, to be elevated to the top post, ousting Ian Murray, the left-wing president of the Fire Brigades Union. With that, the Labour leader took control of the officers group too.

Bit by bit, Starmer's team was edging the machinery of the Labour Party in an increasingly centrist direction. There is little question that these changes cemented Starmer's power and control. Important for any political leader, in Starmer's case it was critical in order to steer the party in his direction. But some have argued there is a downside; this approach eats up goodwill. 'People feel trampled on. While you are winning that is fine, but when things get tougher, it might be harder,' said an NEC source.

The changes were not just organisational. Early appointments to Starmer's team were also clues to a likely shift in policy. Alongside his long-time aide, Stuart Ingham, Claire Ainsley, the former head of the Joseph Rowntree Foundation, joined as policy director. In her book *The New Working Class*, Ainsley had argued that Labour needed to redefine the voters it was trying to reach. What it meant to be working class had changed, she insisted, and was not only white British people. Nor was this group located in just one part of the country (the Red Wall, for instance). The new working class was now multi-ethnic and included many women living in towns and suburbs across the country. These voters tended to be slightly to the left on economics and slightly to the right on immigration, but not as far to the right as the Conservatives imagined.

When Ainsley's book was published in 2018, her ideas about an industrial revolution, skills, day-one employment rights, points-based immigration and regional economic growth (which all sound very familiar now) were firmly aimed at Labour. But it was the Tories who first showed greatest interest. Robert Halfon – then MP for Harlow and chair of the Education Select Committee – had set up a group linking Tories to working-class trade unions, and he brought an annotated copy of Ainsley's book to the discussion. Conservative HQ also invited Ainsley to a meeting as they scoured for ideas. It was Steve Reed who introduced her to Morgan McSweeney; her ideas chimed perfectly with what Labour Together was trying to achieve.

The new team invited YouGov's Marcus Roberts along to an early shadow cabinet session to run through some numbers. The pollster told them that Starmer's strategy should be to try to win everyone, everywhere and on everything. He believed it was not possible to come back from a defeat on the scale of 2019 with anything other than a strategy for a landslide. McSweeney did not disagree, but he and Ainsley believed strongly that the key to unlocking Labour's voting coalition was the working-class voters lost in 2019 and now clustered in marginal seats.

For some, the focus on working-class voters across the UK, many of whom had voted to leave the EU in 2016, may have felt like a moral endeavour aiming to reconnect the Labour Party with the very people it was set up to represent. But that was certainly not the only motive. Starmer's laser-like focus on the working class was also an electoral calculation; without these votes Labour had virtually no chance of winning nationally. This was McSweeney's voter efficiency, focusing disproportionately on building up support in marginal seats where the party was just short of a majority, even if it meant the size of their mandate slipped back in safer urban areas.

The group knew they needed the Tories to fail but agreed that such a failure would not be sufficient for Labour to win. YouGov polling underlined just how far the Conservatives were ahead of Labour on defence and security, the economy, taxation, immigration, and law and order. It suggested Labour should avoid the comfort blanket of campaigning mainly on the NHS, that these votes were already in the bag. The votes of people nervous about whether they could trust Labour on the economy and defence, however, were not.

According to the polls, one thing was unquestionable: Corbyn's 2019 manifesto had been packed with popular policies. Some 64 per cent questioned said they supported a higher rate of tax for the super wealthy, while 60 per cent wanted those earning over £80,000 to pay more. Around 54 per cent wanted companies to give a third of places on their boards to workers, and 50 per cent were in favour of water nationalisation, compared to just 25 per cent who opposed the idea. But when asked which politician they trusted most with the economy overall, 34 per cent said Boris Johnson and only 16 per cent Jeremy Corbyn, while 33 per cent believed Tory promises were unaffordable compared to 53 per cent who said the same for Labour. Roberts argued that the Tories were favoured on the economy not despite the popularity of Labour policies, but because of them;

voters simply did not trust that so much good stuff was deliverable without the cost falling on their shoulders.

At the time, the issue of Scotland and how hard Labour should fight to rebuild support there was a live debate. North of the border the party had been electorally crushed in recent years, losing 40 out of 41 seats it was defending in 2015, with political heavyweights like the Scottish party leader, Jim Murphy, booted out. Douglas Alexander had hoped to become foreign secretary in Ed Miliband's government, but instead lost his seat to 20-year-old Scottish National Party (SNP) candidate Mhairi Black, who became the youngest MP to be elected to Parliament in hundreds of years. In 2019 Labour's 18.6 per cent vote-share in Scotland was its lowest in a Westminster election for more than a century, ranking fourth on seat numbers behind the SNP (who secured a landslide with 48 seats), the Tories and the Lib Dems, in that order. Labour had held only a single Scottish seat.

Some in Labour were pessimistic about the prospects of recovery because of the challenge of finding a message that would allow them to fight on two fronts: the Tories to the right in England and Wales and the SNP to the left in Scotland. But McSweeney did not share these doubts. By then he had moved north of the border with his Scottish wife, Imogen Walker. Her later decision to fight to become the MP for Hamilton and Clyde Valley was perhaps a sign of where both of them stood on the argument. McSweeney would later be one of the loudest voices in pushing for the party to ditch Richard Leonard, its leader in Scotland under Corbyn. In the end, after facing rebellions Leonard stepped down and before the 2021 Scottish elections was replaced by Anas Sarwar.

There was another thing that McSweeney was obsessed with. He believed that Starmer must pursue a single-term strategy; to try to win in five years rather than ten. It wasn't that he necessarily expected Labour to win that quickly, but he believed that saying anything else could breed a lazy mindset, in which difficult decisions were left until nine years into the project. Take Brexit, for example.

On Christmas Eve, 2020, Boris Johnson completed an EU–UK trade agreement with president of the European Commission, Ursula von der Leyen, and then brought it back for a vote in Parliament just six days later. No one on the Labour side thought that Johnson's deal was a good one, and sources claimed that three former party leaders – Lord Kinnock, Tony Blair and Gordon Brown – urged Starmer to oppose it. But Starmer was convinced that he had to put this row to bed and show the very voters his party was gunning for that Labour would not stand in the way of their democratic vote to leave the EU. A ten-year strategy, might have led Labour to the much more comfortable position of voting 'no' on Johnson's imperfect deal.

It was up to Rachel Reeves, then shadowing Michael Gove and focused on Brexit, to persuade colleagues that Labour should vote in favour, and once again she impressed. It was tough going, with fury from the left led by John McDonnell but also from closer allies like Ben Bradshaw. Inside the shadow cabinet, senior figures, including the shadow chancellor Anneliese Dodds as well as the shadow secretaries of state for Wales and Scotland, raised their concerns. But there was also strong support, particularly from MPs who represented high Leave-voting communities including Ed Miliband on the front bench and Yvette Cooper and Hilary Benn on the backbenches. The key argument was that while this, in the eyes of the Labour Party, was not a good deal, the choice was between backing it or effectively supporting the UK's crashing out of the EU with no deal at all.

Still, it was quite a shift from Starmer's pro-EU stance in his party leadership bid, and for many in Labour walking through the lobbies to hand the Conservatives a huge majority on their version of Brexit it was a difficult and emotional moment.

But long before all this unfolded, a different problem had landed on Starmer's plate. Within days of his becoming leader, on 12 April 2020 an 860-page internal report into Labour's handling of alleged anti-Semitism was leaked to the media. The *Guardian* reported that this document had been intended to be submitted as an annexe to the Equalities and Human Rights Commission (EHRC) inquiry into the affair.[1] The findings clashed with the claims of whistleblowers, who in a BBC *Panorama* programme said their attempts to deal with such allegations had been scuppered by political interference in the process.

According to the *Guardian*'s Rowena Mason, the 'leaked report' had found no evidence of anti-Semitism complaints being treated differently to other forms of complaint nor that any current or former staff member had been 'motivated by anti-Semitic intent'. Instead, the report highlighted deep-rooted hostility towards Corbyn, which had created a 'hyper-factional atmosphere' that 'affected the expeditious and resolute handling of disciplinary complaints'.

But most explosive was the inclusion of some 10,000 separate emails and thousands of private WhatsApp messages which unveiled the scale of the anti-Corbyn mood among some Labour staffers, who had described their more left-wing colleagues as 'trots'. Corbyn's strategy chief Seumas Milne was derided as 'Dracula' and his chief of staff Karie Murphy as 'Medusa' and 'crazy woman'. The report claimed that such staffers had relished the prospect of Labour election losses that might help oust Corbyn and piled money disproportionately towards their favoured 'moderate' candidates – charges strongly denied. 'At its extreme, some employees seem to have taken a view that the worse things got for Labour, the happier they would be,' claimed the report.

Starmer faced a dilemma in dealing with this leak. It unquestionably highlighted rancour towards Corbyn and raised questions over whether elements of the Labour machine opposed to Corbyn's leadership had worked against party interests. But the decision to both commission and leak the study was also seen as incredibly hostile; it was like Labour's left flank pulling the pin out of a grenade and lobbing it behind them as they walked out the door. There were also the potential legal ramifications of so much personal data being placed in the public domain.

Some of Starmer's closest team urged him to just ignore the 'leaked report' and move on, but he decided to commission a new inquiry from Martin Forde KC to investigate the contents. Two years later, the Forde Report would find structural problems in the party's disciplinary processes with regards to anti-Semitism that were exacerbated by factionalism, with 'a cycle of attack and counterattack'. Forde concluded that both left and right of the party were guilty of 'weaponising the issue' and failing to recognise the impact this had on the Jewish community and the moral standing of the Labour Party. He said both camps in this internecine war wanted to win with as many of their 'favoured MPs' as possible, so 'the two sides were trying to win in different ways'. The Labour Party made a public apology and committed to respond to Forde's 165 recommendations, including that to review its disciplinary processes to ensure 'this is never allowed to happen again'.

Some say that this experience hardened Starmer's approach to tackling any form of perceived anti-Semitism from the very start. And he did not wait long to take steps that shocked many in his party.

On the morning of Thursday 25 June 2020, Rebecca Long-Bailey was drinking a cup of coffee when she spotted a tweet by the *Independent* newspaper sharing an interview with a constituent she admired, the actor Maxine Peake. The shadow education secretary and former leadership rival to Starmer quickly scanned the copy and retweeted the link, writing: 'Maxine Peake is an absolute diamond ...'

It was just a month after the shocking murder of George Floyd in Minneapolis, Minnesota had sent a wave of protest crashing across America and surging out to the rest of the world. The passion of this Black Lives Matter movement was felt by Starmer too as he and his deputy Angela Rayner took 'the knee' in the LOTO boardroom.

Floyd had choked to death after the white police officer Derek Chauvin knelt on his neck for 9 minutes and 29 seconds, ignoring his dying plea: 'I can't breathe.' In her *Independent* interview, Maxine Peake claimed the tactics used by Chauvin had been 'learnt from seminars with Israeli secret services', a charge emphatically denied by Israel and which Starmer considered to be an anti-Semitic trope. When Long-Bailey posted her tweet, the Labour leader was on a visit in Stevenage accompanied by BBC political editor Laura Kuennsberg. His adviser Paul Ovenden had spotted the tweet and flagged it to his colleague Ben Nunn, who in turn showed it to Starmer during the train journey home. Starmer said he wanted the post deleted by the time his journey was over, or Long-Bailey was gone.

What happened next is slightly disputed. Long-Bailey has described how her 'heart sank' when she got the call from a senior adviser in Starmer's office, telling them that she never intended to endorse anything that could cause hurt. She later wrote in the *Guardian*: 'I know how painful the issue of anti-Semitism has been for the Jewish community and I have been part of the efforts to eradicate it from our party.'[2] She said that Starmer's team had drafted a clarification for her and, after some discussion, suggested she attach it to the original post so the context would be clear. But that simply made things worse. Starmer saw it as a retweet that would share the *Independent* piece even more widely. She was asked to delete both posts.

It is not clear why Long-Bailey did not immediately do just that, and she has confided to friends that in hindsight she wishes she had. But at the time she argued that it was necessary to issue a clarification explaining what had happened and that then she would delete the posts. She believed a press notice was being drawn up along those lines and so waited to act.

Allies of Starmer have since told me how much they liked Long-Bailey, seeing her as friendly, smart and deserving of her place on the front bench. One said they really admired the work she did later to support veterans who suffered health complications as a result of radiation exposure dating from British nuclear-weapon testing in the

50s and 60s. But for them her behaviour that day fell short of what was necessary, and it was because, in their eyes, she did not want to embarrass her friend Maxine Peake.

Starmer was in no mood for patience, telling colleagues he could not have a situation in which an instruction from the leader to a shadow cabinet member was ignored. After his train journey, his mind was set, and he rang Long-Bailey to tell her she was no longer needed on his front bench. One of his staff members told me their reaction was: 'Wow! He is serious.' Starmer's ruthless streak was on show once more.

Was it was always his plan to oust Long-Bailey? I don't think so. For a start, Starmer knew that it felt like a harsh move. That evening he called his political director Jenny Chapman, who had been involved in trying to find a resolution that would have kept Long-Bailey in place, and asked: 'Are you OK?' She admitted it had not gone the way she had hoped, to which Starmer urged Chapman (who was picking up dinner in a supermarket as they spoke) to go home, pour herself a glass of wine and know that tomorrow was another day.

But it is worth mentioning that there had been tensions between Long-Bailey and Starmer on policy that were quite revealing as to the Labour leader's instincts. The question that had dominated her short stint as shadow education secretary was the impact of the pandemic on schools. In May 2020 the National Education Union set out five conditions that they believed should be met before schools were reopened, including much lower Covid cases, a national plan for social distancing, and much more comprehensive testing.[3] When Long-Bailey signed up to the conditions, Starmer was unhappy as he believed that schools should reopen at the earliest possible moment, and sources said the pair clashed over the policy behind the scenes.[4]

But while ousting Long-Bailey was not planned, Starmer was perhaps interested to hear from senior advisers that the incident had shifted underlying polling figures in his direction. YouGov's Marcus

Roberts was amazed when he saw Starmer's personal ratings rise as a result of a scandal that he considered to be an 'SW1 Westminster bubble story'. 'I still don't understand it,' he told me. 'But there was an increase in the number of people who saw Keir as a strong and decisive leader.'

Perhaps that public response was on Starmer's mind when five months later he was confronted by an even bigger scandal.

'There was no plan to oust Jeremy Corbyn,' said a source. 'There was no plot.'

Perhaps. But the night before the Equalities and Human Rights Commission (EHRC) released its findings of its investigation into anti-Semitism within the Labour Party, Starmer's communications chief, Ben Nunn, told colleagues that he believed there was a 70 per cent chance that Corbyn would say something the next day that would result in him being kicked out of the party.

It was 28 October 2020 and Labour had just seen the final version of the EHRC report and now knew that, while it did not accuse the party of institutional anti-Semitism, it included some damning conclusions. That evening, when Starmer spoke to Corbyn, it was said that his tone was more 'in sorrow than anger' as he made clear that he was not seeking to make Labour's public response to the report confrontational or all about Corbyn. The former leader was being supported by members of his previous team, who no longer had formal roles but maintained a bond with their old boss. They had not seen the final conclusions and so Seumas Milne called deputy leader Angela Rayner (who had once served under Corbyn) to ask if it was possible to share the report or Starmer's likely response, so that Corbyn could prepare a statement. At 1 a.m. they had received nothing – and by then a problem was brewing.

After finding a poll that suggested people thought a third of Labour members had been suspected of anti-Semitism, some of those supporting Corbyn argued that the public's perception of this issue was distorted – they believed the real number was 0.3 per cent.

It is worth saying that Channel 4 News's FactCheck has raised questions about how both figures had been calculated.[5]

Corbyn found this apparent disconnect deeply frustrating and contended in his planned response that while anti-Semitism existed in the Labour Party and was 'absolutely abhorrent', the scale of the problem had been 'dramatically overstated for political reasons.' Sources familiar with the discussions insist there was no desire to be 'provocative' and that if they had seen Starmer's statement in advance they may have left that line out.

The next morning at 10 a.m., the EHRC report was made public. Its conclusion stated that there was a culture within Labour which 'at best, did not do enough to prevent anti-Semitism and, at worst, could be seen to accept it.' It judged that there had been political interference in the handling of cases, and it highlighted a breach of the 2010 Equality Act in two instances, one involving the former London mayor Ken Livingstone, which cited unlawful harassment including the use of anti-Semitic tropes.[6] Another eighteen cases were considered 'borderline' as there was insufficient evidence to conclude the Labour Party was legally responsible for the individuals. It urged Labour to build a culture of 'zero tolerance' by making it clear to members that anti-Semitic conduct would not be tolerated.

Exactly thirty-six minutes later, Corbyn issued his statement. According to sources, Starmer was furious that the day would now be overshadowed by the former leader, and not his unreserved apology. At 11 a.m. he was due to address journalists, who were sure to ask only about one thing, and there was no time to consider how to respond. So, Ben Nunn suggested he simply say that he had not yet seen Corbyn's statement. Of course, Starmer had seen it and some wondered if one line in particular was consequently added to his speech: '[those who deny that] there is a problem are part of the problem ... Those who pretend it is exaggerated or factional are part of the problem,' the leader warned.

Of course, the language appeared explicitly to call Corbyn out, but sources insist that these words had already been written in advance. When Starmer stepped off the stage, Nunn suggested that his prediction about the former Labour leader being kicked out may have been correct.

In interviews for broadcasters just after midday, Corbyn was then seen to 'double down'. Ultimately, it was the general secretary David Evans's decision to suspend the former leader, who learned his fate as he walked out of the community centre in Crouch End where he had been speaking to journalists. Key figures on the left were furious; John McDonnell called the decision 'profoundly wrong'; Len McCluskey declared it was 'an act of grave injustice'. The next step for Corbyn would involve the NEC as he asked the party to 'kindly think again'.

In the days and weeks that followed, allies of Corbyn believed that they had hammered out a way forward with the leadership. A Zoom call was arranged involving Seumas Milne, the left-wing MP Jon Trickett, and from Starmer's office, Simon Fletcher and Morgan McSweeney, during which they discussed a statement which Corbyn would post on social media. The NEC panel would then decide between two possible sanctions, both of which would see Corbyn re-admitted as a Labour member. What the group did not discuss was the question of his parliamentary whip which allowed him to sit in the House of Commons as a Labour MP. His allies simply assumed that this would follow as a matter of course. Instead, Corbyn was re-admitted to the Labour Party but blocked from returning to the Commons as a Labour MP, and much later he was banned from standing for the party in the 2024 Election.

Senior Labour figures say that this was the moment that Starmer's 'unity' project died; a project that a current cabinet minister privately described as his failed 'Kumbaya' experiment.

In my opinion, Starmer had originally wanted to achieve at least some form of 'unity'; he had no grand plan from the outset to throw Corbyn out of the party. But once he took the decision, it provided him with a feisty response to the repeated Conservative attack about his time serving his predecessor. And ultimately, it would allow

Starmer to draw a contrast between his actions and those of Rishi Sunak, who did not distance himself nearly so far from his own problematic predecessors – Boris Johnson and Liz Truss – despite the damage they had inflicted on the Conservative Party in terms of its reputation for trust and competence.

But if this shift in attitude began in November 2020, sources say he had not properly thought it through by the time of the Hartlepool defeat on 6 May the following year.

Even then, Hartlepool 2021 was not the worst of it. On that same day, Tracy Brabin, Labour MP for Batley and Spen – the seat formerly represented by the murdered and much-loved MP Jo Cox – was elevated from MP to mayor of West Yorkshire. And that meant there was about to be another by-election. A lot of people from inside Labour and across the community were urging the late MP's sister, Kim Leadbeater, to stand. She was not a Labour member as she was working for an organisation that was deliberately non-partisan.

The Jo Cox Foundation was created in the name of a wonderful MP and friend who believed passionately in the benefits of working across political divides, arguing people had 'more in common' than that which divides them. Gordon Leadbeater told his daughter that he and his wife were nervous and apprehensive, but believed she would be a brilliant MP for their local area and that he didn't want her to regret not doing it. In the end Kim Leadbeater decided to go for it, building a team that included chief of staff Lance Price and Matthew Doyle, working on communications. Doyle was a safe and experienced pair of hands: he had worked for years for Tony Blair, running Labour's press office in the 2005 general election, then carrying on in government as a special adviser.

After the Hartlepool defeat, Starmer knew he was hanging on by a thread and his political future would now be defined by whether Leadbeater won or lost, in a little under two months' time. Everyone knew that the Batley by-election was going to be close, in a race that gave an early indication of disillusionment among Muslim voters. Leadbeater had to contend with George Galloway who landed in town to contest the seat with an entourage from his Workers Party of Britain and a claim that if he were to win it would be 'curtains for Keir Starmer'. It was at times a deeply unpleasant campaign in which Leadbeater was once chased and heckled by men from outside the constituency who wanted to know her views about LGBT rights and the Kashmir conflict. Leadbeater claimed that some people had come into the seat to deliberately cause trouble. The stakes were high and so senior figures were sent to the seat week in, week out, including the new shadow chancellor, Rachel Reeves.

Meanwhile, anxious members of Starmer's team discussed the possibility of a leadership challenge should Batley and Spen be lost. They feared that Angela Rayner might want to have a go (her aides felt the rumours were being deliberately planted by figures on the right of the party), or the mayor of Greater Manchester, Andy Burnham, if sympathetic MPs could help manoeuvre him into a seat. In preparation for any attacks they prepared a set of 'war rooms' with a ninety-six-hour action 'grid' starting at 10 p.m. on polling night, Thursday 1 July, until 10 p.m. the following Monday. The communications team were due to ramp up media activity at 5 a.m. on the Friday morning, with announcements on Saturday and a meeting with MPs on the Monday.

Luckily for Starmer, though, he had the best candidate possible. Leadbeater was local and popular, and on 1 July 2021, she won, but only just. '323 votes,' said one senior figure from Starmer's inner team. 'That is how close we came to being challenged.'

Having just about survived, Starmer began to shake things up in earnest. With Deborah Mattinson now in place on strategy, Starmer turned his focus to communications. Ben Nunn had told him some months earlier he wanted to resign and spend more time with his family. So, Matthew Doyle had been sounded out. Doyle saw considerable challenges but, he said, something in his 'political gut' told him Starmer would not be satisfied as leader of the opposition; he saw someone who wanted to be prime minister and so would agree to the decisions needed to edge him closer to Downing Street.

Matt Faulding, previously deputy director at Progress, was recruited at the same time and his first task was to wade through some 10,000 complaints still unresolved, many involving anti-Semitism. He and the party's legal director, Alex Barros-Curtis, brought in over twenty investigators who had worked on complaints inside banks and credit card companies, to focus in on Labour's cases. The vast majority were dismissed but after hours-long sessions by NEC panels a large number of Labour members were suspended or expelled. It was a process that critics on the left of the party saw as a factional purge, but which Starmer's supporters said was about clearing the party of any anti-Semitism.

McSweeney also took a new role, one which everyone knew would make the best use of his skills: campaign director in charge of running elections. Sam White – another returnee from the New Labour years – took over as chief of staff, and Jenny Chapman, who had accepted a peerage the December before, moved to the House of Lords.

With this new team, Starmer decided to complete the organisational changes that he had started as soon as he became leader. McSweeney and White had talked about this idea when they met up at Edinburgh train station to discuss their new roles. The pair walked all day, around the town and up the steep climb to Arthur's Seat, weighing Labour's challenge. White's view was that only one thing mattered for Starmer – whether his Labour Party looked like a credible alternative for government. He believed that a Conservative collapse was inevitable and when that happened, Labour had to be ready.

To this end, the pair discussed the possibility of pushing through a motion in support of organisational rule changes at the party's autumn conference in Brighton later that September. This package of reforms would: stop MPs from being deselected at short notice (a threat which they believed made politicians more preoccupied with the Labour Party membership than with voters); end the system whereby people could sign up to Labour for £3, as thousands had done in order to vote for Corbyn; require six months' membership to vote in a contest; and give MPs far more power over the choice of a new party leader. By raising the threshold for the number of MPs required to get a candidate onto the ballot paper, the group felt it was unlikely that someone with Corbyn's politics would ever be selected again.

McSweeney and White pitched the idea to Starmer, who demanded the evidence to support their proposal. Once he had been persuaded, they told him that if everything went according to plan, he would win this conference vote by 50.5 per cent to 49.5 per cent.

Some of those close to Starmer saw his decision to go ahead with this move as hugely significant. They argued that it pushed against his reputation as cautious; it rather demonstrated that he was politically 'brave'.

'He bet his entire leadership on this vote,' said one.

After all, Starmer's chances of securing the rule changes through a vote at party conference was slim; but trying and failing could potentially deliver a fatal blow to his authority.

Things didn't start well. At a meeting of key trade union leaders ahead of the conference there was furious shouting as some argued it was wrong to spring such significant changes at such short notice. Starmer's best hopes lay with three unions – USDAW, Unison and GMB. The group were helped by both Unison and GMB electing more 'moderate' general secretaries, Christina McAnea and Gary Smith respectively. At a second meeting with Starmer, this time at the conference itself in Brighton, the fury was vented in both directions. Smith was outraged at briefings suggesting his union had done a deal with the Labour leadership. McAnea said she was leaving the decision to her union's 'Labour Link committee'. The anger was enough that during the next few days the baker's union (BFAWU) disaffiliated from Labour. But before that, on 27 September, furious that the party would not agree to a £15 minimum wage as proposed in a new paper on workers' rights, Andy McDonald – one of the only remaining shadow cabinet members from the left flank of the party – quit the front bench. Responding to the news of McDonald's resignation, Jon Lansman, founder of the left-wing Momentum pressure group, told BBC News: 'He [Starmer] promised to unite the party and actually, unfortunately, he's driving wedges within the party.' A day later, Simon Fletcher, the former Corbyn aide who had lent Starmer's leadership campaign credibility on the left, wrote an article for the *Guardian* in which he admitted that he regretted this decision.[7]

Not that any of that stopped Starmer. He pushed on with his plans, first trying to assess the likelihood of his winning the vote on reforms by getting his general secretary, David Evans, to trigger a conference vote on his own position. When that was won, the party carried on to the Rule Book changes. In the end Starmer won narrowly, securing 53 per cent, after a last-minute decision by McAnea's Unison to back him.

Starmer's gamble had paid off, but he'd won it by a nose. Just eighteen months after becoming the leader who had said Labour's 2017 manifesto should be its 'foundational document', he had kicked Corbyn out of the party and forced through rule changes that would make it incredibly hard for any Corbynite to be elected again. When asked by the BBC's Laura Kuenssberg that week, 'What is more important to you, unity or winning?' Starmer did not hesitate. 'Winning,' he said. 'I didn't come into politics to vote over and over again and lose and then tweet about it.'

Watching in the wings, his communications chief, Matthew Doyle, told colleagues he knew then that he had made the right decision in coming back.

Knowing that this battle had won him some political enemies on the left, Starmer prepared for his conference speech in a slightly different way. The team holed themselves up in a spare room in the Hilton Brighton Metropole, where White, Mattinson, Ainsley and Ingham would watch the leader practise the speech, which was being written by Tony Blair's former adviser, *The Times*'s columnist Phil Collins. As well as watching his delivery, they would throw in fake heckles, to see how he might respond.

And so, when the time came to deliver it on Wednesday 29 September, Starmer was ready. Angry activists waved red cards shouting out demands for a different position on Brexit; to free Julian Assange; and for a higher minimum wage. One woman, in a red top with a transparent face-covering to protect from Covid, jabbed her arm angrily, yelling, 'They want to be paid properly!'

Starmer paused, and then addressed the room filled with party delegates: 'Shouting slogans or changing lives, conference?'

8

The Reset

One of the criticisms levelled at Starmer's political operation has been that it is a boys' club. But, while the sheer number of senior women who played critical roles in Keir Starmer's elevation to prime minister puts paid to that notion, many of them have not received quite as much attention as the men. Obviously, we know all about the high-profile figures on the front bench like Rachel Reeves, Angela Rayner, Shabana Mahmood, Louise Haigh, Liz Kendall, Lucy Powell, and so on. And most people probably know exactly who Downing Street chief of staff Sue Gray is, let alone that she is arguably the government's most powerful figure. You might have been aware of strategy director Deborah Mattinson, and possibly Ellie Reeves, whose role as deputy national campaign coordinator will become an increasingly large part of this story.

But how many of the general public know of Hollie Ridley, the 35-year-old from Essex who directed Labour's entire field campaign (and was described to me by one pollster as 'perhaps the best field director in the world')? What about McSweeney's deputy, Marianna McFadden, whose foresight, planning and one-page day-by-day campaign summaries would guide the entire leadership team through the 2024 elections? Or Helene Reardon-Bond, a working-class Londoner who survived the jump from Corbyn to Starmer and then stayed in position, deputising to three chiefs of staff before helping to transition her party into government? Or Claire Reynolds at the Labour Women's Network who drove up the number of female candidates?

There are plenty of others, including Steph Driver, Sophie Nazemi and Jess Leigh in the communications team; Katie Martin and Vidhya Alakeson, whose drive to transform the party's reputation with business I'll come back to; and former policy director Claire Ainsley, who as far as I'm aware was the first woman in that role.

Then there is the woman who was at Starmer's side throughout the election campaign as director of the leader's office, perhaps better described as his 'gatekeeper' – namely Jill Cuthbertson. She really had seen it all before when Starmer's new chief of staff Sam White called to ask if she'd ever thought about coming back. In truth, she had thought about it almost every day but was acutely aware that Labour was 18 points behind in the polls. And Cuthbertson knew, from painful experience, how things could get much worse.

In 2010, she had worked as a 'runner' for then prime minister Gordon Brown, ensuring he got whatever he needed, whether it was a spare suit or his regular lunch of two ham sandwiches, a KitKat, a banana and a bottle of sparkling water. She was with the Labour team in late April on a general election visit to Rochdale, when Brown bumped into Gillian Duffy, a 65-year-old former council worker who had popped out for a loaf of bread. In an exchange recorded for broadcasters, she told the prime minister that her family had always voted Labour; as a teenager her father would go to Manchester's Free Trade Hall to sing *The Red Flag*. But these days, Duffy admitted, she was ashamed to say she was a Labour supporter. In a long discussion about pensions, policing, student funding and more, Duffy noted: 'You can't say anything about the immigrants ... but all these Eastern Europeans are coming in, where are they flocking from?'

At the end of their conversation, the pensioner declared Brown a 'nice man' and said she would vote Labour after all. Cuthbertson, meanwhile, was sitting in the team's back-up car comforting a colleague whose home had been burgled that morning when Brown walked away from the conversation without removing his microphone. With broadcasters still listening and recording, the politician threw Labour's entire campaign into turmoil by telling a colleague, 'That was a disaster [...] she was just a bigoted woman.'

Four years later, Cuthbertson had joined Ed Miliband's 'advance team', racing around the country ahead of the Labour leader to check everything was in place for each visit. But during the 2014 local elections, the team had not managed to recce New Covent Garden Flower Market in central London fully before Miliband's arriving there at 6 a.m. Cuthbertson turned up at 4.30 a.m. and rushed around trying to find stallholders who would talk to Miliband for broadcast, but a number said they were voting UKIP (Nigel Farage's United Kingdom Independence Party) and weren't keen. One man suggested he might do it if Miliband bought a bunch of flowers for his wife, but then a café-owner said yes, so Cuthbertson decided to go with that. When her boss arrived, he told her he was starving. 'There is a bacon sandwich in the car,' she said. But Miliband was too hungry to wait and decided to order the same snack in the nearby cafe, taking a big bite just as the *Telegraph* photographer Jeremy Selwyn started to snap. The resulting awkward photograph spawned internet memes, a debate around gaffe-prone politicians and, on the day before the 2015 election, even made the frontpage of the *Sun* (which definitely wasn't supporting Miliband). So it was not without a sense of trepidation that she returned the leader of the opposition's team.

After Miliband's election loss, Cuthbertson had worked on the Remain campaign. On 16 June 2016 she was in Gibraltar helping to organise a major rally, at which David Cameron was due to speak, when the team on the ground heard the devastating news of Jo Cox's death. The planned event was immediately cancelled and Cuthbertson joined colleagues to help to clear the square. It was there that she met Mo Hussein, an adviser to the then Conservative secretary of state for energy and climate change – soon to be home secretary – Amber Rudd. Hitching a ride back to the UK on Cameron's plane, Cuthbertson didn't know it then, but she had just met her future husband. When years later she met Keir Starmer at Cafe Renoir on Kentish Town Road to discuss the possibility of joining his team, Cuthbertson told him, 'Full disclosure, I am married to a former Tory spad [special adviser].' Starmer replied, with a laugh: 'I shared a room with [the Conservative peer] Andrew Cooper at university, it doesn't bother me.'

Cuthbertson's skills were in operations and logistics; always thinking of how the images surrounding Starmer would help tell Labour's story on the evening news. If Starmer was caught in the rain without an umbrella, it would be her fault. The leader told Cuthbertson that he had a three-part strategy that would aim to drive Labour through the 'Kinnock, Smith and Blair' phases in just five years. He argued that the idea was to modernise the Labour Party just as Neil Kinnock had between 1983 and 1992; highlight Conservative failures as John Smith had done before his sudden death from a heart attack in 1994; and then sell Labour's offer to the country, as Tony Blair had so successfully achieved in 1997.

By then the first 'Kinnock' phase was well underway, but the second and third were reliant on a much better understanding of and how to reach the voters Labour needed to target. McSweeney, Ainsley and Ingham had already turned the focus to winning back working-class voters in towns. Strategy director Deborah Mattinson now went a step further in working out exactly who these voters were. She observed that one reason for underperformance was lack of focus on the voters who mattered most; trying to be 'all things to all people' and, in the end, pleasing none. She commissioned pollsters Opinium to deliver a major segmentation of the electorate in order to identify the key voters in the crucial battleground constituencies. Analysing this study, she identified the group that she would call 'hero voters'.

During the summer Mattinson and Starmer met in her London garden to go through the results and discuss their implications. She remarked that there was now greater voter volatility than ever before, which meant that these voters tended to change their minds and so were very much in play. Further data analysis revealed that they were located in the seats that Labour needed to win, and historically preferred the party but had drifted away, with many voting Conservative in 2019.

When the House returned in September, Mattinson presented her findings to the shadow cabinet. She said that these voters felt that Labour was utterly divorced from them, it didn't understand their lives. They felt Labour was made up of urban graduates who had looked down its nose at them; sneered at them, even. And they were right to think that, said Mattinson. But she pointed to reasons to be hopeful. For one thing, she explained, attitudes shifted fast – take the example of Conservative support taking a nosedive after Dominic Cummings's day trip to Barnard Castle before rocketing up again with the vaccine breakthrough.

A central argument that day was that Labour's problems, though deep-seated, were fixable. 'One reason why our messages are not landing is because we are trying to cast the net too widely,' read one slide in Mattinson's first presentation. 'This means we have a thin appeal across a wide coverage. So, we don't offend anyone, but we don't excite anyone either.' Mattinson said that the party must do even more to tailor a message to its 'hero voter'.

Some of Starmer's top team mocked Mattinson's name for this group and resisted the move to 'wean' the party off talking to every-one, too. They were afraid this tactic would alienate the party and, for some politicians, their own constituents. But Mattinson pushed back, stating firmly that the reason for the name was that Labour had disrespected these voters; to win them back, the party had to treat them like heroes.

Over time, Mattinson would carry out further research showing that while the group was not homogenous, it did follow certain trends. In another slide presentation, Mattinson revealed that those who lived in Conservative-held target seats tended to be non-graduates who had voted Leave in the EU Referendum; earned £30–£35,000 per household; largely were homeowners; and mostly worried about economic security. They spanned all voting ages and tended to be in skilled manual-work or junior managerial jobs. They were often socially conservative and fearful about crime, wanting tougher prison sentences. They were very family oriented, extremely patriotic, concerned that their communities had been left behind and dogged by a sense of unfairness – that hard work didn't pay.

Mattinson said Labour needed to put in place clear and effective lines of attack to persuade 'hero voters' that Conservative 'incompetence' had had a negative impact on their lives, and then offer a positive vision. But she argued that before any of that, these voters needed to believe that Labour was different to the party they had rejected in 2019; her polling suggested that big spending, however individually popular the policies might be, would hamper the urgent need for people to believe that this represented change. The first step must be to boost Labour's reputation for economic credibility, she said.

Rachel Reeves told me that when she was appointed shadow chancellor, Starmer had made clear what he wanted: 'He said by the time we got to the election people had to look at him and see a prime minister and look at me as someone they could trust with the economy.' So that was exactly what her team were thinking about at the autumn 2021 Labour Party conference. Her new chief of staff, Katie Martin, had already helped to introduce a new regime in which shadow cabinet members started hearing the word 'no' more often than 'yes', their policy ideas now eliciting the simple question, 'Where is the money coming from?'

Martin and communications' adviser, Heather Iqbal, launched Reeves's conference media-push with an op-ed in the *Sun on Sunday* (a placement derided by some on the left) and an interview in *The Sunday Times* with the headline: 'Fired-up Rachel Reeves takes her axe to Corbyn's "magic money tree."'[1]

'If you want to pay for things, you've got to explain where that money is going to come from,' she told the paper's Tim Shipman and Caroline Wheeler. The journalists suggested that there were so many questions at the time about Starmer's lack of personality and policies, some thought that if his conference didn't go well, he could well face a visit from 'the men in grey suits' suggesting he tender his resignation.

For Reeves and her team, this marked the first year of what would become a conference routine: gathering in her room the night before her speech with pizza and red wine (just one glass for Reeves) to go through the script. That year, with the fiscal credibility part of the jigsaw laid down, they had another objective. Climate-change fell under Ed Miliband's shadow business brief and was an issue the entire Labour Party wanted to tackle. In shadow cabinet conversations there had been some excitement about what was happening in the US, where Joe Biden was pushing forward the most ambitious climate legislation ever passed but in combination with a modern industrial strategy. With discussions focused on Biden's Inflation Reduction Act, which over ten years would pump $800 billion into the US economy, a corresponding UK target of £28 billion didn't sound crazy. It had been the brainchild of Ed Miliband, then shadow secretary of state for business, energy and industrial strategy, who had been close to Reeves since she backed him for the leadership and served in his shadow cabinet. Miliband had been involved in a Labour Together report, along with colleagues such as Shabana Mahmood and Lucy Powell, in which they had concluded that the party's terrible loss in 2019 had been partly driven by a failure to provide a bold-enough economic offer to working-class communities. The idea behind this new policy was to combine climate ambitions with a compelling story about jobs and industrial change.

Some have told me that at the time there were mild tensions between Reeves and Miliband (particularly when he insisted the party was still in 'favour of common ownership'),[2] so they were keen to have a policy on which they could unite. With interest rates still incredibly low, an investment plan with a green outcome seemed perfect. Moreover, now that Reeves had set down pledges on fiscal credibility, it would give her something with which she could also woo a hall of Labour members, and at the time these plans did fall within the fiscal rules. Reeves' recent experiences of Labour conferences had been somewhat unpleasant and so she was nervous about the reception she would receive. In 2018, one delegate had called her a 'purple Tory' while another asked, 'why don't you fuck off and join the Conservatives?'

Before Reeves stepped up to the podium for her first speech as shadow chancellor, her colleague and old friend, Jonathan Reynolds, leant into her and whispered, 'You were born to do this, it is going to go brilliantly.' In a red dress, Reeves set out plans for an additional '£28 billion of capital investment in our country's green transition for each and every year of this decade.' Raising her voice, she added, 'I will be a responsible chancellor. I will be Britain's first *green* chancellor. Conference, that is what a Labour government will do.' The hall rose to its feet, as hands slammed together. They loved what they had heard.

Some senior Labour figures claim they had not been briefed on the figure that would be assigned to this policy, but it had certainly gone through Starmer's policy team, and Starmer himself was standing on the stage clapping as hard as anyone in the audience, with a beaming smile on his face.

Also enthusiastically applauding was Angela Rayner who had experienced a somewhat tumultuous conference. A recording had been leaked to the media of her describing Conservative ministers (and specifically Prime Minister Boris Johnson) as a 'bunch of scum, homophobic, racist, misogynistic, absolutely vile ... nasty, Etonian ... scum', and of course the comment drew fury from Conservatives. Shadow cabinet members were quick to insist they would not use the same language. Sources tell me she was devastated by what she had said, and knew that it would take some time to repair the harm she'd done to her reputation, but in public at least she refused to apologise for her remark, telling Sky News, 'If the prime minister wants to apologise and remove himself from those comments he's made that are homophobic, racist and misogynistic then I will apologise for calling him scummy.' Later that year, after the murder of Conservative MP Sir David Amess, she would apologise 'unreservedly' for her comments. But at the other end of the spectrum, Andy McDonald's resignation as shadow employment secretary meant that she was given full control of the flagship workers' rights package the party would pledge to deliver within 100 days of a Labour government.

At this point in Starmer's leadership, his policy team of Claire Ainsley, Stuart Ingham and others had developed plans for an industrial strategy, a learning and skills council, and education and mental health reforms, along with the climate investment pledge and employment protections. Gordon Brown's commission on devolution was also underway. And part of the strategy to reach these 'hero voters' also hinged on a sense of patriotism, with Labour wrapping itself in the flag but also making a firmer offer on defence from its shadow defence secretary, John Healey. Ultimately the party would commit to spending 2.5 per cent of GDP on defence but without setting a time frame, opening it up to questions of how credible the pledge was.

The 2021 conference also marked a turn towards Starmer's next big reset; another reshuffle he hoped would be less shambolic than the last. This time the inner team, including McSweeney, Ainsley, Matthew Doyle, Starmer's chief of staff Sam White, and political director Luke Sullivan, met secretly at Deborah Mattinson's house to prevent any leaks. Sam White bought a bag of magnets onto which they could write MP names and departments and then place them on the large metal fridge. In discussions dubbed 'Project Deborah's House' or 'Project Magnet', the group crowded around her kitchen table eating crisps and drinking wine. They worked through dozens of permutations, including names that would not lead to job offers. Hilary Benn's name was on the fridge, but he did not join the shadow cabinet until 2023. There was also some 'blue-sky thinking' about how to make an impact and signal that they were serious, by bringing big players back onto the pitch. At one point, 'Lord David Miliband' (former Labour foreign secretary) was scrawled on a magnet which they moved under different departments, the suggestion of a peerage added to indicate a way back.

With the names and positions decided, Starmer began rejigging the shadow cabinet on 29 November 2021 and, this time round, Luke Sullivan and Starmer's chief whip Alan Campbell and made sure that everything ran smoothly. It would involve some hard decisions: Starmer was sad to demote his close ally Nick Thomas-Symonds from shadow home secretary to the less prominent post of shadow secretary of state for international trade, but he was determined to refresh his top team.

When Yvette Cooper, who already had an influential role chairing Parliament's Home Affairs Select Committee, did not immediately say 'yes' to becoming shadow home secretary, Starmer dispatched Sam White to speed up her decision making. After his calls went unanswered, he turned up at her office in person to wait for an answer, making clear that if she wasn't sure, the Labour leader would assume it was a 'no'. Cooper was in. By the end of the day Starmer had promoted Wes Streeting and Bridget Phillipson – both seen as figures who would drive a reforming agenda – to shadow health and shadow education respectively; David Lammy became shadow foreign secretary, while Lisa Nandy went to levelling-up; Peter Kyle entered the shadow cabinet, taking up the Northern Ireland brief, and, with a reputation for fiscal constraint, Pat McFadden came in as shadow chief secretary to the Treasury. Starmer also split Ed Miliband's former role, shadow business and energy secretary, into two new posts. Given Miliband's passion for climate policy he took the latter, and Jonathan Reynolds became shadow business secretary, a position from which he would drive Labour's planned industrial strategy. Starmer, fond of a football metaphor, would argue that he was simply putting his best players on the pitch but, as the newspaper coverage that followed the shake-up made clear, this was the rise of the party's centrists. As Labour-watcher Paul Waugh (now the MP for Rochdale) concluded: 'Starmer's ruthless reshuffle confirms it – the Blairites are back.'[3]

Jonathan Reynolds's promotion would help turbo-boost the work already underway by Reeves to change Labour's reputation with business. Since joining the party earlier in the year, the shadow chancellor's chief of staff Katie Martin had been focused on this task, organising a series of breakfast meetings at Franco's on Jermyn street. Consequently, in a nod to the shadow chancellor's favourite dish, they dubbed their efforts the 'smoked salmon and scrambled egg offensive' (with echoes of Labour's wooing of the City in the early 1990s, jokingly called 'the prawn cocktail offensive'). These meetings would help set in place their priorities in policy development, including an emphasis on growth, sweeping planning reforms and a shake-up of business rates, as businesses made clear that this is what they needed.

When Vidhya Alakeson joined Starmer's team as director of external relations, she believed that such efforts with business leaders needed to be formalised across the party. Until then there were few channels through which Starmer could reach out strategically to outside organisations. If someone wrote to him, they may have ended up with a meeting, and the odd roundtable had been arranged. But she felt that Labour's relationship with business had been neglected and so, in a three-phase process, they began to turn things around. One source described phase one as urging bosses to 'look in the whites of our eyes'; another called it the 'we are not mad' phase. In this the team were helped by a series of slip-ups by Boris Johnson in which he managed to offend company bosses. In once such incident, at an event with diplomats, when someone raised employer concerns about a 'Hard Brexit', the PM was reported to have said, 'fuck business'. And then, at a Confederation of British Industry event in the North East, there was the bizarre and rambling speech in which he extolled the joys of Peppa Pig World at Paulton Park, over 300 miles south in Hampshire.

And so, Starmer's team got to work organising regular business breakfasts, dinners and roundtables. Previously Starmer had hardly met any FTSE 100 bosses, but by the end of Vidhya Alakeson and Katie Martin's push, he, Reeves and Reynolds had met almost all of the FTSE 250. Then they held bigger events, culminating in a 2024 reception at the Oval cricket ground with 400 business leaders, including bosses from Google, Goldman Sachs and Microsoft. Starmer and Reeves also headed to the World Economic Forum in Davos, dressed in snow boots while they charmed billionaires, arguing that the 'lifeblood of economic growth is private-sector investment'. *Tatler* magazine suggested their aim was also to persuade mega-rich donors to help fund their election bid.[4]

The second phase of these efforts involved business conferences followed by much more focused policy work, in which industry figures were invited to discuss Labour ideas and how they might impact on their companies. Again, there was a sense that their policies had not been stress-tested with outside stakeholders such as business owners, but also trade unions and other industry organisations. After a chaotic few years, this was music to the ears of British businesses, who for the first time in years now lined up to attend the Labour Party conference.

Inevitably, some on the Labour left felt uncomfortable with their party's courting of the super-rich and felt the party was moving further away from its radical roots. They feared that these conversations with business would have an impact on Labour's pledges on workers' rights, rail nationalisation, and plans to put a stop to future oil and gas contracts. Such objections put pressure on the party, with opposing views from trade unions, particularly over changes to employment rules, hammered out over time.

A high point for Katie Martin came when Reeves's links to the former Bank of England governor Mark Carney bore fruit. When Carney agreed to endorse Reeves, Florence Wilkinson (who had filmed Starmer over the years) was dispatched to record Carney's message and hurriedly cycled across London to an agreed location.

The resulting video was supposed to play as a big reveal ahead of one of Reeves's conference speeches, but when it failed to do so, Starmer (sitting next to Reeves) told her to get up on stage quickly and start speaking. Luckily, the technical hitch was solved and Carney's words, which had been pre-briefed to journalists, boomed out right at the end.

Martin also supported Reeves's first communications chief, Heather Iqbal, in transforming the shadow chancellor's personal image. Focus groups suggested that voters needed convincing of her economic credentials. To highlight Reeves's intelligence, Iqbal focused on her background as a child chess-prodigy and urged her boss to shoehorn her experience as an economist at the Bank of England into every possible conversation.

'We joked that we have to say, "Bank of England economist", like Sadiq Khan says "son of a bus driver", until people rolled their eyes,' said one source.

The team wrote a note about the type of background images that should accompany all of Reeves's media appearances: boardrooms in the City, the New York Stock Exchange, or the front door to the Bank of England. They did not worry about the optics appearing elitist because all their research suggested people did not consider the shadow chancellor to be 'out of touch'.

Reeves also built a fearsome reputation with shadow cabinet colleagues who, when pressed on why they weren't making more spending commitments, would retort, 'Have you met Rachel Reeves?' At the Labour Party's so-called 'Clause V' meeting to hammer through the policies that would make it onto the party's election manifesto, Reeves commented that Wes Streeting had just fifteen minutes to present his section on health, warning (with a smile) that 'for every minute you go over, it will be £100m less for the NHS.'

With voters, Starmer faced different challenges. The first was a personal one. His title 'Sir Keir'; his background as a leading lawyer; and his north London constituency risked evoking in the minds of some voters an image that was distant and somewhat elitist. His team knew that this was not a fair representation of Starmer, who had grown up in a working-class family and been knighted because of his work in the legal profession. However, his now well-rehearsed story about being the son of a 'tool-maker' who grew up in a pebble-dash semi and knew what it was like to go without things, was not well-known to start; and in fact he was reluctant to talk about it at all. Matthew Doyle and others, including Steph Driver, one of his closest media aides, persuaded him to lift the veil on his private life. Starmer's long-standing fear was that speaking out would make his wife or children 'fair game' and when he ultimately did start revealing more about himself, it rarely involved them. He would tell aides, 'I talk about them the least because I love them the most.'

At first, Starmer was not happy about his new openness. Once he mentioned his care-worker sister in Prime Minister's Questions (PMQs) and told his team he was 'mortified' when tabloid journalists turned up at her door the next day. He felt he had let her down and should have stuck to his instincts about his privacy.

But over time he has become less reticent. During interviews for our ITV documentary, he told me the story of his father's equal treatment of him and his brother, which he saw as a 'real leveller'. He admitted that Angela Rayner was right to suggest that she 'overshares' while he 'undershares'. Having suffered the trauma of losing a loved one myself, I wondered if the experience of being in and out of hospital with his seriously ill mother Josephine had led him to a more guarded state? Starmer described the terrible experience of seeing her surrounded by monitors, and of sitting by her bed through long nights fearing he would lose her. He spoke of his late dad Rodney's total devotion to his mum, who suffered with a rare form of inflammatory arthritis, but his 'distant' relationship with Keir himself, because of his long working hours and more 'traditional' parenting approach. He almost teared up when he admitted they had never had that conversation to tell his dad how he felt. 'I knew I needed to, but when he eventually went downhill, he went downhill quite quickly,' he said. 'I should have done.' The experience, he told me, had made him deliberately pursue a different relationship with his children, 'talking ... hugging ... sitting with them', and including his now famous desire to keep Friday evenings after 6 p.m. free to be with them.

Despite these concerted efforts, there was still a sense from voters that they didn't know what the party, or its leader, stood for – something that infuriated Starmer. Some of his closest aides had worked with him to try to solve the problem. Peter Hyman had been an adviser to Tony Blair in opposition ahead of 1997, and then after Labour's win was head of the Strategic Communications Unit at Number 10 between 2001 and 2003, and the prime minister's speechwriter. He had then worked as a teacher and then headteacher, co-founding School 21 in Stratford, before returning to the party to advise Starmer. Grappling with this question of what his party stood for, he and others asked Starmer, 'What's your vision?'

Starmer replied that he hated the word 'vision', deeming it vague; inviting policy talking-shops rather than action. Hyman spoke to colleagues and looked to Germany, drawing ideas from Olaf Scholz's Social Democratic Party of Germany (SPD) who had included four 'missions' for the future in their manifesto. They also referred to economist Mariana Mazzucato's book *Mission Economy*, which was inspired by John F. Kennedy's 1962 'moonshot' programme, in which the former US president set out his mission to send an American man to the moon within a decade. But moon-landings were outside Labour's aspirations, so what objectives might work? When they discussed the idea of 'missions', Starmer loved what he heard, with one proviso: he wanted the goals to be big, telling Hyman that he hoped they would elicit a 'sharp intake of breath'.

And as Hyman drove forward the project that would ultimately provide the policy scaffolding for Starmer's premiership, some of the missions laid down did just that. Labour promised to cut both knife crime and violence against girls and women by half; deliver clean power by 2030; return NHS waiting lists to the levels of the previous

Labour government; and secure the highest sustained growth in the G7. I remember my colleague Robert Peston arguing that the growth goal was eye-watering, but exactly how would Labour achieve it?

The critique Starmer would repeatedly face along the way was that these final outcomes may be all well and good, but could he lay down the details of the route that Labour would take to get there? Hyman's pitch was that missions were about moving away from so-called 'sticking-plaster politics' and quick fixes and instead embedding longer-term thinking into governance; not just setting out policies but encouraging ministers to work together across departments and to devolve power. Ultimately, the plan was to turn pledges into retail offers, but only after underlying arguments had been made.

In developing the party's priorities, Hyman asked Starmer what he cared most about? The Labour leader had recently visited Burnley, the 2019 constituency win that had come as the biggest surprise to the Tories. Starmer told Hyman that what mattered to him more than anything was to be able to say to the people of Burnley that Labour could and would match their ambitions, and that they would no longer have to leave their Lancashire town to achieve great things. And so, breaking down barriers to opportunity through childcare, education and skills reform would be the most personal to Starmer, but economic growth was seen as the most important for the country if Labour was to win. The other three priorities would be framed around making Britain a clean-energy superpower; taking back the streets; and building an NHS 'fit for the future'. Some saw the missions as an intellectual project that did not capture the imagination of voters but Starmer never veered from the plan. One adviser told me that holding off on a 'retail offer' was about discipline, arguing 'even if Keir Starmer tattooed the policies to his chest, voters are not paying attention yet.'

Eventually the party put forward a schedule for six 'first steps', including tough spending rules to deliver economic stability; 40,000 more health appointments each week; a Border Security Command to target the gangs operating boat crossings via the Channel; creating the publicly-owned Great British Energy to invest in green technology; cracking down on anti-social behaviour; and recruiting 6,500 new teachers. Labour would also frame other flagship policies under the structure; for example, shadow transport secretary Louise Haigh would pitch policies including rail nationalisation as helping drive growth, fostering the green revolution, and creating opportunities by providing affordable and reliable transport to work. The party would go on to promise not to raise Income Tax, VAT or National Insurance in its first term in power but did set out plans for some more targeted tax increases, including forcing private schools to pay VAT to help fund changes in the state system.

Hyman's argument was that voters were saying: 'We no longer trust the Tories, but what would you do? And can you be trusted to deliver?' Missions provided 'clarity and credibility', he argued, and provide a platform 'on which we will build our election campaign over the next twelve months', in an unapologetic pitch to take on 'the bureaucracy, the NIMBYs and the cynics too, to achieve the real change the country needs'. Communications director, Matthew Doyle, told journalists that Labour was moving into a new phase that he described as, 'If not them, why us?'

Did Labour fully answer that question for voters? Many would argue that the sheer size of the party's victory means the answer to that question must be 'yes'. But there are plenty of critics who observe that Starmer never achieved anything like the levels of enthusiasm that had been felt for his party during its last rise to power almost thirty years earlier. They point out that Labour's victory would be built on a low-turnout and highly fragmented vote. On election night, even as Conservative MPs stepped up onto the stages from which they would hear of their fate, many insisted that this was not a positive vote for Labour, but the end result of spiralling Conservative decline.

PART III
The Tories

9

Boris

On 8 January 2021, Labour's deputy director of communications, Paul Ovenden, received a call from someone who thought they might have something interesting to share. The person had been told by a friend about an alleged Christmas party at the Conservative Party's Westminster headquarters, and that Johnson himself had sent out invitations to the event (a claim which is still unproven). The original source had no idea that they were passing information to the Labour Party, nor that this would be just the first tip-off in what would become known as the 'Partygate' scandal.

Ovenden sent a text message to a journalist: 'I have a story. Very good.'

Ovenden, who would later set up and run Labour's 'Tory attack unit', was a former hack who had worked on the *Sunday Telegraph* with political editor Patrick Hennessy, who went on to work for London's Labour mayor. Ahead of the 2010 election, Hennessy tasked Ovenden with reaching out to Conservative candidates, and in doing so he had built himself a network of contacts that would be useful in the future. Years later, his obsession with trying to drum-up attention to Conservative sleaze, from Downing Street wallpaper to Russian donors and these mysterious lockdown parties, would sometimes attract an eye-roll from colleagues who simply did not think these issues were landing with voters. But Ovenden pushed on, convinced that these scandals were reminiscent of the sleaze allegations that dogged John Major's government in the 1990s. His stories from inside government and the Conservative Party would later lead to claims of a nefarious 'red throat' leaker passing information to the Labour Party, although in reality there were a number of 'moles'.

This first Partygate tip-off was not enough to get the story over the line, but it did set Ovenden on a quest to investigate the matter and to gather information on a number of other potential scandals. His efforts would take a variety of turns, from compiling a sixty-page document about the financial affairs of one cabinet minister to picking up from a shaking employee a brown envelope containing bullying allegations about a colleague. He also helped shadow environment secretary Steve Reed and adviser Owain Mumford to highlight the controversial approval of a property scheme by the then housing secretary, Robert Jenrick, after he sat next to the developer at a Tory fundraiser.[1] The approval of the scheme was later reversed.

But Labour's secret squirrelling was not Johnson's only problem. First was the breakdown in relations with his former Vote Leave advisers. Lee Cain had left on 11 November 2020 after a furious bust-up with Johnson's wife Carrie over the appointment of a new press secretary. Cain believed that, contrary to the advice of the Civil Service, Carrie was trying to parachute a friend into the role. The prime minister had suggested making Cain his chief of staff, but there was too much bad blood and so he declined. Even more problematic was that two days later, Johnson's chief strategist, Dominic Cummings, also walked away, taking with him many of the PM's secrets and considerable resentment about the way in which Johnson had been behaving.

Second, the *Mirror*'s political editor Pippa Crerar, who earlier had broken the story about Cummings's trip to Barnard Castle, had herself received a tip about Tory parties during lockdown. Speaking to several sources, she had a sense that something was going on, although at that point she did not have quite enough evidence to crack it open. Meanwhile, in April 2021, ITV News's UK editor Paul Brand and his producer Nathan Lee received a call asking if they would like to watch an interesting video. The tape was a two-hour long recording of Johnson's press adviser Allegra Stratton and her team practising media briefings in a new room they had kitted out in Number 9 Downing Street. A couple of things caught their attention, including Stratton appearing to joke about a 'cheese and wine' Christmas party. 'The fictional party was a business meeting … and it was not socially distanced,' she announced, as others in the room broke into laughter. Brand and Lee discussed the tape with their senior colleagues Amber de Botton and Imogen Barrer, aware of its potential significance. But at first, the source was too nervous to release it.

As Keir Starmer hit a low in 2021 following the Hartlepool disaster, the Conservative political director Ross Kempsell, now Baron Kempsell, who had taken a leading role in that by-election, warned against underestimating the Labour leader. The former journalist who had worked for the Guido Fawkes website and previously written for *The Times*, issued advice in which he argued that Starmer was a 'presentable and acceptable' alternative for 'Tory-persuasion voters'. Internally, Kempsell argued that this middle-aged, suit-wearing party leader who was willing to stand in front of a Union Jack, would come across as non-threatening and ultimately would be defined in contrast to Corbyn. The Tory mantra that Keir Starmer was no Tony Blair was true, he said. But he did not need to be Blair to win. Meanwhile, Sunak's closest aide and chief of staff in the Treasury, Liam Booth-Smith, also argued to colleagues that while Starmer was not setting the world on fire, his approach appeared to be placing strategy ahead of tactics, including by pulling his punches over the government's handling of the pandemic. Sitting in the Downing Street garden, Booth-Smith told another aide, Henry De Zoete, that Starmer looked deadly serious.

In the eyes of Conservative insiders looking back at this period, one mistake was the failure of the party to communicate 'aggressively' just how much they were doing to intervene in people's lives. Among those working inside Numbers 10 and 11 Downing Street at the time, there was a sense of frustration that there was little longer-term credit for the £350 billion bailout for workers at the height of Covid. But the second problem they point to is the issue that drove a wedge between the prime minister and the chancellor: 'The thing that fundamentally broke Boris and Rishi was the social care tax,' said one senior figure from the time.

By the middle of 2021, the NHS was on its knees as a result of the pandemic and needed an urgent injection of support. By turning its focus so heavily towards Covid patients, other serious illnesses had been pushed to the back of the queue, with some devastating consequences. I will never forget my interview in August 2021 with 27-year-old Sherwin Hall, a young dad with a six-year-old and new baby, who struggled to get medical attention for the excruciating pain he was suffering in his groin. He turned up at hospital twenty times begging for help but was told scans were backed up and delayed. When Hall finally received a scan, doctors found dozens of tumours, and told him his chance of survival was below 5 per cent. Just a few months later, in December, Hall died. And many others were still languishing on waiting lists. Johnson wanted to clear the backlog but also deliver on a pledge he had made in the 2019 Conservative manifesto: to fix the crisis in social care and ensure no one would ever have to sell their home to pay for support.

Sunak's friends have described him as a 'fiscal purist' who strongly believes that the government must demonstrate how it plans to fund state spending. Although the then chancellor felt the pandemic borrowing splurge was justified, he believed more discipline was required in its wake to maintain market confidence. Ministers have described Sunak arguing in cabinet meetings that every time the public want more money for the NHS, 'we should say "fine, but here is a levy to pay for it."' His point was not to argue in favour of tax rises but rather spending restraint. Sunak, therefore, was deeply frustrated by Johnson's demands. He presented the prime minister with a package that could cover spending to deal with the NHS backlog without raising taxes. But Johnson was insistent that he wanted his promised social care policy. The PM would have been relaxed about extra borrowing to fund the plans, but that was not on offer from this chancellor. Sunak told aides that he was not willing to pile a £10 billion liability on the state without a new funding stream and so pitched the idea of a health and social care levy of 2.5 per cent on National Insurance Contributions (NICs), which people would see on their payslips and know what it was being used for. Some say he was trying to 'call Boris's bluff' and expected the PM to back down – but he didn't. One cabinet minister from the time described it to me as a 'power play in which everyone lost'.

One of the big issues with the chancellor's proposal was that in delivering one manifesto promise, the government would be breaking another. In 2019, the Conservative Party had made a 'tax guarantee' not to raise Income Tax, VAT or NICs. The weekend before the policy was announced, Sunak's chief of staff urged him to ditch the levy even if it killed the PM's social care policy, warning that Johnson would claim further down the line that 'Rishi made me do it.' Sunak was frustrated and considered quitting as chancellor but his argument was that he was simply setting out how to fund a package; the political decision to go ahead was down to Johnson as leader.

At a cabinet meeting to secure collective agreement, Sunak threw his weight behind the plan. The then trade secretary, Liz Truss, declared that the party should not do it, particularly since the party had long dubbed National Insurance a 'jobs tax' that hit hard-working people. For advisers in Number 10 this was the beginning of strained tensions between a prime minister who wanted to spend big and a fiscally cautious chancellor. Sunak was placed on 'resignation watch'.

In the event, the policy was very popular, with support from 58 per cent of the public, while only 22 per cent opposed it.[2] On 6 October 2021 at the Conservative Party conference in Manchester, a confident-sounding Johnson delivered a bombastic, joke-filled speech to rally party activists. To defend his coming tax rise, the leader invoked the former Conservative prime minister Margaret Thatcher, contending that she 'would not have ignored this meteorite that has just crashed through the public finances' and allowed borrowing to rise further. He poked fun at cabinet colleague Michael Gove who had been pictured dancing in an Aberdeen nightclub, suggesting he was testing out sweaty venues following the relaxation of Covid restrictions. 'Let's hear it for Jon Bon Govi!' he cried. And he hit out at Labour. 'Did you watch them last week in Brighton,' he said of the party conference at which Starmer forced through his bold rule changes. 'Hopelessly divided,' he continued. '[…] a seriously rattled bus conductor, pushed this way and that […] by a Corbynista mob of Sellotape-spectacled sans-culottes.'

In the car on the way back to Downing Street, Johnson spoke to Ross Kempsell, his speechwriter at the time. They were both stunned by how well the conference had gone and how well the party was faring in the polls, despite everything that was happening. But they also wondered: was this sudden elation a warning sign?

That very month, Pippa Crerar had received a call from a source who wanted to meet her in person. This source showed her what she has since described as a 'metaphorical brown-paper envelope'. This looked like more evidence of parties, but ones that may have taken place inside Downing Street. Crerar's interest was piqued, not least because of the tip-off she had received nine months earlier, in January. But the information she had was still not enough, so she began hitting the phone. Speaking to over a dozen sources, half of them in depth, it would take more than a month for Crerar to gather the evidence she needed.

On the morning of Tuesday 30 November, the chief executive of the UK Health Security Agency Dr Jenny Harries used an interview on Radio 4's *Today* programme to urge people to be careful that Christmas, 'not socialising when we don't particularly need to.' When later that day Crerar took a seat in the Number 9 Downing Street briefing room, she had these words on her mind. So she was surprised to hear Johnson's official spokesman contradict Harries and suggest that the PM 'did not want people to cancel those events.' This was the spur that Crerar needed. She gathered together all her source material and broke the story.

Under the screaming headline, 'Boris Johnson "broke Covid lockdown rules" with Downing Street parties at Xmas', Crerar revealed three allegations: that in November, 'when the country was in the grips of the second lockdown', the PM had given a speech at a leaving do; there had been social gatherings in his Downing Street flat; and just days before Christmas 2020, members of his team had held a bash in Downing Street, with wine, a Christmas quiz and a Secret Santa.[3] Crerar reported what a source described as a 'Covid nightmare', with claims that forty or fifty people were crammed 'cheek by jowl' into a room.

Crerar included a statement from a Downing Street spokesman in response to her stories about parties, which stated simply: 'Covid rules have been followed at all times.' And that is what some who have been close to Johnson consider as the 'original sin' on Partygate – the lie.

Some who were in Downing Street at the time insist that they genuinely believed that the rules had been followed, and certainly they claim that Johnson thought that. But following detailed investigations by civil servants and then the police, we now know it wasn't true.

Inside the Labour Party, Paul Ovenden was ready for this story to break, having been thinking about the claims he had heard for some months, and he knew that Starmer would not have to wait long to get stuck in. Alongside Stuart Ingham, Ovenden was a key figure in prepping the Labour leader for his weekly Wednesday PMQs sessions in Parliament. Each week on Monday, they would discuss likely issues, draw up a script on Tuesday, then lead a practice session in the LOTO boardroom with various colleagues, including Tom Webb who would play the current prime minister. Starmer would joke that they had the 'best job in the world because you can call your boss every name under the sun without any comeback.' That week, they knew the best tactic was to draw on Starmer's legal brain; how could they force Johnson to place his denials on the record in Parliament?

'As millions of people were locked down last year, was a Christmas party thrown in Downing Street for dozens of people on 18 December?' asked Starmer. In his first mistake in a scandal that would consume his premiership, Johnson replied, incorrectly, of course, 'All guidance was followed completely.'

The next day Johnson was filmed receiving his booster jab at St Thomas' Hospital in Westminster. Afterwards, I was there to carry out what is known as a 'pool clip' – when broadcasters take it in turn to question politicians for interviews that are then shared. 'You said no rules were broken. Why don't you make this story go away and tell us what happened?' I asked. Johnson immediately swerved the question.

In the ITV News headquarters on Gray's Inn Road in London, Paul Brand, Nathan Lee, Amber de Botton and Imogen Barrer began furious conversations with lawyers about the leaked tape showing Allegra Stratton and colleagues laughing about a 'fictional party'. By seeming to prove that Johnson was not telling the truth, they knew that what they had could be explosive. The nervous source of this video had seen the prime minister's response to the *Mirror*'s allegations and had started to change their mind. 'You can run it,' they now said.

At 5 p.m. on Tuesday 7 December 2021, Robert Peston and I were invited to chat with Keir Starmer in the LOTO boardroom. Labour had taken a lead of 6 points over the Tories and a confident-sounding Starmer talked about the fact that no one had thought he could turn things around within one term, but that he planned to try. As we were leaving, we told him that a big story was about to break and he might be asked for an interview.

At 6.24 p.m. Paul Brand tweeted: 'EXCLUSIVE: Video obtained by ITV News shows Downing Street staff joking about a Christmas party on 18 December last year.' In light of Johnson's denials, the story, the reaction, the fury exploded.

The next day was PMQs, and Starmer gathered with his close team as usual. That Wednesday, they would once more press on Partygate, trying to lay a trap for Johnson. Starmer believed the PM's instincts to deny any knowledge of having broken any rules could result in a charge that he had misled Parliament. At midday, however, the prime minister tried to get in first. 'I was also furious to see that clip,' he told the House, apologising unreservedly.

Starmer pointed out that the anger was so widespread that Johnson's government had even been mocked by Ant and Dec. 'The prime minister has been caught red-handed,' he boomed. 'Why doesn't he end the investigation right now by just admitting it?'

'Because, I've been repeatedly assured that no rules were broken,' Johnson snapped back.

But again, the assurances were wrong. As is well known, Partygate would morph into a scandal that would start to suffocate Johnson's leadership. An investigation he announced that day would later be taken over by Sue Gray, who would be propelled from a behind-the-scenes enforcer in charge of the government's propriety and ethics team to the most famous civil servant in the country. Separately, the police would also launch an investigation. The difficulty for Johnson was that the Partygate revelations kept coming. On ITV's *News at Ten* Robert Peston revealed details of Number 10 press officers drinking wine together on Fridays; in the *Mirror* Crerar published a picture from a Christmas party in Conservative headquarters; the *Telegraph* offered revelations about boozy parties on the eve of Prince Phillip's funeral; and there was more from Paul Brand and colleague Amber de Botton, who brought in a number of significant scoops. One of their stories, which revealed an email inviting Downing

Street staff to a 'bring your own booze' reception in the gardens during the first lockdown, caused a particular storm.

All the while, the government's denials continued, giving the sense of a cover-up. Sometimes a story led to strange conversations. On the day after the *Guardian*'s Rowena Mason published a picture of Johnson, his wife and advisers, sitting in Downing Street's garden on 15 May 2020, drinking wine and eating cheese, I was in Downing Street for another pool clip. Johnson was talking about a dangerous spike in the Omicron variant of Covid, urging people to be cautious and get vaccinated.

'Do you understand why people are angry, and maybe less likely to do what you say?' I asked, referring to the photograph and the way it had made people feel since, at that time, they could not even have that many people at a loved-one's funeral.

'Those were people at work, talking about work,' he replied.

'So, you were having a work meeting, without laptops, without any notes or paper – do you normally have wine and cheese at a work meeting?' I retorted.

'Those were people at work … talking about work,' he repeated.

By 10 January 2022, Labour had a 10-point lead in some polls, with a large majority of the public thinking Boris Johnson should resign; the PM was in trouble with his own party and appeared broken when grilled on behalf of broadcasters by Sky News's impressive political editor Beth Rigby. One MP representing a Red Wall seat in the Midlands, who would go on to be a Johnson-supporting tub-thumper, told me he thought it was time for a 'managed exit' for Johnson. The politician representing his neighbouring constituency agreed. As MPs saw the scale of anger in their constituencies, this sentiment spread.

Later in the month came 'the pork pie plot', when Alicia Kearns (whose constituency was home to the famous Melton Mowbray pork pie) hosted a meeting of discontented Red Wallers and others who had become MPs in 2019. Graham Brady, chair of the Tory backbench 1922 Committee, started to receive a steady stream of 'no confidence' letters, raising fears within Downing Street that Johnson could be forced to face a vote. What could he do to shore up support?

The answer? 'Operation Save Big Dog'. A team was set up in the office of Johnson's then chief whip, Mark Spencer, whose job it was to corral his party's politicians and get them voting in line with the prime minister. This group included key Johnson allies such as MPs Nigel Adams and Chris Pincher, along with political advisers Ben Gascoigne (known to the group as 'Gazza'), Charlotte Owen, and Johnson's adviser and speechwriter Ross Kempsell. Transport secretary Grant Shapps, who would later be dubbed the 'spreadsheet assassin', was brought in to do the numbers. According to a source, the basic aim of this supplementary whipping operation was to 'analyse MP sentiment'. Shapps would assign a score to Tory MPs ranging from 1, which indicated total loyalty to Johnson and would lead to an invitation to the 'support group', to 0 for those who had submitted a letter of no confidence. Letters from 15 per cent of Conservative MPs would trigger a vote.

Each day at 9 a.m. and again at 2 p.m., the team would gather in the chief whip's office with supportive MPs. Pincher would read out a list of colleagues' names, and they would be carved up depending on who felt best placed to reach out to whom. The politicians in the room would then spread out and aim to 'bump into' colleagues to start organic conversations to gain insights into their opinions about Johnson.

'Operation Save Big Dog' (an informal name revealed by the *Independent*'s Anna Isaac) grew out of a more strategic 'hearts and minds' approach to MP outreach put in place by Charlotte Owen when she moved from Johnson's political office in Number 10 to become a special adviser. She felt that the prime minister's team had not put enough effort into relationship-building, which she considered critical to party management. When Johnson's leadership was rocked by the Partygate allegations, Owen became the point-person to whom MPs would feed data to help the team build an overall assessment of just how much trouble the prime minister was in.

As part of the effort, Owen implemented simple steps, such as the PM marking colleagues' birthdays, weddings and other special occasions. Once, in what some present dubbed 'the worst pub quiz of all times', Owen even took a group of MPs to the pub in order to compile a list of the names of their colleagues' partners. And on Saturday evenings, the Tory leader would host Zoom calls for dozens of colleagues. The aim was to boost morale in the party but also to encourage Conservative MPs to withdraw their letters, and many did.

The group believed that Lee Anderson, the outspoken Ashfield MP (now Reform UK MP for this same constituency and Nigel Farage's chief whip), was one of the 'pork pie plotters' and had submitted a letter. When Anderson mentioned he had good friends visiting from Ashfield, Owen encouraged him to bring them along to Number 10 for a private tour. Afterwards they headed to Johnson's parliamentary office where the PM (perhaps after an encouraging text message) flung an arm around Anderson to shower the MP with a bit of love in front of his friends. Owen et al. believe he later withdrew his letter, and Anderson went on to become a vocal Johnson supporter, only later leaving the party under Sunak.

Those working with the PM said they could feel the situation shift, as if they were headed into a 'nosedive that we pulled up from at the last moment'.

In February 2022, the Operation Save Big Dog efforts were followed by a staff shake-up. Senior figures linked to Partygate were sent walking, while new faces came in. One of those was the prime minister's latest communications director, Guto Harri, who had worked with Johnson when he was London mayor.

At 5 a.m. on 24 February 2022, Russian missiles began to strike Ukraine, with explosions in the capital Kyiv, the cities of Kharkiv and Odessa, and the Donbas region. As the war began, Johnson rose to the occasion, developing a positive relationship with President Zelensky that matched Britain's place as a special ally. One of

Zelensky's advisers described the British prime minister as a 'hero', and some Ukrainian towns proposed naming streets after him.

The advent of a war in Eastern Europe changed the mood in Parliament too. A Conservative MP who had previously argued that Johnson's premiership needed to come to an end, sent me a message, saying 'The situation in Ukraine has changed a lot for me. Both because that's where I think all the focus should be and secondly the PM, in my view, has handled it very well.' This MP also approved of the recent personnel changes inside Downing Street, concluding that he now believed that plunging the party into a leadership election would not be a 'reasonable thing to do'.

That spring, things started to get rocky for Rishi Sunak. In early April, journalist Anna Isaac broke an exclusive story in the *Independent*, claiming that the chancellor's multi-millionaire wife had 'avoided tax through non-dom status.'[4] Next, Sky's Sam Coates asked: 'Did he have a US Green Card declaring himself "permanent US resident" during his first year as chancellor?' The answer was yes. It's hard to overstate the impact these stories had on Sunak's squeaky-clean reputation; suddenly the 'furlough chancellor' who had saved the nation was seen as rich, elite and out of touch. His colleagues in Number 11 were suspicious about the source of these allegations, with some rumours circulating questioning if it could be via someone close to Boris Johnson. But sources have also told me that, in light of the story, Johnson himself urged his team to 'rally around' Sunak. There was certainly a sense that the scandals would dent any future leadership hopes for the chancellor.

Some say that Sunak's chief of staff was 'as ambitious or more ambitious' for the top job than his boss. Liam Booth-Smith stood out in Tory circles, having grown up with his mum on a council estate in Stoke-on-Trent, where Labour had long been in power. Booth-Smith saw this political dominance as a 'one-party state' but did not feel that things had improved in his hometown. After university, he worked in think-tanks focused on local government before moving into government to advise the Tory communities secretary, James Brokenshire. It was there that Booth-Smith hit it off with the junior minister Rishi Sunak and this workaholic pair became firm friends.

It is clear that by 2022, Booth-Smith and other members of the chancellor's team were already thinking big for Sunak. Before Christmas that year, when Johnson was facing a slew of Partygate claims, members of his team registered the official website, 'ReadyforRishi.com'. But after the leaks, the team decided to step back.

At a meeting at Dorneywood, the country home that senior ministers can use, Sunak and his team agreed that they did not know what the future held, but for now they needed a rethink focused on rebuilding his brand by doing good work and concentrating on voters rather than the Westminster village.

But just as the team felt that things were settling down, the police investigation into Partygate drew to a close with the shock news that both the PM and chancellor would be receiving a fixed penalty notice for a gathering in the Cabinet Room to cut a cake on Johnson's birthday. Sunak was horrified, not least as he believed he had simply turned up to a meeting five minutes early. A friend described Sunak's response as 'mortified, enraged, pissed off' and, once again, ready to resign. In conversations, including with former Tory leader William Hague, Sunak argued that even if the fine felt unfair, surely it made it untenable to remain in such a high-profile position because of the impact on public trust?

Some of Sunak's aides see his decision to stay in the role as a mark of 'loyalty' to Johnson, arguing that the chancellor wanted to quit but that doing so would suggest that the PM ought to follow suit. He agreed that there was no way to resign without implicating Johnson too.

I've seen evidence that when government lawyers were preparing papers for the Covid Inquiry they highlighted a number of events in Johnson's diaries that they believed might constitute a breach of the rules. These included an overnight stay of an adviser in Chequers in

October 2020, which they warned may not have been in line with the tier system of restrictions unless 'reasonably necessary' for work. Also flagged was a dinner with a donor in Downing Street that November, the day after the country went into national lockdown, with the query, 'Was it reasonably necessary to meet indoors for work purposes?' Questions were also raised about meetings in the Downing Street flat. Sources said the diary was passed to police officers, who declined to investigate, and so Johnson was cleared of any potential charges relating to these events.

Thursday 5 May 2022 brought local elections in England, Scotland and Wales. The Tories lost almost 500 seats and control of eleven councils, but it was a mixed picture for Labour, too. While the party had made gains in a number of councils, it had failed to break through in Newcastle-under-Lyme, where the Tories had not only retained control but gained 2 additional seats.[5] At Labour HQ, senior figures wanted to shake up the way the party campaigned and operated at council level, both in opposition and in power. There was a sense that where Labour-run councils were underperforming, it would make it harder to win general election seats. General secretary David Evans, along with campaign director Morgan McSweeney, established plans to tackle the issue by introducing a system in which poor performance would be reported to the party's NEC. In response, Labour could establish a 'campaign improvement board' that could force tough action – including the option of 'removal of [Labour's] group leader'. The move was deeply controversial for some in the party who saw it as Starmer taking centralised control of councils in a way that could stifle local representation. To them, this was yet another example of the Labour leader's ruthless streak. But Evans and McSweeney saw underperforming councils as a key driver of voter sentiment and feared that failing to take action would cost the party seats in a general election. Besides, there was 'world-class' training from the Local Government Association to help councils, but some Labour groups were not taking that up.

For example, they knew they had a growing problem in Birmingham City Council. Indeed, I'd reported warnings of a coming financial crisis at this council linked to a historic failure to pay women and men equivalent wages for equivalent jobs. The party stepped in to force out Labour's group leader and deputy – which in turn resulted in the pair having to step down as council leader and deputy. The decision to reappoint the roles caused anger locally. Birmingham was nevertheless forced to issue a Section 114 notice (similar to declaring bankruptcy), resulting in higher Council Tax bills and service cuts, which for Labour almost certainly made political fights in this Midlands city tougher in the years ahead.

But before any of that could get underway, Starmer had a more personal problem to face. On the afternoon of Friday 6 May, as results were still coming in, Starmer headed to Carlisle to celebrate Labour gaining the council. Back in HQ, communications chief Matthew Doyle received a call from *Telegraph* journalist, Tony Diver. Durham police were reopening an investigation into the evening just over a year earlier during the Hartlepool by-election, when Starmer and colleagues had visited the Durham MP's office where they had taken a dinner break of takeaway curry and a beer.

It was Tory Ross Kempsell, author in 2021 of that note for Johnson warning that Starmer was a political threat, who had led the party's efforts on so-called 'Beergate'. He was by then director of the Conservative Research Department (which included research into Labour), and searching through newspaper cuttings from the previous year, he had come across the *Sun* article referring to that night. Kempsell believed it was justified to focus on the potential scandal because of the way Starmer had toughened his stance on Partygate. To Tory advisers, the Labour leader's meal looked comparable to Johnson's birthday cake, for which he had been fined. And when they sought legal advice, it suggested that police forces varied on the matter in question but that most would judge Starmer's dinner break as a breach.

In Carlisle, Starmer was horrified. He rushed back to the party's Westminster HQ, stopping briefly to tell broadcasters he would cooperate fully but believed he had done nothing wrong. Next, he gathered together key staff members for what has been described to me as a tense meeting with close aides including Doyle, Steph Driver, Sophie Nazemi, and his chief of staff, Sam White. Starmer told them that, if found guilty, he felt he was going to have to offer to resign, a suggestion which invited a variety of views. White played devil's advocate, warning that this decision would mean handing over his fate to someone else. Despite a clamour from the media to say more, Starmer wanted to take the weekend to think it over properly.

Over the following days, Starmer rang a number of colleagues. Jill Cuthbertson was at home with Covid at the time, so had watched a fairly positive reaction to the local election results unravel from afar. When he rang her, she was clear: if he was found to have broken the rules, he would have to go. The Labour leader also reached out to close friends like Parvais Jabbar who raised the incident when I asked him for examples of things that sum Starmer up. He said this episode 'speaks volumes' about the PM. 'I clearly remember at the time how upset Keir was at that allegation,' he told me. 'Many said he didn't need to [offer to resign] but for Keir, this went to the very core and heart of who he is. For him, his integrity was important and he would not allow this to be questioned.'

Sam White knew that, morally-speaking, Starmer was wedded to the principle of abiding by the law, so having this called into question was 'huge' for the Labour leader. He supported Starmer's decision to think it through over the weekend but was convinced they needed to go into Monday morning with a clear decision. And so, that Sunday evening he turned up at his boss's house. Over a couple of beers in Starmer's front room, the two men systematically argued every scenario and likely fallout. White's view was that while the way to relieve short-term media pressure would be to promise to resign were he found guilty, there were a lot of potential downsides, and so he must think it through. This wasn't a normal decision; it was existential. Firstly, White reiterated his initial reaction; that Starmer's future would lie in the hands of the police whose decision-making on breaches of lockdown restrictions had not always been entirely clear-cut, with a guilty outcome ending his leadership. Secondly, shadow ministers and MPs might start to consider leadership campaigns that could be destabilising even if he was found innocent. And thirdly, voters already thought he had more integrity than Boris Johnson, so there was little upside to the risk. But Labour's lawyers thought that if Durham Police properly applied the law, Starmer would be cleared. By the time White left Starmer's house late that night, the Labour leader had decided what to do and they formed a plan. The next morning, Starmer made an announcement that he would resign if fined, which would similarly apply to Angela Rayner, who was also being investigated.

Starmer was said to be sanguine about colleagues considering the possibility of a leadership contest, with many urging the shadow chancellor Rachel Reeves to be prepared just in case. If it was going to happen, many female MPs wanted to make sure that not all the frontrunners would be men.

White has since argued that Beergate was another example of Starmer behaving in a way that does not fit the 'Ming vase' theory of his leadership. He maintains that this was a huge risk; just like the minute's silence at conference, the radical NEC rule changes, and the staff restructure. But in White's opinion, this gamble wasn't like the others. The downside-risk was existential. The upside gains were negligible. It was a damage-limitation exercise with extremely high stakes. While they awaited the police's deliberation, there would be a 'sword of Damocles' hanging over the Labour Party.

As for Prime Minister Boris Johnson, he still could not shake Partygate allegations, and later that May Sue Gray published her final report with its lurid details of parties, including one where there was a fight and someone vomited. Warning of 'failures of leadership and judgement in Number 10 and the Cabinet Office', the report stated that both political and official leadership teams 'must bear responsibility'.

Meanwhile, tensions over tax were once again mounting between Johnson and Rishi Sunak; the PM wanted to cut Corporation Tax to help boost growth, but the chancellor remained cautious. Sunak insisted that the move could cause economic catastrophe and that inflation would explode. In late June, Johnson and Sunak met with their senior advisers at the PM's office in Parliament. Sunak put forward a document called 'Plan for a Strong Economy' in which he tried to satisfy Johnson's itch with supply-side deregulation including on planning and a longer-term trajectory to tax cuts, but only when it was sensible to do so.

Some present said this meeting between Johnson and Sunak felt more 'performative' than their previous encounters and when it was over, advisers on both sides emerged convinced that this political relationship was running out of road. Behind the scenes, Johnson's team had been throwing around other names as a possible chancellor, including Liz Truss, Kwasi Kwarteng, Dominic Raab, Grant Shapps, and once Priti Patel, though the prime minister was not yet seriously considered moving Sunak on. But after that meeting, Booth-Smith was said to have told his boss, 'You won't be chancellor for long.' And a senior adviser to Johnson agreed that Sunak was unlikely to remain in place if the PM survived the summer. But then, another scandal hit.

Boris Johnson had just jetted around the world for a series of high-profile events that placed him on the world stage. He'd travelled first to Kigali in Rwanda for a Commonwealth Heads of Government meeting, then to Germany's Bavarian Alps where he rubbed shoulders with French president, Emmanuel Macron, before heading to Madrid for a meeting of NATO leaders. Accompanying him, communications chief Guto Harri felt the prime minister had 'smashed it', positing that the tour felt like 'what being a world leader was all about'. So, when the duo returned to Britain on 30 June, the news that MP Chris Pincher had resigned as deputy chief whip after a drunken incident at the Carlton Club, did not strike them as a brewing catastrophe. However, Johnson immediately spoke to his chief whip (then Chris Heaton-Harris) about what had happened and how to respond. The story had been broken earlier by the *Sun*'s Noa Hoffman and Kate Ferguson who revealed an allegation that Pincher had groped two men. Johnson soon faced a howl of anger for failing to go further and neglecting to withdraw the whip from Pincher quickly enough, a move that would suspend him as a Conservative MP. Moreover, rumours about Pincher's behaviour had swirled for some time and so Johnson came under pressure to reveal if he had heard any such claims before appointing him to his role. Downing Street's contention that the prime minister had heard 'speculation', but nothing regarding official complaints, appeared to be blown out of the water by the bombshell intervention of a former senior civil servant. Lord Simon McDonald insisted the PM had previously been briefed in person about a formal complaint; a revelation that caused fury among Conservative MPs, who began to bay for Johnson's head.

Five days later the story was still rumbling on and Johnson's allies once again were trying to shore up the support of MPs. Around sixty colleagues were gathered in his parliamentary office, with Johnson himself tucked away in a side room, when he received a text message from Sajid Javid saying he was about to resign from cabinet. The health secretary then posted a tweet, which landed just as the BBC aired an interview in which Johnson apologised for appointing Pincher. Nine minutes later, came fresh news about which Johnson had not been forewarned. Rishi Sunak had just resigned. In a tweet, he stated his reasons: 'The public rightly expect government to be conducted properly, competently and seriously. I recognise this may be my last ministerial job, but I believe these standards are worth fighting for and that is why I am resigning.'

In the face of the cabinet resignations, Johnson emerged into his throng of supporters and delivered a rallying speech about Sunak's decision: 'Now we can cut taxes!' he hollered. His allies roared with delight.

But it wasn't over; the next day the resignations started pouring in thick and fast. Johnson's inner team gathered in Downing Street to resurrect Grant Shapps's spreadsheet and carry out a reshuffle, including the appointment of Nadhim Zahawi as chancellor. Once again Charlotte Owen began to make a list of loyal MPs, while the PM embarked on an intense day, with PMQs at midday, followed by a series of grillings in a hearing of the Liaison Select Committee. In Downing Street, advisers gathered around a white board on which they desperately tried to fill ministerial gaps, but they also created one.

Johnson had not trusted Michael Gove since the day in 2016 when he blew up his first leadership bid by announcing his decision to run against him. Earlier, Gove had called on Johnson to resign but had not himself stepped down as secretary of state for levelling-up. Guto Harri was irate and told the PM that even if it felt as though they were all going down on the Titanic, Michael Gove should not drown with them – he should be shot on deck. So, he was the one cabinet minister to be sacked.

That evening, I was standing in Parliament's central lobby waiting to speak to restless MPs when I got a call from Guto Harri. Johnson's communications director told me, 'He's carrying on!' I was shocked and tweeted that an 'absolutely defiant' prime minister was not stepping down. Looking back now, Harri compares that last rallying push to the finale of a famous opera. In La Traviata, the protagonist Violetta falls seriously ill with tuberculosis. On her deathbed, when the disease appears to have wholly consumed her, her lover Alfredo turns up to beg for her forgiveness. The couple are reunited and Violetta experiences a sudden surge of energy in which, for a moment, a rapt audience wonders if they are about to get a happy ending. But then, Violetta collapses and dies.

Perhaps that Wednesday evening as his team gathered around the white board and completed filling in all the ministerial positions, it felt as though a miraculous last-minute recovery was indeed possible for Johnson. But later that night, as Johnson prepared to head up to the Downing Street flat, he sounded more resigned when he bid goodnight to his closest aides, as if he knew that the odds were stacked against him. When Ben 'Gazza' Gascoigne left Downing Street and was heading up Whitehall, he called a loyal cabinet minister and confided that sadly he felt it was coming to an end.

The next morning at 5 a.m., 7 July, an adviser messaged Johnson to admit things weren't looking good. The prime minister replied that he was already writing his resignation speech. At 6.30 a.m. Johnson's bleary-eyed allies, devastated and unslept, arrived in Downing Street to a round of bacon butties. They described his mood as 'sanguine' as he prepared to head out to deliver his resignation. In a speech lasting just over six minutes, Johnson thanked the millions who voted Conservative in 2019, many for the first time, declaring that they had provided his party with an 'incredible mandate'– the biggest Tory majority since 1987, and highest vote-share since 1979. Johnson talked about Ukraine and levelling-up, before making clear that he was deeply frustrated by his colleagues' 'eccentric' decision to change government when his party was only slightly behind in the polls. (According to YouGov, the gap widened to 11 points on the day of Johnson's resignation but was much closer in the days before and after.)

He opined that in Westminster the 'herd instinct is powerful and when the herd moves, it moves'. Johnson bowed out by concluding that no one is indispensable in politics, referring to his party's 'Darwinian' nature, which convinced him that the Tories' animal-like survival of the fittest instinct would soon spit out its next prime minister. Johnson (who as a child had famously dreamt of being 'world King') said it was the best job in the world, but 'them's the breaks.' And with that, he turned and disappeared back into Downing Street.

The next day, Durham police announced that after gathering a substantial amount of documentary and witness evidence it would be taking no action against Angela Rayner or Keir Starmer. It marked the end of a tumultuous period during which the Labour leader's political fate was tied to that of his deputy; an experience that aides claimed brought the pair closer together than ever before.

A senior Labour figure once wondered to me if the Conservative Party's biggest mistake was to oust Johnson. 'They panicked,' he said. 'They took a proven winner off the table and [ultimately] replaced him with a loser. Sunak lost the leadership election, local elections and several by-elections.' There are certainly some Conservatives who agree.

Former cabinet minister Jacob Rees-Mogg told me that his party had made a 'catastrophic mistake in thinking it could change the top person without consequences. [...] It was an arrogant decision. Of course, we had problems, Boris should not be confused with the Archangel Gabriel, he shouldn't. But he had a mandate.' He talked about one Tory MP in a Red Wall seat who suggested that they won in 2019 because of his own brand and not the prime minister's. 'The fellow was not even a household name in his own household, let alone his own constituency. It's unbelievably arrogant,' Rees-Mogg added, pointing out that the politician was no longer an MP, having lost in 2024.

One of Johnson's closest allies, Nigel Adams, told colleagues that removing their leader was 'the biggest act of political self-harm in modern history'. But others I've spoken to strongly disagree, arguing that Johnson would have been ousted sooner or later, with the Privileges Committee ultimately ending his time as an MP. There were many reasons for Johnson's downfall, and many individuals behind the various stories that ultimately felled him. But the former Vote Leave adviser who had helped carry Johnson to that stunning 2019 victory, certainly played a part. After his exit from Downing Street, Dominic Cummings publicly attacked Johnson, accusing him of lurching from side to side like a 'trolley'. But Cummings also had a hand behind-the-scenes and his belief that Downing Street would lie in response to certain allegations helped to manipulate the ultimate outcome for Boris. Some of the original Vote Leave team were said to have shared Champagne-bottle emojis when Big Dog was finally forced out of office.

Partygate caused immeasurable damage to the Conservative brand, resulting in a disastrous loss in trust from which it would be difficult to ever recover. But at least the party retained its reputation for economic competence.

10

Liz

A few weeks after the 2019 Conservative election victory and cabinet ministers Matt Hancock and Thérèse Coffey, the health secretary and work and pensions secretary, were performing a karaoke duet of 'You're the One that I want', the chart-topping record from *Grease*. In a packed room, Tory MPs had just discovered that their colleague Angela Richardson had an incredible voice; watched Lee Anderson morph into Elvis; and cheered as trade secretary Liz Truss plumped for Madonna's 'True Blue'. Coffey and Truss had been close friends for many years, and this was one of their famous Christmas karaoke parties held in their ministerial rooms.

So, it was perhaps not a surprise when three years later Truss, by then foreign secretary, asked Coffey if she would run her campaign to become Conservative leader and prime minister. She had considered standing for the position some years earlier, but back then Coffey had confided in her friend that she did not believe she had any chance of winning. This time, they both knew that the odds had changed dramatically. It was Wednesday 6 July 2022, just one day before Johnson finally resigned. Coffey knew that if she could get Truss into the final two candidates, then she would likely win in a contest of Conservative members.

On that same day, Rishi Sunak was with aides at a suite in London's Conrad Hotel, which he'd booked to avoid the cameras that had been congregating outside his home since his resignation as chancellor. He had just released a polished video to accompany his own leadership launch, leading to claims that his bid had been in the offing for some time. His allies claim instead that they had simply hung up a black curtain in the hotel suite and produced the footage within twenty-four hours of Johnson's resignation.

In a series of votes, Conservative MPs whittled down the candidates, knocking out Jeremy Hunt and Nadhim Zahawi, then Suella Braverman, Tom Tugendhat, Kemi Badenoch and then Penny Mordaunt, until only Sunak and Truss were left. The pair went through to a summer campaign in which 172,000 Conservative members would crown a new prime minister. But it didn't take long for Sunak to realise he had little chance of success.

Early on, he gathered together his close team including Oliver Dowden (known as 'Olive' to colleagues and friends), as well as key aides, to look at the polling. It wasn't hopeful, suggesting that Truss was on 49 per cent and Sunak 26 points behind. Sunak's problem was twofold. First was the ingrained sense among Tory members that his resignation as chancellor marked the moment that Boris Johnson (whom many of them still loved) had been knifed. The second was that Sunak wanted to pursue a fiscally cautious agenda; not nearly as appealing to this selectorate as Truss's tub-thumping agenda for growth. Sunak's closest aide Liam Booth-Smith felt that Johnson had 'poisoned the well' and was said to be frank about the polling figures: even if they were wrong, Sunak would need to convert every undecided member. He simply could not see a path to victory, but the former chancellor did not give up, scrapping for votes throughout the summer months.

Truss, meanwhile, looked like a shoo-in and began preparing for government. She would gather colleagues for policy discussions at her London home in Greenwich and later overlooking a lake on the first floor of Chevening, the country house traditionally used by the foreign secretary. As agreed with the government, many of these sessions would be attended by senior civil servants including cabinet secretary, Simon Case, and would act as 'access talks' to prepare for early September, when Truss looked increasingly likely to emerge as the new PM. It was here that the group would start to put together the doomed mini-budget, as Truss set out her desire to take on twenty-five years of economic orthodoxy with unapologetically bold policies from day one.

Some would urge Truss to consider pairing her planned tax cuts with a retrenchment on spending to show fiscal restraint, but she feared the political impact, having experienced just how painful those decisions could be when she was chief secretary to the Treasury. Others argued that supply-side reforms such as changes to planning ought to come first. Truss supported those moves but sources described her as being in an incredible rush to get things done. 'She felt things had to happen yesterday,' said one person present.

Among the civil servants who would join discussions were senior Treasury officials Cat Little and Clare Lombardelli, who were said to warn Truss that if she carried out the measures without a forecast from the Office for Budget Responsibility (OBR), it would result in negative 'consequences'. In the early sessions, Truss's political advisers also urged that the forecaster should be involved as well, but the cast-list would later be narrowed to only those who were ideologically supportive of the direction. Those present say that Truss repeatedly insisted that she did not want to be beholden to what she saw as the 'abacus economics' of the OBR, and instead wanted to try to drive growth through more dynamic changes, which she believed would be triggered by tax cuts. The discussions did not sit comfortably with everyone. There was a feeling that some in the room were nervous at the speed of reform, including MPs Simon Clarke and Chris Philp, who was once described by a Truss aide as going 'white as a sheet' at one particular proposal.

The group were acutely aware of the cost-of-living crisis, with inflation crossing 10 per cent and energy bills spiralling. A lot of their time was spent hammering out the details of an Energy Price Guarantee that would cap bills at £2,500 a year, on top of a £400 discount for all households that winter. The problem was that this was a huge spending commitment on top of the tax cuts that Truss was eager to introduce. During the campaign, she spoke of reversing Rishi Sunak's National Insurance rise (aka the social care tax), suspending green levies and halting a planned increase in Corporation Tax from 19 to 25 per cent. But behind the scenes she wanted to go further, and to lift a cap on bankers' bonuses. Truss saw the move in economic terms, arguing that with potentially just two years in power, this fiscally neutral measure could drive growth. But it was the politics of the policy that bothered her communications director Adam Jones, who urged her in meetings to ditch the idea. He held that the optics were so bad that even bankers were not calling for the change, which he feared would leak and allow Labour to frame the budget as helping the super-rich. But Truss was insistent, asserting that it would send a bold signal that she was prepared to do the right thing even if it was unpopular.

Not that every idea got across the line. Sources tell me that a number of radical plans were put forward at these meetings, including from Jacob Rees-Mogg who was slated to become Truss's business secretary. He often pushed the idea of a 'flat tax' in which Income Tax, Corporation Tax and Capital Gains Tax would be equalised at just 20 per cent, costing the Exchequer around £41 billion. Rees-Mogg claimed that removing a series of tax reliefs, including those applied to pensions, would make the policy fiscally neutral. But some, including the cabinet secretary Simon Case, were said to argue that the proposal was 'undeliverable'. Others wanted to scrap Inheritance Tax.

Two people have described to me an even more leftfield idea, shared in the front room of Truss's London home during a conversation about securing Britain's energy security. Rees-Mogg began with a question: 'What is the big problem with nuclear power?' His answer was that people believed it was unsafe. He mused about the possibility of drawing power from nuclear-powered submarines in order to provide the energy needs of a British town, while also proving the source to be safe. One person present described the conversation akin to Rees-Mogg suggesting they plug Trident (our nuclear deterrent) into a coastal city like Liverpool. Another source also claimed that Merseyside was mentioned as a possible trial site. But when quizzed, Rees-Mogg told me he was referring to nuclear power in submarines, not warheads, and insisted that in any case he would have suggested his home county of Somerset, rather than Merseyside. One source said that in response there was a stunned silence, until a civil servant leaned over to a member of Truss's team and muttered, 'You know that won't work.'

Reflecting on that time, there are some who think that one of Truss's weaknesses was that she governed in 'silos' or 'cells', only inviting advisers or colleagues to the narrow set of meetings specifically linked to their briefs. Consequently, there was a lack of communication across her team, which made it harder to challenge decisions.

In parallel to the discussions on the economy was another set of talks about personnel. Truss had already decided that Kwasi Kwarteng (who was seen as a fellow libertarian) would be her chancellor. Coffey was summoned to her friend's house in Greenwich to discuss her own role. Coffey's dream would have been to be appointed foreign secretary but that had already gone to James Cleverly. 'What about the Home Office?' she asked, but was rebuffed. Truss argued that Coffey wasn't right-wing enough. Instead, she was appointing Suella Braverman, in return for her backing in the leadership race. She asked Coffey if she would be her deputy prime minister and health secretary, a large delivery department in which the minister could build on her experience leading the Department for Work and Pensions. In truth, Coffey was a little disappointed. She had written down the roles she would least like to do, and health secretary was top of the list. Coffey confided to friends that she feared being pilloried because she would be seen as 'too fat', because she had once been photographed smoking a cigar and because of her voting record against abortion rights.

Sources say that Truss was considering offering Rishi Sunak a role as secretary of state for education and skills, but he made clear that he was not interested in serving under her. Did Truss make a mistake in selecting a cabinet that only made space for one of Sunak's supporters, Michael Ellis? Some argued strongly that it would be better to have figures like Michael Gove and Grant Shapps, who could cause trouble on the backbenches, inside the tent, but Truss told advisers that she did not trust Gove or rate Shapps.

Truss was elected Conservative leader (by a slightly tighter margin than expected) and on Tuesday 6 September flew to Balmoral where a fragile Queen welcomed her fifteenth prime minister.

The next day, the new prime minister and her chancellor showed their willingness to take on what they saw as the 'Treasury orthodoxy' by sacking the department's most senior civil servant, Tom Scholar. Truss declared that she would not hold the Number 10 morning meeting in which prime ministers had traditionally run through the day's diary and the newspapers' coverage of the government. She was determined not to be pushed around by headlines and asked for the newspapers to be sent to her advisers rather than directly to her. To some, the loss of this meeting was another example of her 'cell' approach to governing and that made communications difficult.

On day three, Truss was in front of Parliament's green benches announcing her energy package when someone passed her a note that made clear to her that the Queen had little time left to live. The new prime minister gathered with her team in her parliamentary office to write a speech that would fit the moment. When the cabinet secretary, Simon Case, who had previously worked in Kensington Palace as private secretary to Prince William, received the call with the bad news it was met with an atmosphere of utter shock, with Truss struggling to hold back tears.

On Monday 19 September, 2,000 guests descended on Westminster Abbey for the state funeral of Queen Elizabeth II; among them six former British prime ministers and 100 world leaders.[1] It was an emotional day for the country, marked by pomp and ceremony. But with the sense of a premiership curtailed to two years, Truss barely took a breath. Almost everyone I speak to who worked closely with Truss during that period believes that she moved far too quickly when the mourning period was over.

The night of the funeral I was among the journalists who flew with the prime minister to New York for the United Nations General Assembly (UNGA) meeting. Here her communications director Adam Jones was proven right – the plan to lift the bankers' bonus cap had leaked to the *Financial Times*. When I had my chance to interview Truss, we were at the top of the Empire State Building. Shaking slightly because of my fear of heights, I challenged her with the perception that she was helping the rich in the middle of a cost-of-living crisis. Just weeks earlier I had travelled the country hearing heartbreaking stories, and I put to Truss the experience of pub-owner Stephen Hey who told me he went to bed and woke up 'frightened' after his electricity bill rose from £12,000 to £56,000. Truss responded with the argument she had used in Chevening: that in her pursuit of growth she was prepared to be unpopular.

The next day she announced £2.3 billion military aid for Ukraine, then on Thursday she had Coffey unveil a major plan for patients. And then in the House of Commons on Friday 23 September, Kwarteng brought forward the mini-budget. There were no spending cuts to accompany it, nor the supply-side reforms discussed at Chevening. And there was no time for her advisers or Treasury officials to 'roll the pitch' with the public, the markets, or even fully with her cabinet. As for the biggest headline-grabber, the decision get rid of the 45p top-rate of tax, her closest advisers were only told a day or two before and it was not mentioned on the morning of the budget to the top ministerial team. The first time the cabinet heard the plan was when Kwarteng announced it in Parliament to those roaring cheers of Tory backbenchers.

But the markets did not cheer and soon the chancellor's suggestion that there was 'more to come' would add fuel to the fire. When the Asian markets opened on Monday 26 September, they forced sterling to drop further, and then yields on ten-year bonds – the interest rate at which the government borrows – climbed through one day to the next to reach the highest level since the 2008 financial crash.[2] Even the International Monetary Fund took a view, claiming the mini-budget would fuel the cost-of-living crisis. This unusual intervention was seen as deeply political, even by Truss's more moderate aides who themselves were critical about the measures. But the potential impact on voters' mortgages was immediately and painfully apparent. That week saw coordinated statements from the Bank of England and the Treasury as Kwarteng set a date for a 'fiscal plan' that would set out a disciplined approach to spending. Not that it eased the febrile mood at the Conservative Party conference. Even after the 45p U-turn, and despite a speech to delegates that was warmly received, the fraught, nervous energy was palpable.

Panicked by party disunity, Truss wondered what to do. And then it emerged that she was facing an even bigger problem, which no one had her warned about. A tinderbox, concerning Liability Driven Investment funds, or LDIs, had been set alight below her feet.[3] It turned out that pension funds had invested heavily in LDIs which aimed to reduce economic volatility by investing in turn in long-term gilts or government bonds. But gilt prices fall when interest rates spike, and that meant that their plummeting value had generated an unexpected crisis in pension funds. These were forced to urgently sell the gilts and other assets, pushing their price down even further. On his podcast, *The Rest is Money*, my colleague Robert Peston said the Bank of England had only learnt of these forced gilt-sales on the Monday after the mini-budget and had put in place a time-limited rescue plan, pledging to buy £65 billion in government bonds to stabilise the markets until 14 October. As this deadline approached, panic was spreading through the Bank of England and Treasury because the crisis was being escalated by a mechanism that no one seemed to have previously understood. Does that mean that the resulting financial crisis was not Truss and Kwarteng's fault?

Peston has pointed out that neither were pre-warned about the risk, arguing that when the 'Establishment' banged them out of the door of Number 10, relieved to see the back of them, it did not suit the narrative to question the poor performance of the Bank of England. After all, it was the role of the Bank to pre-empt such disasters and 'in a healthy democracy, if voters' confidence in the system is to be sustained' the serious mistakes made by powerful institutions must not be swept under the carpet. But no, he continued, that does not absolve the then prime minister and chancellor from blame. Ultimately, it was their measures in the mini-budget, which was seen as an unfunded stimulus at a precarious time for the economy, that caused the initial crash in the price of UK government bonds.

Kwarteng has recounted how he urged Truss to slow down, particularly after the consequences of the mini-budget became clear. He has since characterised her mood as 'impatient and impulsive'. Behind the scenes, she told him, 'I've only got two years.' 'You will only have two months if you carry on like this,' he replied. Meanwhile, Coffey was getting calls from Conservative MPs who had supported Truss and were arguing that Kwarteng was the problem. They told her, 'We voted for Liz, not Kwasi', and urged that he be sacked. It is no coincidence that Truss's decision to remove her chancellor and reverse all the mini-budget measures came on the day that the Bank of England's rescue plan ran out of road, although some argue that the Bank could have given the government a bit more time. But was it a mistake to remove him?

Kwarteng told Truss she was wrong if she believed that sacking him would give her more staying power. He argued that she was instead shortening her premiership. 'They are going to come after you, you're finished,' he said. Others agreed, with one Sunak-supporting MP who had been banished to the backbenches, sending me a message which read: 'Sacking KK would be like blowing her own foot off.'

When Truss showed Kwarteng the statement that she planned to deliver to journalists announcing that she would increase Corporation

Tax after all, and that the OBR would be involved, he warned her that the one question they would all ask was as follows: if she had sacked him for her mini-budget, why was she still in post? And at a press conference that day, that is exactly how it unfolded. Ben Riley-Smith from the *Telegraph*, the *Sun*'s Harry Cole and BBC's Chris Mason all asked a variation of that very question. And then ITV's Robert Peston wondered out loud if Truss would apologise for trashing the Tory's reputation for economic competence?

The *Sunday Times* reported that Kwarteng had given the prime minister three weeks. In fact, she had just six more days. The decision to appoint Jeremy Hunt as chancellor had come after internal discussions about who would be accepted by Conservative Party MPs. They needed someone who would be seen as a 'grown up'. Coffey had been discussing her policy area with Hunt because he had been the government's longest serving health secretary, and so his name emerged. Nadhim Zahawi was also discussed. The problem with appointing Hunt and allowing him to reverse all the mini-budget measures was that it was seen by many as Truss relinquishing all power and handing over control of her government.

And then, yet more scandal. There had been tensions with Braverman over the issue of immigration. The new home secretary cared deeply about this issue and wanted to bear down on numbers – but there was a problem. Immigration was one of the few things that in future forecasts the Office for Budget Responsibility would actually 'score' as delivering growth. Some in the leadership team feared that a hard-line tone on immigration might spook the OBR into downgrading its estimates. When Braverman used a personal email account to send the draft of a written ministerial statement suggesting 'liberalising our immigration rules' to a high-profile back-bencher on the right of the party, Sir John Hayes, Truss tried to sack her. Braverman stepped down first and was replaced as home secretary with Grant Shapps. Coffey felt Truss may have fared better with a home secretary chosen on the basis of their ability to deliver rather than their ideology – an argument she had made at the start.

Reflecting on what went wrong, Kwarteng told me that he takes his responsibility and admits that he should have challenged Truss more. But pointing to President Harry S. Truman's insistence: 'The buck stops here', he said, 'My thesis is that it is a study in psychology. There were extraneous factors and you can talk about LDIs or conspiracy theories or the deep state, but ultimately it is about the psychology of the leader; the psychology of the protagonist is central to what happened. It is a study in flawed leadership. Liz was extremely hardworking, extremely tough on herself and very driven, but she was not patient and not very reflective. It was frenetic and never in control. She had to do things immediately, yesterday. She would not have lasted more than six months, whatever happened, she would have blown up on something. But still, seven weeks is nothing; it is such an extraordinary thing to have happened.'

In hindsight, the mini-budget should have waited until November, he concluded, with the supply-side reforms underway and a serious discussion about spending cuts.

However, he also argued that Truss's 'intuition was right' that it would be difficult to unlock growth if the government 'slavishly' followed the OBR's diktat of requiring every spending increase to be funded by a tax rise. He stood by the argument that tax cuts could have dynamically driven growth but accepted that there was a major failure of delivery. To Kwarteng, the better way to proceed would have been a slower process with clear spending restraint to calm the markets. Others who worked closely with Truss have emerged somewhat resentful about that period; particularly given, in their opinion, she stopped listening to advice.

For her part, Liz Truss has been unapologetic, blaming the 'powerful economic establishment' for her downfall, and doubling down on her attacks on the OBR. One paper distributed by her office asked 'Why should anyone trust the OBR?' claiming its forecasts are 'wildly inaccurate'. The document hits out at 'lazy political attacks' on the Truss government, arguing that the real blame was failure to properly regulate 'leveraged LDI pension funds'; the announcement of a gilt sale on the eve of the mini-budget; and the way the Bank of England lagged behind the US Federal Reserve, raising interest rates to 2.25 per cent in September 2022 when they had reached 3.25 per cent in the US.

For Truss, the final straw was nothing to do with economics, however; bizarrely it was a parliamentary vote on fracking after she had announced plans to lift a moratorium on the technique. On Wednesday 19 October 2022, Labour issued a motion to formally ban drilling for shale gas in England, which raised the prospect of a Tory rebellion among climate-focused MPs. Conservative whips told colleagues that this would be seen as a 'confidence measure'. That meant that voting with Labour would be seen as equivalent to a vote of 'no confidence' in the Truss government as a whole and would result in MPs being stripped of the Conservative whip. At a session of the cabinet that morning, the minister for energy security and net zero, Graham Stuart, argued that it was wrong to lift the fracking ban, because there were still questions over its viability and safety. He was wary of creating a political battle over an issue on which the party did not have a firm answer. But Truss and her business secretary, Jacob Rees-Mogg, believed it was a pro-growth measure and so overruled Stuart, who was asked to close the debate in the House on behalf of the government.

As he was doing so, he received a text from Downing Street's director of political strategy, who told him it was essential that now, from the dispatch box, he should state that 'this is not a confidence vote'. Stuart did just that, but the move caused chaos. The Tory whips were aghast that their instructions were suddenly being overturned and forty Tory MPs failed to back Truss, with claims that others who were wavering were being physically pulled into the voting lobbies. One Conservative MP was left in tears. Some claim that the chief whip and her deputy resigned from government in the aftermath.

That Wednesday evening following the vote, in Parliament's central lobby a furious and emotional Conservative MP Charles

Walker claimed that for Liz Truss, it was time up. 'This is an absolute disgrace … I think it is a shambles and a disgrace. I think it is utterly appalling. I'm livid.' With his tone becoming increasingly irritated, Walker hit out at colleagues who had helped propel Truss to Number 10. 'I hope it was worth it for the ministerial red box,' he said, gesturing for emphasis. 'I hope it was worth it to sit around the cabinet table, because the damage they have done to our party is extraordinary.' Walker said colleagues were worrying about their constituents' mortgages but now also their own because many faced losing their jobs. As he revealed that he would be standing down voluntarily at the next election, he added, 'Unless we get our act together and behave like grown-ups, I'm afraid that many hundreds of my colleagues, maybe 200, will be leaving at the behest of their electorate.'

The next morning, when Thérèse Coffey went to see her best friend, Truss had already seen the chair of the backbench 1922 Committee, Sir Graham Brady. She asked him, 'Is there a way out?' He thought not. Coffey wanted to persuade Truss to hold on for a few days or at least until that evening, but her mind was made up. After forty-four days in charge, she resigned, and completed her term in just forty-nine, earning her the record as the shortest-serving prime minister in British history. The Tories had slipped to just 19 points in a YouGov poll; 37 points behind Labour on 56.

Was this the moment that Keir Starmer's journey towards Downing Street became unstoppable? Perhaps. But with that animal-like survival instinct that Boris Johnson had identified, the Conservative Party was determined to give it one more try.

It was Friday 21 October 2022. By the following Monday, a new party leader and prime minister would be in place, but only after a frantic weekend of political blood-letting.

11

Rishi

'We've agreed!' boomed Boris Johnson, gleefully clapping his hands together as he emerged from a room with Rishi Sunak.

'I'm going to be prime minister! And Rishi will be chancellor, foreign secretary, deputy prime minister, and anything else he wants!'

The group who had been waiting outside for the pair laughed.

'Come on guys, toss a coin for it,' joked the Conservative MP for Selby and Ainsty, Nigel Adams.

'No! Let's arm-wrestle,' said Johnson.

Sunak smiled as he took in the scene. And then he slapped Johnson on the back. 'I'll see you at the debate on Tuesday,' he said about the first planned membership hustings, before walking out.

It was October 2022 and the pair had just spent two hours huddled together at Johnson's office in Millbank Tower down the road from Parliament. At the start of a fraught race for a new Conservative Party leader following the demise of Liz Truss's brief and disastrous premiership, Johnson had launched an audacious bid. But just over three months after they ousted him for failing to be straight about yet another scandal, could he really persuade Tory MPs to have him back?

When news of Truss's resignation first broke, Johnson had been enjoying a Caribbean holiday with his family. Tempted by what looked like bubbling support for his come-back, including encouragement from six cabinet ministers, he called Charlotte Owen who was by then working for Truss in Downing Street. His former aide headed to a quiet area and told him he should give it a go. Johnson then called Conservative MP James Duddridge to say he was 'up for it'. 'I'm going to do it, Dudders,' he reportedly told him.

Knowing that Penny Mordaunt had already announced her candidacy and that Rishi Sunak seemed likely to join the race, there was an urgency to his decision, and so Johnson cut short his trip and headed home to London.

Arriving in Westminster, he faced two problems. The first was a new rule imposed by the Conservative's 1922 Committee by which candidates would need the backing of more than 100 MP colleagues just to get onto the ballot. To Johnson's supporters this was effectively match-rigging; an unfair rule-change deliberately designed to scupper him. But could he do it?

Sources from the 1922 Committee told me that the answer was 'yes'. As soon as Johnson made up his mind and threw his hat into the ring, a small support team had geared back up, with Nigel Adams, Ben 'Gazza' Gascoigne, Ross Kempsell, Owen and the MP Amanda Milling immediately hitting the phones. In one day, they had powered through fifty nominations, and were able to keep going towards the target. One MP told me that after a long and persuasive call with Johnson they 'duplicitously' signed his nomination papers despite having already publicly backed Sunak. Adams carried the list to a member of the 1922 Committee – Bob Blackman – who agreed: Johnson was over the line.

But his team was never convinced that 100 backers would be enough. They had privately set a higher bar of 150 for Johnson to overcome to be able to comfortably fill enough ministerial positions to ensure a functioning government. On that second, self-imposed, hurdle Johnson fell short. On Sunday 23 October, close allies gathered around him to offer their advice.

'The reality is, you will be prime minister by the end of the week if you carry on,' said one, arguing that in a vote of Tory members the former leader would trounce any opponent, and certainly Sunak who, of course, had previously fallen short against Truss. 'The problem,' they added, 'is that when you go back, it will all start again, all the plotting, all the undermining, all the shit.' When Johnson subsequently arranged a Zoom call to tell his support team about his decision not to go forward after all, some of them cried.

The meeting with Sunak had been an attempt to secure a 'unity pact', but it had failed. Too many others were fed up with the 'circus' that they believed Johnson had brought to their party and the government, with some breaking cover. The MP and Foreign Office minister Jesse Norman posted on Twitter: 'Choosing Boris now would be – and I say this advisedly – an absolutely catastrophic decision.'[1] Former Tory leader William Hague went further, telling *Times* radio it was the worst idea he'd heard in forty-six years as a Conservative member and would cause a 'death spiral' for the party. Another minister texted me, writing: 'I am PRAYING that Boris doesn't get to 100. It would tear the party asunder.'

In the end, Johnson accepted that his party needed unity and he could not deliver it.

Sunak's team were no doubt relieved, but they still did not think they had it in the bag. The former chancellor wanted to reel in some eye-catching support from the right of the party and turned almost as far to the right as he possibly could, to Suella Braverman, who had only just been sacked by Truss over the misuse of her personal email. Braverman had recently described how desperate she was for a policy first announced by Boris Johnson, to deport asylum seekers arriving on Britain's south coast in dinghies to Rwanda, to pass into legislation: 'I would love to have a front page of the *Telegraph* with a plane taking off to Rwanda, that's my dream, that's my obsession.' She was certainly persuadable to join the Sunak bandwagon, but she said she would only do so if he would agree to meet her demands.

Braverman set out six points in a document that I have seen. It begins by calling for tougher action on both illegal and legal migration; asks that the graduate visa route should be shut down; demands that the salary threshold for skilled workers should be increased from £25,000 to £40,000; calls for Britain's membership of the European Convention on Human Rights to be reviewed; asks for a tougher stance on trans rights, including 'unequivocal and enforceable' guidance for schools on the 'binary nature of biological sex'; and insists that the Home Office must be broken up. Believing a deal had been struck, Braverman published an article (in the *Telegraph*) backing Sunak as the only candidate who could unite the party and 'put our house in order'.[2]

With this unexpected endorsement, Sunak looked unbeatable, and pressure mounted on Penny Mordaunt, who was just short of the numbers needed, to pull out of the race. Two minutes before the 2 p.m. close of nominations on Monday 24 October, she duly did so.

It was a frantic day for Sunak – and for me! After months of political drama I had finally gone on holiday, but I could hardly miss this latest twist. So I left the family for a whirlwind twenty-four hours, boarding a flight in Italy, arriving at Gatwick at 2 a.m. I spent the night in a hotel airport before spending the day racing around Westminster from the parliamentary room, where Conservatives banged appreciatively on tables to welcome the announcement of Sunak's victory, to Conservative Party HQ, where Rishi's grinning supporters lined up to greet him. That evening I did a piece to camera for the news bulletins, did a 'live' from outside Downing Street at 10 p.m., then jumped onto a motorbike taxi to the west London studios to do *Peston*, before finally boarding a middle-of-the-night flight back to my holiday.

The mood outside CCHQ had been giddy as as they listened to their new prime minister talk of the 'greatest privilege of my life, to be able to serve the party I love and give back to the country I owe so much to.' Warning of the 'profound economic challenge' ahead, he promised to serve with 'integrity'. Mel Stride, soon to become

Britain's work and pensions secretary, crouched down to speak to me through the bars that wrap around the building, and said, 'I guess we are all excited aren't we? It's a new beginning.' The future justice secretary Alex Chalk was similarly delighted. 'He's got amazing abilities, he's highly intelligent, he's got bags of integrity, he's got judgement … he's going to be great,' he gushed.

Did Rishi Sunak himself have any doubts about taking over as prime minister at this juncture? Just over a week earlier, he had gone for a drink near Westminster with a friend who argued that Truss's premiership was wobbling and he should be ready to step forward. I'm told that Sunak replied that he was not interested in becoming PM because it would only be short-lived, to which the friend warned he had no choice. 'This is your destiny,' he said.

I pressed him on this point later during an interview. 'You must have thought, I'm coming in for two years?'

'Well, I certainly didn't do this job because I thought it would be easy,' he said. 'I did it out of a sense of duty […] the country was in a tough spot and I thought, given my […] economic experience, that I could make a difference.' But the challenge was daunting. Sunak's mentor, the former Tory leader William Hague, who had represented Richmond in North Yorkshire before him, described it to me as 'taking over an army on the battlefield when it has been fighting itself.'

It is perhaps inevitable that once settled into Number 10 Downing Street the new prime minister began to hope and believe that there was a way to carve out a path towards election victory. In fact, he told colleagues that this could be 'the greatest political turnaround in history.' But how on earth could he close the yawning gap that had opened up between his party and the opposition in the polls?

Sources have suggested to me that in the first month there was a lack of a plan, with Sunak focused on responding to events in a crammed timetable, which saw him head to Egypt for the COP 27 climate summit and then to Indonesia for the G20. I accompanied him on the second trip to Bali and when we sat down for an interview my focus was once again on the cost-of-living crisis, and a looming challenge for the new prime minister – public-sector pay demands.[3] How could he possibly resist more money for teachers and nurses, when City bonuses were on the rise?

'The enemy we have to face down is inflation,' Sunak said, as he urged City bosses to also consider pay restraint.

The PM hated inefficiency, with a reputation for wanting to minimise time away from the office, even suggesting skipping press conferences at the end of major summits to allow a swift exit. He considered missing his first COP 27 meeting; a signal of both his impatience and perhaps a lesser commitment to net zero goals than Boris Johnson. After a month, staff members were looking for ways to limit travel, pointing out that in his first few weeks the prime minister had spent dozens of hours in transit, and much of his time locked in meetings about the economy. Interestingly, there was a suggestion that he should not spend more time talking about the small boats crossing the Channel with asylum seekers, but instead focus on issues like education, crime and levelling-up. As for the strategy, everyone was told to wait for a briefing from Isaac Levido, whose services Truss had briefly dispensed with, but who would now be redeployed as a consultant by Sunak.

On 3 December 2022, the prime minister invited just a few members of his inner circle to a strategic away-day in his country home, Chequers. The group included the deputy prime minister; Oliver Dowden; Downing Street chief of staff Liam Booth-Smith and his deputy, Will Tanner; director of communications, Amber de Botton; and Will Dry, Sunak's special adviser focused on data.

Also attending were Ameet Gill and Paul Stephenson, who had formerly been senior strategists in the Conservative Party, and who came together in the wake of the EU Referendum to launch a successful consultancy, Hanbury Strategy. Both knew the PM well. With them was Joe Slater, director of Stack Data Strategy, which had spun out of Hanbury and was now being used to carry out internal Conservative polling. Stack's speciality was Multilevel Regression and Poststratification (MRP) modelling, the technique that was everywhere in 2024, combining large-scale polling data with other information including demographics to predict a seat-by-seat result if an election was held that day. In late 2022 and through 2023, Stack ran 20,000-strong polls for Sunak every quarter, rising to one each month in the run-up to the 2024 election. But the guest of honour was Isaac Levido himself.

At Chequers, the group gathered around a long, thin table in a wood-panelled room, heavy curtains framing huge windows onto the gardens. It was a half-day session on a Saturday and those present were dressed casually. Levido did not pull his punches. He told Tory high-command that voters were enraged with their party. The path to victory the prime minister was searching for did exist, but it was very narrow, extremely steep, and required ruthless determination and party unity, he said. The latter was always going to be a tough ask for Sunak, who was still blamed by a number of MPs for deposing Johnson. And although Sunak had embraced some of Truss's allies, others remained bitter about the way they had been spat out of top government roles. Some even blamed the financial instability that had followed the mini-budget, at least in part, on Sunak's warnings that it might happen. I remember sitting in the green room after recording *Peston* with a Conservative MP who looked exasperated as they admitted, 'God, I hate this government.'

But at the time of that December meeting in Chequers, things felt relatively stable and, despite very poor headline figures, they could see reasons to be hopeful. In a presentation, Stack's Joe Slater described what would happen if there were an election right then. The Conservatives would slip back from its 365 seats in 2019 to just 170, he said. It was a grim outlook, and significantly worse than the lowest point ever reached during the Partygate scandal. But there were two sources of optimism.

The first was the sheer number of people who had not yet decided how they would vote. One senior adviser now looks back and thinks the team were wrong to draw so much hope from this particular data set, arguing that 'on reflection' they now believe that many of these voters had already decided one thing for sure – that they would not vote Conservative. They now think that this group was assigned as 'don't knows' because they were grappling between Labour, the Lib Dems, Reform UK, and staying at home. But Levido certainly believed that significant numbers of these voters, many of whom had backed the party in 2019, could be won back.

The second reason for optimism was Sunak himself. Although that wild popularity of the furlough years had been blunted by scandals including his wife's non-dom status, the prime minister was still much more liked than the Conservative Party itself. To illustrate the size of that gap, Slater had carried out a theoretical exercise of re-running the seat numbers based on Sunak's personal polling versus those of Starmer. If Sunak's popularity could be transposed to the Conservative Party, the number of MPs surviving in an election would be 280, enough to prevent a Labour majority.

The data paved the way for a 'presidential style' strategy. Levido told the room that he knew they wanted to win a general election, but first they needed to take a step back. People were fed up with politics and slogans; instead they wanted to understand a government's priorities and have politicians willing to be held to account. And so Levido suggested a 'communications device', in which Sunak himself would identify five or six achievable priorities, and then set these out in a promise to voters that he would work tirelessly to deliver them. The strategist made clear that focus groups showed that people wanted to hear specific, measurable and binary targets. Finally, Levido warned that this was just step one of the strategy but that Sunak must be patient, and not expect the polls to tighten during 2023. His final thought was not one the politicians in the room wanted to hear, fearing that a continued lag in the polls would cause jitters among twitchy Tory MPs.

The group then embarked on a long discussion about what these half a dozen priorities should be. Analysing feedback from Stack's quarterly surveys, one issue in particular was overwhelming: not only was 'the cost of living' the number-one concern for voters, but it had also been dominating what people cared about for a longer time period than any other topic before it. People had been hit hard; they were suffering stagnant wages as their energy prices spiked, supermarket bills ballooned, and, for many, mortgage rates went through the roof. On top of that crisis was an attitude that politicians were hearing time and again on the doorstep; that Britain was broken, and nothing worked. The combination of years of austerity followed by the post-Covid squeeze had left councils on their knees, with local services pulled back, the courts creaking, school buildings deteriorating and the NHS stretched to what felt frankly beyond breaking point.

Halving inflation was therefore agreed as the first priority, with two more on the economy, one on debt and one on growth, which was less about public desire and more about satisfying a restless Conservative Party. They wanted this list to look like the priorities of Sunak the prime minister and not Sunak the chancellor, so next they turned to the NHS and their belief that reducing waiting lists was achievable. The Tories knew that voters' struggles to secure NHS appointments added to the sense of a societal breakdown. And they knew the political impact could be sharp, with some later arguing that many pandemic governments had fallen as a result of 'Covid-compromised incumbency'. The trouble looming with public sector workers and the prospect of strikes would surely make things worse, but in Chequers there was a strong belief in Sunak's ability to fix these problems.

Next, Levido and Paul Stephenson turned to the need for 'red meat' policies, including on immigration. After all, a number of the undecided voters that the Tories needed to win back were flirting with Nigel Farage's Reform UK because they were furious about a lack of action to stop asylum seekers arriving in Dover on dinghies. 'We need to stop the boats,' someone suggested. Some of those present argued that with such a promise they would be setting down an impossible target, and wondered if the aim should be to reduce the number of crossings rather than eliminate them entirely. They played around with the language, but it was argued that voters tended to see this issue in binary terms, and with softer words they would be outflanked. 'We knew we couldn't stop them, but we had to show bloody-minded intent,' said one person, arguing that the public would have expected nothing less. The problem was that this ambitious pledge would push a problem the PM had been trying to avoid discussing, right to the top of the agenda.

This punchy three-word slogan would come to dominate Sunak's premiership in a way that perhaps still haunts him to this day. It is an indisputable fact that his government failed to 'stop the boats', so should he have promised to do so, in a speech asking people to 'judge us on the efforts we put in and the results we achieve'?

I've discussed this issue with a number of people close to the Sunak machine. One source remains steadfast that this was the right and only possible strategy, maintaining that Tory voters would not have accepted weaker promises on illegal migration. Laying out this level of ambition showed a 'laser-focused determination', they said. But others now wonder if the party simply shone a torch directly in the direction of an intractable problem that was always impossible to solve. 'We made the issue salient and then we failed to deliver it,' said an insider. A third figure comes down in between. 'The salience was already there but it was a mistake, and not just a tactical one, it was a strategic error. We spent ten years chasing the UKIP dragon,' they said. 'You can't do that and then not deal with those voters' primary concerns.' Those concerns were not just illegal migration but also legal migration, and yet they argued that a post-Brexit points-based system, introduced by Boris Johnson, had resulted in the immigration numbers soaring.

Before Sunak set out his plan to the public he decided to seek one more opinion. The PM went to the London home of his closest aide, chief of staff Liam Booth-Smith, to meet the architect of the Vote Leave victory and the controversial former chief strategist to Boris Johnson, Dominic Cummings. Cummings was not one for cautious prioritisation and suggested that the prime minister shake things up – on migration but also on the NHS strikes that were by then rolling out.

In a written plan, Cummings urged Sunak to:

- Immediately move to solve the strikes by giving NHS workers the same pay rise as the private sector, which at the time was 6.5 per cent (well above the 4 per cent that had been offered to health workers and higher than the 5 per cent they later settled for).
- Link MPs' wages likewise to the private sector, allowing the government to tell voters, politicians will only get a pay rise if you do.
- Reverse the increase in National Insurance Contributions that had broken the 2019 manifesto promise and take the radical step of lifting the salary threshold at which people start paying the 40p top rate from around £50,000 to £100,000.
- Pass primary legislation to repeal the Human Rights Act and start withdrawing from the European Convention on Human Rights and the Strasbourg Court.
- And, finally, declassify government papers that revealed how human-rights legislation prevented ministers (in Cummings opinion) from tackling terror threats and locking up paedophiles.

Cummings argued that action on NHS waiting lists was absolutely critical, and that as well as stopping the strikes the PM should have set up a taskforce on his first day in Number 10. He suggested that it was easier for Sunak to maintain the 'Vote Leave' coalition built back in 2016 – linking northern and Midlands' towns to the Tory shires – than it was for Labour to rebuild its pre-2010 voting alliance.

Perhaps Booth-Smith's decision to host the meeting with Cummings at his home pointed to his desire to blow things up, but the PM was not convinced. On the question of the ECHR, for example, Sunak felt it would lead to huge internal division and party-infighting. It is certainly true that the issue triggers passionate views on both sides. One of Sunak's cabinet ministers once messaged me, writing: 'Withdrawal would be nuclear; it would detonate the Tory Party.' Not that Cummings cared about any of that; he hated MPs. 'If Damian Green defects to the Lib Dems,' he once told a friend about the Tory MP who chairs the more liberal One Nation wing of the party, 'then fine, fuck off.'

But Sunak did not want anyone to fuck off. So he decided to stick to the original plan. Levido briefed the cabinet at Chequers but was irritated that the media seemed to have caught wind of their meeting, with photographers gathered outside. 'The path to victory takes determination, pulling together. But there are cameras in the field because everyone knows this meeting is happening,' he shouted, in his Australian accent. 'Labour is having these meetings but no one knows about them, because they are deadly serious about winning.'

Members of the cabinet were also nervous about the polls, and the Stop the Boats promise, with conversation around Chequers about the risks of failing to achieve it.

Sunak announced his five priorities on 4 January 2023. But his first win was outside of them, with an EU deal – the Windsor Framework – which finally solved some of the seemingly intractable problems that Brexit was causing on the Irish border. Thanks to a perception that he was the man who could tackle thorny challenges, Sunak's popularity, although net negative, tipped upwards. At the various annual summits that year, world leaders would congratulate him. By April, Labour's poll lead was down to 15 points with YouGov, and close to single digits with other pollsters.

On Wednesday 1 March, Joe Pike, then a political reporter at Sky News, reported an exclusive story that Sue Gray, famed as the Civil Service enforcer and author of the deeply critical report on Partygate, was joining the Labour Party as chief of staff.[4] Many saw this as a brilliant move by Starmer to help prepare his opposition party for government. Gray had a fearsome reputation in Whitehall, having worked in government since the late 1970s (apart from a break in the 1980s to run a Northern Irish pub with her husband, country singer Bill Conlon), and was referred to as 'Deputy God', a riff on her time as right-hand woman to cabinet secretary Gus O'Donnell. Former Cabinet Office minister Oliver Letwin once remarked: 'It took me precisely two years before I realised who it is that runs Britain … unless [Sue Gray] agrees, things don't happen.' For Labour to absorb that wealth of knowledge was a coup for Starmer. But for others, the appointment brought into question the impartiality of Gray's part in a scandal that had ultimately helped to topple Boris Johnson. As the news exploded into the public domain, the former PM's allies reacted with fury. 'The Gray report was a stitch up,' said Nadine Dorries. When one of her Cabinet Office colleagues saw the news alert flash up on their phone they didn't believe it, and quickly messaged Gray to give them a call. They waited eagerly as the words, 'Sue Gray is typing' bubbled into the top of their WhatsApp screen, but then dropped out, and she never replied again.

MPs and some newspapers screamed blue murder. 'PM urged to block new job for parties inquisitor,' said *The Times*. 'Is this proof the Partygate probe was a Labour plot?' asked the *Daily Mail*.

Gray was eventually cleared for her new role, but it later emerged that a Cabinet Office investigation concluded that in discussing the role with Starmer without telling her Whitehall colleagues, she had breached the Civil Service Code.[5]

The report itself was not published, but I have seen extracts. It concluded that Gray did not declare something that was clearly a conflict of interest and against published guidance. There was no suggestion she was 'partial' in her actual decisions or that she shared any information with Labour, but it made clear that her line manager should have known to avoid any accusation of lack of impartiality or lack of openness, pointing to a four-month gap between Starmer's initial contact and Gray's resignation. Senior civil servants have told me they believe that the inquiry into Gray was driven politically by senior cabinet ministers, including Oliver Dowden. Nevertheless, it was a civil servant who concluded that officials are expected to act with integrity, openness and impartiality. 'During the period in question, it is my view that SG fell short of these expectations and as a result acted in breach of the Civil Service Code as well as her contractual obligations.'

As for Sunak, his honeymoon was not to last. The prime minister was facing backbench MPs and a home secretary restless about one particular issue. That spring Sunak invited members of the Common Sense Group of backbench Tory MPs most exercised about immigration into Downing Street for a chat. They wanted the PM to bear down on foreign student numbers and were surprised when Sunak replied that the move would damage universities in the Red Wall. Some of those present shared puzzled looks. They wondered if the PM 'didn't get it'. Meanwhile, the government had introduced the Illegal Migration bill that would make it illegal for anyone to arrive in Britain by small boat, and allow for their immediate detention and removal to a safe third country (with the Rwanda deal the most advanced). Sources tell me that Braverman almost quit over the introduction of the legislation. She and her team were convinced that the bill needed additional teeth to protect it from challenge. Others felt the changes she was demanding were pushing the boundaries of legality. In the end, Braverman secured several concessions but eventually accepted what was on the table when Sunak's political strength was bolstered by the EU deal. However, she felt she had been brow-beaten into this softer version of the bill, and Home Office sources claimed she feared the courts would not allow the Rwanda plan to take off.

But then suddenly Partygate was back. Parliament's Privileges Committee published its reports into claims Johnson had misled MPs when he insisted that there had been no parties in Downing Street. The Committee members, who had done a tour of Number 10 to assess the credibility of Johnson's insistence that he knew nothing about what happened, concluded that he was guilty of 'repeated contempts of Parliament'. Its recommendation that he be suspended for ninety days opened the door to the possibility of a recall petition that would ultimately mean Johnson would lose his parliamentary seat, and so he jumped before he was pushed, resigning as an MP on Monday 12 June.[6]

Less than three weeks later, in what perhaps felt like a shot across the bows, the Court of Appeal overturned an earlier High Court decision in favour of the Rwanda policy and instead concluded that Rwanda was not a safe country to deport asylum seekers to, meaning the government's flagship might be torpedoed.

The chaos hit hard, with the polls widening once more, and Labour securing a 25-point lead by 6 July. That month a much more frustrated Sunak gathered his close team once again to hear from Levido. Everyone I've spoken to about the meeting at the Londoner Hotel in Leicester Square describes it as frustrating. This time a much larger cast piled into a thin basement room with no natural light. Almost like a tip of the hat to the growing sentiment that Britain was broken, the train on which the prime minister had been travelling had broken down and he had to be driven from his constituency home in North Yorkshire, arriving late, in a notably agitated mood. The numbers had already been presented while the group waited for Sunak but were rolled out again when he arrived.

One notable frustration was that the polls had tightened a couple of months earlier after the Windsor Agreement, briefly raising hopes that the Tories could be in a competitive position by the end of that year, but the re-hashing of Partygate had blown things apart again. Stack's Joe Slater revealed a seat analysis suggesting that an election then would have the Conservatives falling down to 150 constituencies, worse than the December assessment. One problem for Sunak was that Labour's strategy to achieve a more efficient vote by focusing on marginal seats meant that Stack was now predicting that Starmer only needed a 5.3 per cent lead in the polls to secure a majority. Sunak felt exasperated by the level of scrutiny he was under and wanted to apply a similar approach to his opponent.

The group discussed the Labour leader's potential weaknesses, including his past closeness to former leader Jeremy Corbyn and his role as a human rights lawyer; questions over what he stood for; and finally, whether it was worth attacking him as too old, and lacking in vigour. At one point Starmer's weight even briefly entered the conversation. There was a widespread belief in the Tory Party at the time that for all their problems there was little enthusiasm for Labour or Keir Starmer. At party conferences I would hear Conservative MP after Conservative MP cloak themselves in what looks in hindsight like a comfort-blanket mantra.

Levido tried to urge Sunak to hold his nerve, stressing that he had warned that the polls would not tighten in 2023. But the prime minister had seen the polls do just that after he agreed a deal with the EU on Northern Ireland, so no longer believed Levido's reassurances. Sources tell me he was hitting out at the strategist, arguing that the plan wasn't working. One person at that meeting described him as 'petulant', with an attitude that confirmed to them that he was not up to the job and was destined to lose the election heavily.

Sunak was feeling impatient. His team knew that the strategy so far had shown him to be steady, safe and focused on the details. They knew that these were positive attributes. But they did not believe they were election-winning ones. And MPs were telling Downing Street that they could not sell the prime minister's five promises on the doorstep – they needed a vision. When aides scoured the polls, they could not escape one attitude that was starting to look formidable: a deep desire for change.

YouGov's Marcus Roberts has argued that voter perception of how different these Tories were to those that had come before them was always going to be critical. If Sunak was seen as a fresh start, he would have far more chance than as a Tory leader heading up the party after thirteen years of government. But making that jump was strategically difficult. Some of Sunak's allies look back now and wonder if he could have done more to distance himself from Boris Johnson, and perhaps even more importantly Liz Truss. One source told me that there were discussions about whether it was possible to throw her out of the party, but there was no mechanism for such a move and besides the whips believed it would simply lead to a coup against Sunak and create a 'martyr' of Truss. But certainly, aides believe Sunak should have spoken out more spikily against his predecessor.

Levido agreed that eventually Sunak would have to break away from the status quo, but he wanted to do it more slowly, and had in his head that the shift should come in January 2024, when people were thinking about New Year's resolutions. Sunak's closest aides disagreed. By then Amber de Botton had left, replaced as communications director by Nerissa (Nissy) Chesterfield, who worked closely with Cass Horowitz, head of strategic communications and digital. Together with the PM's chief of staff Liam Booth-Smith and James Forsyth, who was also one of his closest friends and his political secretary, they planned for a quicker shift in strategy. Some in the press described the change as letting 'Rishi be Rishi'. The idea was to try to move away from Sunak's difficult political inheritance towards fresh ideas about which he was personally passionate, and that were genuinely long term – something he believed in.

That was why in October 2023 they ended up with a conference speech that many found quite surprising. Gone was Sunak's promise to 'stick to the plan, because the plan was working,' and in its place was a speech that concluded thus: 'Be in no doubt: it is time for a change. And we are it.'

In a speech that promised to break up a thirty-year political consensus (a time period that meant he was implicitly attacking five Tory prime ministers including David Cameron), and a willingness to make the difficult long-term decisions the team had discussed, Sunak used the C-word thirty times.

One difficult decision was to cancel HS2, the epically ballooning rail project designed to offer a new, high-speed link between London and Manchester, but which was running long over time and budget. Many would say it was a sensible step that would allow other infrastructure projects to exist in the future, but it was a slightly bizarre headline-grabber at a party conference, especially when it was delivered in HS2's intended destination, Manchester. Another policy to effectively ban cigarette sales for all younger generations was something Sunak cared deeply about but was ultimately seen as legacy-building more than vote-winning. Replacing A-levels with a new Advanced British Standard stemmed from the prime minister's focus on education, but this promised future change for children born in 2015 or later could hardly be linked to the party's 2024 prospects. He also wanted to carve a slightly slower path to net zero emissions that he believed was more practical.

Some of the ideas discussed in the run-up to the speech did not make it over the line. One was to scrap GCSE exams completely at 16, and instead hold one major assessment at 18. The argument was that GCSEs were necessary when teenagers could leave school at 16 but with new laws requiring attendance to 18 there was merit in reducing the number of years dedicated to examinations, as they tended to squeeze out fresh learning. There were also calls for harsher sentences for repeat offenders. One person suggested a 'pothole task-force' that would go out and fill potholes in place of local councils (although a source insisted that was raised as a joke). Another idea they had considered, which doubtless would have caused controversy, was whether the government should remove child benefit from the parents of truant children. This proposal had been pushed hardest by Michael Gove, who was worried about the number of children missing school and believed this tough move would help tackle absences.

Sunak's aides thought that by focusing on the prime minister's more personal priorities, the policies could start to move the dial on Conservative support. But these were not truly headline-grabbing ideas, and the speech drew criticism. In hindsight, allies argue that the direction taken was the least bad of a pretty dire set of strategic options. But one pollster argued that it 'trashed his brand as a safe and steady pair of hands'. What came next was particularly damaging for the PM.

First, there was a growing problem with Suella Braverman. Earlier in September, I'd been invited to accompany the then home secretary to Washington, DC where she made plenty of news. In a strident speech that was cleared by Downing Street, she railed about the 'existential challenge' of illegal migration; claimed societies were living with the consequences of failed multiculturalism; and said that being gay was not enough to claim asylum, a comment that earned her a rebuke from Sir Elton John. When I pointed out in an interview that people in parts of the world face persecution or even death for being homosexual, Braverman dug in, claiming that asylum seekers pretended to be gay to try to win protection. After the trip, Braverman's team were ordered to a meeting inside Downing Street by advisers angry that she had called for American bully XL dogs to be banned, a policy outside of her sphere but that had become stuck in government. Some who worked with Braverman claimed the PM's team was never tough enough and should have torn strips off them, but they felt they emerged with a 'score draw'.

Then Braverman horrified colleagues by suggesting on X that homelessness was 'a lifestyle choice'. The final straw was when, in an article for *The Times* that had not been cleared by Downing Street, she accused the police of treating left-leaning protesters as 'favourites'.[7]

The controversy blew up at the same time as Sunak was trying to appease the former Tory leader David Cameron, who was upset by the conference speech and the HS2 decision that he described as a 'once-in-a-generation opportunity' being lost. Mutual friends urged the PM to meet with Cameron and the pair immediately hit it off, which helped cement an idea that Sunak and his team had been considering.

The PM had already been planning a reshuffle, but Braverman's article hurried things along. On the morning of Monday 13 November, Sunak sacked Braverman. And then, in a 'drop my coffee' moment (according to Sky News's Beth Rigby), a car pulled into

Downing Street and the former PM stepped out. Lord Cameron, as he became, was appointed as foreign secretary. It is rare for just two moves in the chess game of a cabinet reshuffle to have quite as much impact as those. Sunak had booted out the woman who was there to prove his right-wing and hard-line-on-migration credentials and invited back the most liberal Tory leader of the Conservative Party for a generation. Moreover, he had replaced Braverman as home secretary with James Cleverly, a Brexiteer and former Truss ally, but who was now seen as far too centrist for some of Sunak's right-wing colleagues.

Some saw it as a brilliant reset, but in truth, Sunak had just caused himself an immense problem. Just months after declaring himself the 'change' candidate, this reshuffle was the equivalent of sharply pulling up the handbrake and making a 180 degree turn in his Downing Street Jag. Insiders argued that there had been no choice but to remove Braverman, as her interventions seemed increasingly and deliberately provocative. And Cameron's appointment was not about political positioning but about having a heavy-hitter on the world stage with little influence on domestic policy, they said. One thought was that, with Cameron able to tour the world meeting counterparts, it would free up time for Sunak to focus on issues at home ahead of the election. Nonetheless, it appeared that a slower and steadier Sunak was back, sticking to the plan. Voters could be forgiven for being confused, and some MPs were incandescent, not least Suella Braverman. She wrote a scathing letter to Sunak accusing him of 'a betrayal of our agreement', referring to the secret email she had sent at the start of his leadership. And then, two days later, the Supreme Court upheld the Court of Appeal ruling, but this time with a unanimous finding, that for the sake of our legislation, it was not safe to send asylum seekers to Rwanda. And so, the Rwanda policy was deemed unlawful, again, throwing Sunak into a cycle of failure over this flagship policy. Many believed it was this failure which inflicted the fatal wound on his premiership and further opened a door to Reform UK.

A few days later a group of MPs met in the office of former Tory leader, Iain Duncan Smith. The gathering included a wide span of dissenting voices, from Liz Truss and some who had served in her cabinet like Jacob Rees-Mogg and Simon Clarke; to the godfather of Brexit, Bill Cash; the chair of the Common Sense Group, Sir John Hayes; and some of the younger MPs in the so-called New Conservative group, Danny Kruger, Miriam Cates and Tom Hunt. Some were in a belligerent mood, calling for a plan to force Sunak out. It was clear that the 1922 Committee chair, Sir Graham Brady had received at least a few 'no confidence' letters. But others, including Truss disagreed. Rees-Mogg reasoned that it would be disastrous to have another change in leader, and that the grown-up option was now to back Sunak, however much they disliked what he was doing. One person present argued that moving on the PM would risk the right of the party being blamed for poor election results. They said it was better to let the 'left' of the party (as they now saw Sunak's wing) 'own the general election defeat', and then the right-wingers could come to the rescue. In the end, many of them didn't survive the election.

Despite being deeply sceptical about the Rwanda policy from a value-for-money perspective when at the Treasury, Rishi Sunak had been persuaded that it must be tried and might be successful in deterring crossings. His deputy Oliver Dowden was similarly cautious, seeing it as the 'least worst' option. So, their new home secretary James Cleverly moved quickly to try to fix the problems, signing a new Treaty with Rwanda designed to bolster against some of the judges' concerns; and passing new primary legislation declaring Rwanda 'safe' and allowing ministers to disregard some human rights laws. The bill was designed to prevent any domestic legal challenge and block interim attempts to intervene from Strasbourg. But it did not go far enough for Robert Jenrick, whom Sunak had placed in the Home Office as immigration minister.

Jenrick had been a Conservative MP since winning a by-election in Newark in 2014. After the surprise Conservative majority in the next year's general election, he became firm friends with two of the new Tory intake, Rishi Sunak and Oliver Dowden. In 2019, the trio had penned a joint op-ed in *The Times* entitled: 'The Tories are in deep peril. Only Boris Johnson can save us.' They were widely seen as rising stars and solid allies, so in 2022 when Sunak appointed Dowden to his first cabinet (and later to the role of deputy prime minister) but Jenrick to a role as minister of state, many assumed it was a part of careful strategy. Surely Sunak wanted his ally Jenrick, largely seen as a Tory centrist, to keep an eye on his boss, home secretary Suella Braverman. After all, Number 10 always feared that Braverman could be volatile.

When Braverman was sacked in the November 2023 reshuffle, perhaps Jenrick expected that his old friend would promote him. Or maybe his time inside the Home Office had just hardened his views on immigration, and motivated future leadership hopes. Whatever the reason, when Jenrick followed Braverman out of government on 6 December 2023, his resignation came as a huge blow to the authority of his once close friend; it was a bitter pill for Sunak to swallow. It came almost exactly a year after Isaac Levido had argued that there was a narrow and steep path towards victory, but to get there everything had to go right.

In 2023, plenty had gone wrong – and it was about to get worse.

PART IV

The Election

12

The Fourth of July

'THEY ... ARE ... NOT ... GOING ... TO ... CALL ... AN ... ELECTION.'

This was the WhatsApp message I received from a Conservative source when I asked, for perhaps the sixth time, if Rishi Sunak might consider going for an earlier date than the widespread expectation of 14 November. They insisted that Isaac Levido, who was going to direct the election campaign on behalf of the prime minister, wanted to 'go long'. When making his decision to come into the Downing Street operation full-time at the start of 2024 (rather than continuing as a consultant), Levido had discussed with family and colleagues the growing likelihood of a heavy defeat. But he still believed there was a glimmer of hope that they could move the dial. Voters needed to feel better, he said, and the best hope for that was to wait until autumn so there was time for the economy to at least start to improve.

But at the beginning of April, the same source suddenly gave me a call, and said that the conversation had started to shift. They described how Sunak's chief of staff, Liam Booth-Smith, had argued that delaying things could simply worsen the threat facing the party on its right flank from Reform UK. Booth-Smith had apparently started to see the merits of another date – 4 July.

Sensing a good story, I immediately rang Downing Street, only to be told that my contact was talking nonsense. 'First I've heard and very much still working on the basis of [an] autumn election,' came the written reply. Then, a few minutes later. 'I've checked with Liam and he says the same btw about autumn … So no idea where this is coming from?' With a shrugging emoji the subject was changed. But, of course, they were just fobbing me off. Confident about my sourcing, I still wrote a piece for the ITV News website asking, 'Could there be a general election in July?'

So why did they drop Levido's initial strategy to stay the course?

In truth, there had always been a series of possible dates on the table, with conversations intensifying around the question at the beginning of the year. The first decision was to rule out the earliest date on Levido's list, Thursday 2 May, the same day as the local elections. The biggest problem was that Andy Street, the mayor of the West Midlands, was desperate to avoid a general election on that day. Street had a strong personal brand and, while gaining re-election was always going to be difficult, his only hope was to make it a vote for him in the election and not the deeply unpopular Conservative Party. Sources said his strategy was 'differential turnout' in which he aimed to drive up voting numbers in his most supportive areas to above the levels in Labour strongholds, 'and he very nearly pulled it off,' said a source. Canning the 2 May date was an easy decision at CCHQ because they were all agreed: a general election then would certainly sacrifice Street and perhaps even Tees Valley mayor Ben Houchen, and so it was off the table.

Before Christmas, Labour's Morgan McSweeney had wanted to pile pressure on Sunak and his team so the Labour's attack chief, Paul Ovenden, had started to 'lay bait'. Labour deliberately began to suggest that behind the scenes the Tories were planning a May election, pointing to their decision to introduce a planned cut to National Insurance Contributions in January, rather than at the start of a new financial year in April, when tax changes normally come into play. On 27 December, Chancellor Jeremy Hunt then added fuel to the fire by revealing the early date of 6 March for his Budget. Asked about this on Sky News, shadow cabinet minister Emily Thornberry said, 'It's the worst kept secret in Parliament that we are likely to be heading for a May election.' Fearing being depicted as 'bottling' the May option, when they had already ruled it out, Sunak decided to say something.

By then he was a regular at events in Red Wall areas like Accrington and Mansfield. The *Sunday Times* had reported that Sunak tried to fast from 5 p.m. every Sunday night to 5 a.m. on Tuesday, so ahead of a rally at Accrington Stanley football club on a Monday, my producer Lili was surprised to see him tucking into a Twix and a can of Sprite. The PM admitted that he was having a sneaky bite of his typical 'pre-game' snack, so he generally felt 'sugared up' for big events.

It was in Mansfield on 4 January that Sunak delivered his carefully worded statement on election timing. 'So, my working assumption is we'll have a general election in the second half of this year. And in the meantime I've got lots that I want to get on with,' said Sunak, with an almost Tiggerish enthusiasm. The words, which led to immediate claims from Labour that Sunak was 'squatting' in Downing Street and had 'bottled it', were meant to nudge people towards the idea of an autumn election, while leaving the July date on Levido's list on the table.

By then, the Conservatives had also ruled out a December election, meaning there were only three realistic options. No MP wanted a campaign to ruin their summer holidays, so August and September were off the table, leaving the original option of holding it in November or alternatively opting for October, or July. The argument to wait until autumn was based on three factors in particular: that NHS waiting lists might start to finally edge down; that economic improvements would actually have begun to have an impact on people's lives; and that in his bid to 'stop the boats', Sunak would be more likely to have overseen a plane finally taking asylum seekers to Rwanda. And, according to Ben Zaranko at the Institute for Fiscal

Studies (IFS), the Tories were right to think that the longer they waited the more chance there was that people would begin to feel better off. Zaranko pointed out that wages were now growing faster than prices and that voters' pay rises would land at different times during the year.

Having spoken to a wide range of people involved in the debate over the election date, it is clear there was a broad consensus that, 'with all things being equal', it would have been better to wait until autumn. But when the team came to discuss the decision in more detail, they agreed that 'all things were not equal'.

The first problem was the polls. By 2024, Stack Data Strategy was running its huge surveys for the Conservatives every month and turning them into seat predictions. Sunak's team believed that policy changes, like a 2 per cent cut to National Insurance Contributions, forcing the Rwanda Bill into law, and a tough package of welfare reforms, ought to be popular and help shift the dial. But from January to May Stack's models were showing the Conservative Party dropping by 10 seats every month; meaning that fifty fewer colleagues looked saveable by May. The prime minister had been urged to be patient during 2023, but it was now the spring of 2024 and there was only negative movement. 'Nothing we did made any difference,' said one source.

This was compounded by trouble on the backbenches. Isaac Levido had always told the party that his strategy suggestions relied on 'unity'; but the Tories seemed as divided as ever with the Downing Street team agreeing 'our biggest drag is the party'. First, MP for Ashfield Lee Anderson was stripped of the Conservative whip after claiming 'Islamists' were controlling London mayor Sadiq Khan – a comment widely seen as Islamophobic and racist. Anderson was popular on the right of the party and colleagues wanted to find a way back for him, insisting that he wanted to stay. But with no resolution by 11 March, Anderson defected to Reform UK – a coup for the party founded by Nigel Farage and a blow for right-wing Tory MPs, who were left furious by the outcome. 'Lee was absolutely not in the headspace to go to Reform when the incident first blew up,' one MP told me, arguing there was little effort by Number 10 or the whips to 'grip the issue'. The MP claimed that while Anderson's politics may not have aligned with Number 10's 'bland centrism', his departure from the Conservative Party sent a terrible message to those MPs who had won seats in the North of England and Midlands in 2019. 'The message was that Lee, who embodied the Red Wall voter, was no longer welcome in our party, or a priority.'

But the liberal wing of the party was twitchy too, nervous of the coming Labour tsunami predicted by the polls.

In April, Dr Dan Poulter, the MP for Central Suffolk and North Ipswich crossed the floor to Labour, saying the Tories were no longer focused on public services. The decision from this part-time psychiatrist only highlighted Sunak's failure to end the junior doctors' strikes that made it almost impossible to deliver his pledge to fix NHS waiting lists. Many Tories urged the PM to try to solve the doctors' strikes but it was an issue on which he dug in heavily. The PM told allies that he was willing to be 'political' but not if it involved making decisions that were bad for the country. In Sunak's eyes, giving in to junior doctors' demands would permanently inflate the NHS bill to unsustainable levels and send a message that going on strike is the best way to secure higher pay. The doctors, of course, argued that they had faced real-term pay cuts for over a decade.

The defections of Anderson and Poulter were damaging, but not entirely unexpected. However, there was speechless shock among Downing Street advisers when just before PMQs on Wednesday 8 May, Natalie Elphicke walked into the House of Commons chamber as usual, and then swung right to take a seat on Labour benches. The minister Steve Baker, who had once been perhaps the most high-profile Brexit rebel in the Tory's European Research Group, tweeted: 'I have been searching in vain for a Conservative MP who thinks themself to the right of Natalie Elphicke … One just quipped: "I didn't realise there was any room to her right?"' And the shock was not just among Conservatives, there was fury within Labour too.

When I highlighted the unimpressed look on the face of MP Dawn Butler sitting behind her new colleague, she replied: 'This was after some serious adjustment.' Elphicke's decision 'rocked the boat', according to one insider, who argued that Sunak's team were left thinking, 'If she can switch to Labour, anything can happen.' They feared a defection a week through the summer months.

But that wasn't the deciding factor. The bigger worry for Downing Street was the sense that major institutions including the Civil Service and the courts had started to prepare for a change in government, which was causing a shift in the ways in which they served the Conservative administration. One aide described the sense that the power needed to achieve change in government was draining away.

Two examples stood out: decision-making over prisons, and the battle to send a flight to Rwanda. On the first, Liam Booth-Smith, was said to be irritated that Labour's chief whip seemed to know more about a difficult policy involving early prisoner release than the Conservatives themselves.

Severe overcrowding in prisons had already forced the police to put in place a system called Operation Early Dawn in which defendants were held longer in police custody before being transferred to court for bail hearings in case there was inadequate space for them in jails. This problem had been caused by court backlogs in the wake of the pandemic which forced up the number of people being held on remand, waiting for a trial. The justice secretary, Cheltenham MP Alex Chalk, had repeatedly warned Downing Street that the situation was at breaking point, and it was only by deploying a measure called ECSL (End of Custody Supervised Licence) under which lower-level offenders could be let out of jail on licence a maximum of eighteen days before their conditional release date, that the pressure could be temporarily eased. Number 10 sources have told me that the effectiveness of ECSL meant they started to view the Ministry of Justice as 'crying wolf'.

However, in May 2024 Chalk said that ECSL was a short-term measure that had been exhausted and without further action the prison service would be forced to trigger the much more serious Operation Brinker, a 'one in, one out' system. Sources in the Ministry of Justice and Downing Street tell me that Chalk kept talking about a 'pray-date' in the middle of June, complaining that if the government failed to act by then, they all might as well 'get down on our knees and pray'. There were fears that Brinker would force the entire justice system to collapse and could result in prison riots.

On Monday 20 May, Chalk went to see Sunak to tell him that there was now no choice but to pass legislation that would allow a more effective early-release plan, under which prisoners on standard determinate sentences would be automatically released at the 40 per cent point of their sentence, rather than 50 per cent. He argued that rapists, violent offenders, and terrorists would be exempt from the scheme. But in the eyes of the PM's advisers, it would still mean taking the unpalatable step of letting criminals, including shoplifters, out earlier than they rightly deserved.

Later that day, Downing Street officials briefed colleagues in the Ministry of Justice that the PM was minded to consider taking the steps required. And so Chalk, who felt it was the government's responsibility to make the changes (and who was also facing an unwinnable fight against Lib Dems in his constituency) was said to be deeply frustrated when the election was announced.

The other problem was Rwanda. A number of people made it clear to me that by May, the prime minister was fast losing hope that any flight full of illegal immigrants would take off before an autumn election. The legislation passed by the government was meant to bombproof the Rwanda plan by disapplying the Human Rights Act to prevent a domestic legal challenge and suggesting that ministers would be able to ignore a temporary intervention from the European Court in Strasbourg. At first, ministers genuinely thought they had 'kitchen-sinked' the legislation to protect it from legal challenge. But it wasn't that simple and by late spring, Downing Street was convinced that the domestic courts would find a way to stymie their plans. Sources believed that judges would want to avoid a bust-up with Strasbourg ahead of a general election that could result in Labour dropping the policy anyway (and even believed that likely delays had been suggested). 'If we had just won an election, I'm convinced this would not have been an issue,' said one senior figure. Senior lawyers involved in cases against the government told me there were 'holes' in the legislation that would have allowed domestic challenges which could have resulted in the embarrassment of asylum seekers being disembarked one by one from a plane ready to fly.

Sunak believed that he had made good progress on legal migration with new rules increasing the salary-threshold for foreign workers and restricting the ability of people to bring spouses in order to bear down on the number of visas issued. But the immigration numbers still felt too high, and paired with this lack of action on Rwanda made the party fear the threat from Reform UK even more. They'd heard rumours that Farage might announce that he was standing as a candidate in Clacton in late May or early June and thought perhaps they could disrupt his plans by announcing an early election day, sooner rather than later.

So the prime minister was afraid of a bumpy summer in which he would have to let serious criminals out of jail; watch boat numbers spike with the diminishing prospect of a Rwanda flight; and suffer more doctors' strikes. All alongside the steady drumbeat of Conservative defections. Moreover, he felt that Labour were getting away scot-free without proper scrutiny and told aides that calling an election would bring one major benefit: focusing voters' minds on the choice before them – Rishi Sunak or Sir Keir Starmer? So, he made up his mind.

The Tory government's decision to go for a 4 July 2024 election has been widely derided because many of the party members did not feel ready and also because the economy was expected to improve. Another factor raised by politicians was the sheer number of levelling-up projects they felt could make a visible and material difference in their local towns that were only due to complete later that year.

Many say Sunak should have waited until the autumn, but when I put this to a senior figure close to Sunak, he hit back with a different take. 'This would be seen as a heretical view and I'm only saying it with hindsight,' he said, 'but I think our problem was not that we went too early, but that we went far too late. The optimal time to go was May 2023, when we had a grace period, had set out a forward-facing agenda, and before people were enraged. Rishi was an unelected prime minister and it would have been reasonable to seek a public mandate.'

While Sunak and his team settled on the date soon after the May local elections, the green light was only fully lit a few days before the announcement. Sources say the prime minister still would have waited if it weren't for the victory of Conservative Ben Houchen in the Tees Valley mayoral race (a reasoning that a senior Labour figure argued was bizarre since Houchen's election saw a hefty swing away from the Tories). They chose 22 May for the announcement in order to make way for a six-week campaign, and because of Sunak's number-one priority; on that day inflation was expected to finally fall to its 2 per cent target.

Only Sunak's close team were involved in the various discussions about the election, including Booth-Smith and the deputy prime minister Oliver Dowden, as well as key figures in CCHQ. The inner team had kept these discussions tight to try to give the Conservative Party an advantage over the opposition. But if Sunak wanted to wrong-foot Labour, he had a problem. Keir Starmer's team had been ready for a general election for some time.

On Thursday 14 March 2024, Labour's deputy director of communications Paul Ovenden passionately outlined to his attack team the reasons he was sure the Conservatives would hold an election in May and laid out the preparations they would need to make. One member of the team joked that his colleague's rant sounded akin to a *Henry V* monologue. Later, they decamped to the Libertine pub, close to Labour's Southwark headquarters. At 6.30 p.m., one of his colleagues handed Ovenden the phone to show him a tweet. Rishi Sunak had just ruled out a 2 May election on ITV News West Country. 'He obviously didn't hear your speech,' they teased. Ovenden shrugged. 'He hasn't ruled out May 9,' he said, to a long groan from the rest of his team.

Even though it did not happen, Labour had been ready to go to the polls on 2 May, with a campaign plan that they were prepared to adapt to 9 May, anytime in June, October, November, or indeed 4 July. In readiness Labour had: shaken up its organisational structure to lay the groundwork for a field campaign that would be more digitally-focused; analysed by-election results to sharpen the policy offer; turbo-boosted candidate selections under a somewhat contro-versial and more centralised system; honed in on a campaign slogan; and started prepping shadow cabinet ministers for government.

In charge of the organising team were campaign director Morgan McSweeney and national campaign coordinator Pat McFadden, who had taken over from Shabana Mahmood when she became shadow justice secretary. Alongside Starmer's strategy, policy, communica-tions and data teams, other key figures were McFadden's deputy, Ellie Reeves; Labour's general secretary David Evans; the executive director nations and regions (or field director) Hollie Ridley; digital director Tom Lillywhite; and McSweeney's deputy, Marianna McFadden (who was married to Pat).

Following a review by the former Civil Service boss, Bob Kerslake, David Evans had marshalled the team under the banner 'Organise to Win'. His restructure was said to be about making the party more 'voter-centric'. Approximately 100 roles disappeared through a voluntary redundancy scheme, drawing criticism from some who argued once again that it squeezed the influence of the left. Ridley wanted the field and digital teams to be more integrated than ever before. In place of the more centralised positions, Labour recruited a network of field and digital 'trainees', whom Ridley and Lillywhite based in the regions and deployed into key constituencies. Lillywhite's digital network was used to develop 'social proof' content designed to encourage vote-switching by showing people that others in their community were doing the same. In a plan called 'Operation Go', around forty-five trainees took filming kits into target seats and created thousands of videos, with 180 ready to post immediately when the election announcement was made. They had also created adverts using candidates that would 'pre-roll' ahead of videos on Facebook or YouTube, targeted into the right constituencies by postcode.

Labour had also reached out across the world to other social democratic parties, with Evans visiting Berlin five times to meet SPD counterparts at their headquarters in the Willy-Brandt-Haus. Starmer's party took inspiration from the SPD manifesto. Both political parties placed a black-and-white image of their leaders (Keir Starmer and Olaf Scholz) on the front page with a splash of red and a simple message. Where the SPD wrote 'RESPEKT FUR DICH' (respect for you), Labour's manifesto had 'Change'. Hollie Ridley would speak regularly to her counterpart in the Australian Labor Party, which in 2022 had achieved its first majority since 2007. There were also meetings with Democrats in Washington, DC and the digital team returned from a fact-finding trip to New Zealand with a presentation on how its centre-right National Party had used humour and TikTok to humanise its leader, Christopher Luxon.

Ridley would describe her role as 'sales', taking pages-long documents from the policy teams and then crunching down the content to allow her regional directors, and through them the field teams, to sell a 'feeling' or 'emotion'. The party tried to create a 'feedback loop' by collecting data from thousands of doorstep conversations in real time, through a new app, and using it to shape policy and communication decisions, as well as to constantly tweak scripts for activists on the ground. There was also a shift away from a 'Get Out The Vote' (GOTV) strategy to 'Maximise The Vote' (MTV). This was an organisational stratagem for Labour, although those working for Corbyn would argue that their methods in 2017 were all about exciting new supporters who had abandoned the party.

Labour's campaign team then introduced a system which they gave the jargony title: 'persuasion pathways', and which they immediately put into practice in local elections. They changed the scripts for activists, so that instead of starting with, 'Who are you voting for?', they would ask the more open question, 'Do you have any issues or concerns?' Then the Labour member would try to assess how likely the person was to vote for Starmer's party. Those who were undecided would be marked down as 'D' and then assigned a number between 1 and 10 based on the likelihood of winning them over. So, a D1 and D2 would be largely hopeless and not worth more effort; while the party would assume a D10 was in the bag. Effort would then be piled into persuading those in-between voters, taking phone numbers and emails for those marked as a D5, -6 or -7. These constituents would then receive a personal call or letter from the candidate, with as much focus as possible on the issues that they had raised on the doorstep.

Furthermore, in May 2023, David Evans came up with an experiment that would result in ruthless targeting. Ridley and others including Labour's regional director, Pearleen Sangha, and London's new political director, the MP Ellie Reeves, would execute this new system. The party knew that 25 per cent of Labour members were based in the capital, but since that year had no London elections, they started bussing activists out into the regions in the run-up to local council elections. 'Exporting London' sent Labour members en masse to Medway, Thanet, Gravesham, Dover, Stoke, Erewash and Swindon, where they targeted specific wards to help boost councillor numbers, with a remarkable result. Labour took control of all of them. The operation was run by 'twinning' London boroughs with a target area elsewhere, a strategy that would be used heavily (and sometimes controversially) in the general election. Before that day came, there were plenty of by-elections this Labour team could practise on.

At first, much of the heady success in by-elections had been down to the Lib Dems, thanks to an impressive machine. In June 2021, when Johnson was still on a high, they shocked Conservatives by ousting them in Chesham and Amersham. Then Ed Davey's party celebrated a huge victory in North Shropshire, followed by a stunning win in Tiverton, Devon. The gains soon started coming in for Labour as well. On 20 July 2023, while the Lib Dems won again in Somerton, Somerset, in Selby and Ainsty the Labour candidate 25-year-old Keir Mather achieved his party's biggest swing in a by-election since 1945 – overturning a 20,137 Conservative majority in this North Yorkshire constituency.

As some in the party were wallowing in this record by-election win, 200 miles south of Selby others were grappling with their shock loss. Labour's failure to take Boris Johnson's vacated Uxbridge and South Ruislip seat, falling 425 votes short, allowed the then prime minister Rishi Sunak to declare that the next general election was not a 'done deal'. That loss was widely attributed to the unpopularity of Sadiq Khan's ULEZ (Ultra Low Emission Zone) reforms, which extended the clean air region in London to include the city's outer suburbs. A decline in support for Labour among some ethnic-minority groups probably also played a part. Whatever the reason, Starmer admitted he needed to reflect.

That weekend, the Labour leader, his shadow cabinet, NEC members, council leaders including those from London, and representatives of all affiliated unions, gathered in a hall at the University of Nottingham for a meeting of the party's National Policy Forum (NPF). If those attending had wanted to bask in the warm glow of the stunning victory in Selby, they were out of luck. Starmer and his campaign director, Morgan McSweeney, were in no mood to celebrate. Instead, they were focused only on their recent loss.

'We are doing something very wrong if policies put forward by the Labour Party end up on each and every Tory leaflet. We've got to face up to that and learn the lessons,' Starmer said.

Uxbridge's unsuccessful candidate Danny Beales (who was narrowly elected in 2024) then took to the stage, blaming ULEZ for the defeat. One shadow cabinet minister noted that there in front of them was the patent tension in Labour's campaign: Khan's 'inner London' strategy had crashed into the national party's 'outer London' one.

At the same time, key unions like Unison, GMB, USDAW and Unite were arguing over Labour's package on workers' rights, with the GMB urging protections on equal pay. There was also intense pressure from the left (and centre) of the party to promise to lift the two-child cap on benefits which the former Labour prime minister Gordon Brown had warned was condemning children to poverty.

But McSweeney believed that Uxbridge should instil more discipline not less, and that Labour should resist any policy that might alienate Tory switchers. A few days earlier, in a BBC interview, Starmer had refused to commit to lifting the child benefit cap, and at the NPF he held firm, arguing the party could not 'keep on piling … up' unfunded commitments.[1] Other policies were also changed in light of Uxbridge. A few days after the result, Anneliese Dodds penned an article stating that while Labour would simplify the process for a trans person to secure a gender recognition certificate, it would no longer support a policy of self-identification. The party also halted its plan to give EU citizens voting rights in general elections and distanced itself from ULEZ. Months later, Reeves said her party would not reinstate a bankers' bonus cap.

Meanwhile, the party was hoping to show the scale of its ambition through its performance in another local by-election which was rapidly speeding towards them. In 2019 Nadine Dorries had won Mid Bedfordshire for the Conservatives with a majority of almost 25,000 and 73.7 per cent of the vote. Although Labour had come second, the Lib Dems began to contend, as they had successfully in North Shropshire, that to win this seat required the support of traditional Conservative voters, who might cross to them but would never go so far as to vote for Starmer's party. But in Labour HQ, they wanted this fight.

Ridley was no doubt delighted when Marianna McFadden first called her Labour's 'field marshal'; everywhere she looked she saw parallels between military and political battles. Ridley had long been fascinated by war, writing a university dissertation on the women of the Special Operations Executive who had risked their lives to bring back intelligence from across Europe. She even named her daughter after a captured French spy. So, when the question of whether Labour should put resources into Mid Beds rang out, unsurprisingly she immediately reached for a military metaphor. 'It's war,' she said, calling for Labour to flood the constituency with Labour insignia to signal that they, and not the Lib Dems, were the key opposition. 'We must gain territory fast, that is our job,' Ridley said.

The shadow Northern Ireland secretary, Peter Kyle had just returned to his flat in Brighton after marking the twenty-fifth anniversary of the Good Friday Agreement in Belfast. It had been an intense and exhausting trip, in which Joe Biden had made a much-publicised appearance. It was a lovely sunny day on Britain's south coast, and the MP for Hove and Portslade had just made himself bagels and scrambled eggs and was sitting with a cup of green tea looking towards the sea, when his phone rang. It was Starmer's political director, Luke Sullivan, asking Kyle's thoughts on Mid Bedfordshire, a true-blue constituency more than 100 miles away. Kyle said the majority was 'gargantuan' so it would take quite some thought to assess the feasibility of cracking it. Sullivan replied that Starmer wanted Kyle to run the campaign. Shocked, the MP replied: 'You can fuck right off,' and hung up. But Sullivan kept ringing and, although it ruined Kyle's day, he agreed to head to Bedford to take a look.

The decision to go for Mid Beds was an interesting one; it was extremely high risk and would involve throwing resources at a difficult campaign that might not pay off. As Kyle criss-crossed the largely rural seat with the regional directors for the East of England Dom Collins and Emma Toal, and the senior regional director for the South East, Teddy Ryan (who happened to be Ridley's husband), he felt growing excitement. There was fury at the Conservatives all over the place, and no obvious revulsion to Labour. Kyle spoke to

Starmer and reported back on what he had found, arguing that Labour could win but if they didn't they would have handed their opponents a stick to beat them with. After a pause, Starmer said, 'Pete, go for it. I will give you everything you need but I expect you to be there, and I expect no mistakes to be made.' Kyle later said that this conversation with Starmer had been revealing, arguing that once again it belied the Labour leader's reputation for caution; he saw this as a bold decision. No one would have criticised Labour for leaving Mid Beds to the Lib Dems, but there would be fury if the two centre-left parties split the vote and let the Conservatives in, and so McSweeney and Ridley came under intense pressure over the strategy. McSweeney was said to be 'exhilarated' by taking on the race but made clear: if the data pointed to a Labour loss the party would immediately pull back all resources. And so, after weeks of pounding the streets, on 19 October 2023 when Kyle, Toal and Ryan realised that their candidate Alistair Strathern had won the seat, they wrapped each other in a hug.

As the successful by-election results kept coming, the party intensified its search for candidates under a new and much more centralised selection system introduced by Starmer. Under his leadership, Labour issued fresh guidance that would take selection powers from local parties and hand it to the leadership. Instead of a longlist of candidates for a seat being drawn up within the constituency, it became the job of NEC panels. This gave the leadership more control over who was eligible for a seat, but the system also introduced tougher sanctions; there were new rules governing social media posts and if a candidate had retweeted anything implying support for candidates from alternative parties, they could find themselves barred from standing.

The selection system was under the stewardship of Matt Faulding, now secretary to the parliamentary Labour Party. He would take an umbrella view of where a candidate list was oversubscribed and constituencies where they had scant interest. His aim was to draw in impressive Labour candidates and suggest appropriate places where they might want to stand. Then a six-week process would get under-way; two weeks for the NEC to longlist around six candidates; two weeks for the local party to narrow it to three or four people; and then two weeks in which finalists were given party members' details and could rally to win over support before a hustings and a vote. This new system was controversial because it effectively allowed Starmer's team to block candidates, which the left of the party felt was intended to eliminate them. Sources I spoke to denied that intent, but admitted they wanted to build a parliamentary party that believed in Starmer's leadership, and with it his (more centrist) brand of Labour politics. That is why some critics saw the system as deeply factional.

To Corbyn supporters like the MP for Normanton and Hemsworth Jon Trickett, this change amounted to 'manipulation, purges and unfathomable methods ... to remove excellent potential candidates, often with deep local roots.' And it upset some on the 'soft left' as well, especially when in the summer of 2023 the party tried to expel Labour member Neal Lawson for his retweet of a call to back Green Party candidates where they could best win in local elections. As the founder-director of the Compass campaign group, years earlier Lawson was one of the people that McSweeney had sought out when he was trying to build bridges with the left of the party; someone long-committed to plural politics who believed in trying to build a 'progressive alliance' between parties on the left in order to defeat the Conservatives. The move on Lawson (which was never realised) was seen by some Labour MPs as a wrong-headed decision. One whom I would describe as centre-left within Labour, and certainly not on the Corbynite radical wing, told me: 'To sustain itself in office, Labour needs to be a broad church. Why shrink it down to a hard right faction?' Lawson himself became disillusioned, writing aghast that the party had thrown out a candidate for retweet-ing a Green Party peer, while welcoming in austerity-supporting Tories like Christian Wakeford, who had crossed the floor. He pointed out that with Labour Together McSweeney had wooed the left from the start, saying the group whose data helped to spur Starmer to the leadership was 'as impressive as it [was] cynical': 'Its polling of members showed that only a candidate who could represent Corbynism could win, but then the ladder would be kicked away on everything that politics stood for, not just the bad but the good as well.'

But sources in the selection reforms hit back, insisting the system was simply about ensuring the highest quality of candidates. Faulding would argue that this included impressive figures from the left, like Miatta Fahnbulleh, the Peckham MP who has gained praise from right across the party – from Faulding himself, to chair of the centre-left Tribune Group Clive Efford (who believes she could be a future leader), to Corbyn's close ally, John McDonnell. And as for Starmer himself, many of his centrist allies argue his politics lies to the left of theirs. But unquestionably, Faulding had helped his boss, by supporting the selections of a Starmerite-looking Labour Party, and the vast majority had been selected long before the election was called.

Separately, Faulding had worked with Claire Reynolds at the Labour Women's Network. The Labour Party had historically used all-women shortlists to improve its gender balance, but for the first time in 2019 the intake was slightly more female than male, so it was considered no longer legally acceptable to enforce the old approach. Instead, Reynolds had tried to force genuine 'cultural change' in which her organisation identified and trained exceptional female candidates who could win selections without men being barred. The Scottish Labour Party, meanwhile, used a system of pairing, with one man and one woman chosen for neighbouring seats. (In the 2024 Election, 190 female Labour MPs won overall, with 100 elected for the first time, making up 58 per cent of all new incoming MPs.)

When Pat McFadden became campaign coordinator in September 2023, with Ellie Reeves as his deputy, his first job was to join activists on the doorsteps in Rutherglen and Hamilton West, just outside

Glasgow and not far from where he grew up. On his first visit McFadden described finding voters who were 'poised' to change their vote. They were angry with the SNP but also saw the Labour Party as part of a past identity they had lost. McFadden praised colleagues for a well-organised doorstep operation, before heading home. A few weeks later, he returned to a much warmer mood among constituents he spoke to and told colleagues that he now believed not only that Labour would win, but win big. He knew that he had to try to export what he'd found in Rutherglen around the country, but at that point Labour still needed to hone a simple message and slogan around which the national campaign would be built.

McFadden and McSweeney gathered close colleagues at the central London office of party donor Waheed Ali, a traditional Soho townhouse decorated with antique furniture. Among those present were the key figures covering strategy, operations, communications and policy including Deborah Mattinson, Jill Cuthbertson, Matthew Doyle, Paul Ovenden, Marianna McFadden and Stuart Ingham, as well as the shadow secretary of state for work and pensions Jonathan Ashworth. It was not high-tech, with McFadden standing at the front with a flip chart and a black marker pen. The team knew that when voters looked at the Conservative Party they saw chaos, but what was their political and economic critique, and what was Labour's offer? Over hours and days of painstaking discussions, the group finally narrowed down a strategy for the election campaign. It would hang on four ideas: it was time for change; the Conservatives had failed; Labour had changed; and it had a plan. McFadden and McSweeney took the pitch to Starmer and his new chief of staff, Sue Gray. Starmer then gathered hundreds of staff and candidates in a London theatre and used the pitch structure for a stump speech to the room. As his team watched closely, they could see that it was working. These four pillars would frame the election campaign.

Not that the new messaging stopped Labour from facing some serious problems. The first came after Hamas's terrorist attack on

Israel on 7 October, in which 1,200 people were killed and 250 were taken hostage, many young men and women filmed in the moment they were snatched from a desert festival. Israel's immediate and brutal response would see tens of thousands killed in Gaza and the Palestinian territories.

The handling of Middle East politics has always been a difficult issue for the Labour Party, and never more than at that time. Starmer's determination that his party stand with Israel in its darkest hour led to an LBC interview in which he appeared to suggest that Benjamin Netanyahu's country had a right to cut off power and water from innocent civilians in Gaza. It took nine days for the Labour leader to respond to the sheer fury among those in his party who had long fought for Palestinian rights, and millions of voters, including many Muslims, who were aghast at the suggestion. After an initial attempt to calm the anger, it took the party months to reach the eventual position of supporting an immediate ceasefire, and this was only in the face of potentially catastrophic dissent that could have seen scores of frontbenchers, including Shadow Justice Secretary Shabana Mahmood, stand down.

Things kicked off for Starmer when what is known as an 'opposition day' in Parliament was granted to the SNP, and Westminster's third largest party put down a motion calling for 'an immediate ceasefire for all combatants'. Labour was ready to shift its position but not quite that far and so laid down an amendment calling for an 'immediate humanitarian ceasefire', with the condition, however, that Israel could not be expected to abide if Hamas continued to threaten violence. Determined to prevent a mass rebellion over the SNP motion, Starmer held a private meeting with Lindsay Hoyle that led to claims the Labour leader had threatened the speaker of the House of Commons – an allegation which was strongly denied. In what was seen as an unusual step the Speaker then chose Labour's amendment first, scuppering the original SNP motion. Parliament descended into farcical scenes, with one clear winner; amid more claims of utter ruthlessness, Starmer had dodged a destabilising rebellion. But this controversy would continue to cause Labour a major electoral headache.

Another complication was Rachel Reeves's earlier pledge to borrow £28 billion per year to invest in green technology, which now, in the face of rising interest rates, was a much less affordable prospect. Although the shadow chancellor had tried to soften the proposed policy by insisting it was subject to fiscal rules, this £28 billion became a rod with which Tories would try to beat Labour day in, day out. I would sit in the press gallery of the House of Commons chamber listening to ministers crowbar the £28 billion figure into the debate, whatever the subject in discussion. Some argued internally that the underlying policy for a green industrial revolution remained important, but the decision to attach a figure to it had become a 'distraction', with every question on the matter focused on £28 billion, when most of the spending had not been allocated.

Labour had already decided to drop the figure after Chancellor Jeremy Hunt's final pre-election budget (due on 6 March) but a series of leaks about their protracted decision-making sent the message that they did not have a grip on the situation. Determined that Labour must not back down on its overall climate pledges and nervous of too many U-turns, Starmer wanted time to listen to the evidence from Reeves but also from Ed Miliband, who was passionate about the policy. So, even when the decision to drop the policy leaked to Jack Elsom in the *Sun* and then Kiran Stacey in the *Guardian*, Starmer continued to stand by it, before a somewhat messy climbdown. The Green Prosperity Plan survived but with a lower price tag, with a National Wealth Fund at its centre to invest in eco-friendly infrastructure projects including those linked to ports and gigafactories, which would be a central plank of the election campaign.

In the fallout from the controversy there were reports that, in a forthright leak inquiry, Sue Gray and the HR department had upset staff by asking if they would show officials their phones. Some claim that the incident marked the start of tensions within the team. But others described Gray's arrival as a breath of fresh air as she reached out to the party's shadow cabinet and regional mayors to make them feel more involved in the operation. In a visit organised by Jill Cuthbertson, Gray also headed to Rutherglen with strategy director Deborah Mattinson, in this lifelong civil servant's first experience of political doorstep conversations. Some of those who accompanied the pair claimed that Gray could spend half an hour with a single voter, needing to be dragged away.

On the £28 billion U-turn, one senior Labour figure admitted to me that the situation wasn't handled in the 'most elegant' of ways, but it did result in the figure being banished which, according to them, had removed 'the central element of the Conservative campaign'.

A further dilemma was how to deal with the clamour from many voters for tougher action on Britain's borders. The party knew it had to be clear that Labour believed in policing Britain's borders, but behind the scenes I'm told that Starmer was explicit that to him, the enemy must be the criminal gangs behind the perilous Channel crossings and not those seeking asylum in the UK. McSweeney briefed colleagues: 'We must never punch down on immigrants, never punch down on refugees, and never punch down on people on benefits.' In discussions the team agreed that while Labour had itself used some derogatory anti-immigrant language in the past, that must never happen again. Starmer's background in human rights meant he was also determined to defend Britain's membership of the European Convention on Human Rights.

As for Labour's own campaign planning, the team had one more crucial decision to make: the slogan. This was crystallised in a meeting in early spring, as the campaign team tried to boil down the four pillars they had come up with to a single compelling message. They knew they had to try to capture the overwhelming emotion crying out for something new that they had perceived all across the country.

'Change for Britain?' suggested one person.

'Change for the future?' added another.

'Time for Change,' suggested a third.

It was then that Pat McFadden and Morgan McSweeney looked at each other and said, 'What about just one word?' The pair discussed the idea and later pitched it to the rest of the team, who agreed.

And so, Labour's 2024 Election slogan would be simply: 'Change'.

13

The Campaign

In mid-May, when rumours of a snap election began swirling around Westminster, it seemed at first like more of the same speculation that had been circling on an almost weekly basis. But when Rachel Reeves's chief of staff Katie Martin heard something that sounded more concrete, she messaged McSweeney. He wasn't sure, but on Tuesday 21 May some people flagged a slight shift in the betting odds.

The next morning, McSweeney bumped into Keir Starmer, in Parliament, saying: 'I think it is going to be today'. By then the party had begun buying up advertising space in both the *Sun* and *Mail* newspapers for the week of 4 July, including digital 'takeovers'. The team moved to print campaign material featuring the new one-word slogan, including a sign to place on a lectern from which Starmer would give his first election speech. Across the country, candidates had each been sent a box with a label that read: 'Break in case of emergency'. Inside were Correx boards, stickers, voter registration cards, QR codes for postal votes, and leaflets. The team wanted an election event in every battleground seat within ninety minutes of the PM's announcement, whenever it came, and had provided enough bumf to get everyone through the first weekend.

Meanwhile, Rishi Sunak's senior advisers had 'gone dark', raising suspicions across Westminster. But just before 11 a.m., The *Sunday*

Times's chief political commentator Tim Shipman wrote on X that he had been sceptical of all previous rumours because people he trusted to be in the loop had told him they were nonsense. 'This time, those people are silent,' he noted.

The prime minister had worked hard to keep the election date under wraps, discussing the question with close aides such as Liam Booth-Smith, Nissy Chesterfield and James Forsyth. Others within a tight circle would include Isaac Levido and immediate colleagues in CCHQ, the MP who acted as his parliamentary private secretary, Craig Williams and from the cabinet only deputy PM, Oliver Dowden, and the chief whip, Simon Hart. Chancellor Jeremy Hunt, who was perhaps already half in the know, having been aware that his March budget was to be the last before an election, found out earlier that day. Lord Cameron was also informed because Sunak needed his foreign secretary to cut short a visit to Albania. But for most of the top cabinet, their first inklings of a potential announcement were from rumours circulating in the media, and a delayed cabinet meeting to be held at 4 p.m. As soon as the prime minister told them the news, any impartial civil servants left the room and in swept Isaac Levido and his team to deliver a political briefing.

Levido told the assembled cabinet that an election was like a court hearing, with opening statements, a long evidentiary phase and then a summing up. The Conservatives were going to put it to the electorate that Sunak had arrived against a backdrop of incredibly difficult circumstances outside his control, dealing with the financial fallout of the pandemic, the inflationary pressures of the Ukraine war and a mortgage crisis that voters associated with Liz Truss. The aim was to persuade the electorate that Sunak had managed to steady the ship and bring inflation under control. Their campaign, he hoped, would then pose the question: Who should lead the country in this uncertain world? And finally, just like Labour, the Tories would say they were the ones with the viable plan. The election must not become a referendum on the Conservative Party, he said, but a choice between two leaders and two alternative approaches to government, particularly on the economy and tax. Sunak's personal standing and his ability to earn the begrudging respect of voters for sticking the course, therefore, would be central to their campaign offer; how they viewed him personally mattered.

Yet another problem was brewing for the Tories, however. Rain clouds hung heavy over Downing Street that day. A wet-weather option had been prepared but there was also a conviction this important address would look better outside the door of Number 10. If they changed the plan, some also feared negative headlines about the prime minister running scared of the rain, not least given that journalists had already been waiting in the downpour for over an hour. Besides, a weather app suggested things might improve – and so Rishi Sunak took the plunge.

You know what came next. Sunak declared that this was the 'moment for Britain to choose its future', as torrential rain streamed down his black jacket and the blaring soundtrack of D-Ream's 'Things Can Only Get Better', the song that marked New Labour's 1997 victory, drifted over from the Downing Street gates where anti-Tory protesters were playing it at full volume. The scene paved the way for a disastrous set of first-day headlines. The Conservatives might have expected a punchy 'Drown and Out' from the Labour-supporting *Mirror*, but perhaps were not expecting 'Things Can Only Get Wetter' from the Conservative-supporting *Daily Telegraph*, which concluded Sunak had gambled big with this snap poll.

One of the big problems was that while Labour (and the Lib Dems for that matter) were poised and ready to go, many Conservative MPs were not. This narrative reached across the world, with a report on CBS News in the US which claimed that Sunak's own party was shocked and confused. The reporter told American viewers about Tory MPs calling this a 'kamikaze decision' and asking 'is this political suicide?' Certainly, a number of Tory politicians had messaged me furiously and in a panic. 'It sent us into a tailspin,' said one. Others spoke of practical issues, like the party's printers having run out of paper. Some planned to send 'pledge letters' to their constituents, but these had to be written using fresh letterheads without an 'MP' label and required staff to stuff the envelopes and get them out, which would take time. Moreover, given how Number 10 ostensibly had steered towards an autumn date, holidays had been booked.

The minister of state for Northern Ireland, Steve Baker, believed that a later election date was 'nailed-on' when he had planned a trip to Greece with his wife and an old friend. He described working furiously through government business linked to Sunak's Windsor Agreement so it would be complete ahead of a vote. Baker was well aware that his seat of Wycombe was a Labour target with a high-profile and experienced candidate in former MP Emma Reynolds, so he had hired a campaign manager a year in advance. But like many of his colleagues he still felt 'bounced pretty hard' by the July date, and decided to stick with his holiday in Greece, from where he would finalise the first batch of election literature. Inevitably, his decision brought negative publicity, although Baker had told me already he felt he was sure to lose. He later said the election 'looked like a surprise to CCHQ', which he found 'unbelievable', and hit out at an 'appalling campaign'. When I put this to a senior figure in Sunak's operation, they replied that MPs 'should have been bloody ready – it was an election year!' But choosing summer over autumn without giving MPs ample notice definitely caused them a headache.

One Conservative politician told me that within hours of the election announcement, they could see the pre-filmed YouTube content being pumped out by their Labour opponent and frantically started messaging colleagues, asking, 'How do you set up an advertising account on Google?'

Another issue for MPs was the rush to get election literature out before Parliament was formally dissolved on 30 May, because from that point on much tighter spending controls were introduced. John Stevenson, the then Tory Carlisle MP, explained that he had pre-booked Post Office slots for June and July to send out leaflets ahead of an autumn election, but in a tightly regulated short-campaign the mailings were far too costly, and so he cancelled them. (Anecdotally Labour and the Lib Dem candidates managed to push out far more material in that period than Conservatives.) The same was true of fundraising events which had originally been in the diary for October and November.

Stevenson wasn't due to go on holiday himself, but members of his campaign team were, including one due to be out of the country in polling week. 'It was disastrous for many MPs. I felt more ready than some, but local campaigns were not prepared,' he said.

Labour, of course, were not in government so they had been thinking of little else than an election. The now former Carlisle MP is chair of his party's Northern Research Group and saw the vast majority of his colleagues also lose their seats. In his opinion, Labour may have picked up 30 or 40 seats because of their extra preparation. 'I knew they were ready as soon as Keir Starmer popped up with a lectern that was already stamped with the word "change"', Stevenson told me.

At Labour HQ, around 200 members of staff gathered around TVs to watch Sunak's speech. Evans, McSweeney, McFadden, Mattinson, Lillywhite and Hyman were there as well as Ridley, who by chance had invited all her regional directors, and general secretaries from Scotland and Wales down to London for face-to-face meetings that day. As politicians including Rachel and Ellie Reeves poured in to join their teams, Ridley was standing beside Labour's senior regional director for the South East, her husband Teddy Ryan. As soon as they all saw the lectern being carried into the street, everyone exploded into a cheer. Many watched in shock as the rain hammered down on the prime minister, with some quietly admitting they felt bad for him.

Starmer headed to an indoor venue across London with Jill Cuthbertson, Matthew Doyle and other communications advisers including Steph Driver. They had originally expected that Sunak would make an election announcement earlier that day, and so had planned for the Labour leader to deliver his response at Gillingham Football Club in Kent, partly because they could get to it quickly, but also because it had a Conservative majority of more than 15,000, which they thought would help demonstrate Labour's ambitions for the campaign. The placards stamped with the word 'Change', had been hidden in Ridley and Ryan's garage, ready for the occasion.

But Sunak's announcement at 5 p.m. limited the time for Starmer to respond if his comments were to make the evening news bulletins, so the team instead opted for a speech in London before heading on to Kent the next day. During his first car journey of what would be a gruelling six weeks criss-crossing the country, Starmer told Jill Cuthbertson, 'I don't know what I would have done if you'd told me to go and deliver the speech in the rain.' 'As if I would have done that,' she said laughing.

From the moment she had arrived in the job, Cuthbertson knew she had to embrace Starmer's love of football (obsession, even). And in this campaign, she knew it would help, because the game provided a connection to local communities, and a safe place to host election events given increased security fears around MPs. Moreover, stadiums had the added benefit of giving the team three weather options: on the pitch in the sunshine; under the stands for a trickle; and indoor boardrooms for a proper downpour. And the backdrop looked great.

As Starmer began his nationwide tour with Cuthbertson, Doyle and Driver often by his side, the campaign team in headquarters started to spread out, taking the seats from which they would direct the campaign. McFadden and McSweeney would spend much of it holed up in a room they nicknamed 'The Cell' from 6 a.m. to after 10 p.m., with other key figures like Evans, Ellie Reeves, Ridley and Lillywhite coming in and out. Some noted that Pat McFadden must have been waking up at 4.30 a.m. because by the time he arrived, he'd already read every newspaper and was prepared for the day. With Doyle and Driver on the road, Sophie Nazemi would run the media team in HQ, a survivor from the Jeremy Corbyn days who colleagues said impressed Starmer with her ability to remain cool in a crisis and deliver.

The first decision was to define which would be their 'core battle-ground' seats. To start, they identified around 100 constituencies to qualify for maximum resources – a visit from Starmer, Rayner and Reeves, a full-time organiser, and the most financial help on offer, including a higher digital spend for activity directed by Lillywhite. As part of the field operation, Hollie Ridley would ensure that extra bodies were parachuted in from safer or unwinnable seats.

In preparation for the election, Labour had already plotted their target seats, assigning each into five main categories – from the easiest wins (groups 1 and 2); those needed to make Labour the largest party (group 3); deliver a majority (group 4); or deliver a large majority (group 5). They expected the Tories to make progress ahead of an election announcement, so the plan was to take the final decision on which constituencies would constitute the core battleground on the day of the announcement, based on the very latest polls. On 22 May, YouGov placed Labour 25 points ahead, although other polling companies were slightly tighter. Assessing Labour's internal figures with the party's director of data, Tom Adams, the team decided to go for a more aggressive approach: groups 3–5 would constitute the core battleground, while groups 1 and 2 would be classified as 'battleground', so would get some additional resources but not as many. Meanwhile, they came up with what some described as a 'mythical' group 6, seats that they had not expected to be in play, but now looked potentially in reach.

Meanwhile, there was a whole new category: they now identified twelve seats as being difficult to hold because of their large Muslim populations and widespread anger about Starmer's response to the humanitarian crisis in Gaza. These seats, which would have five dedicated members of campaign staff, were spread across east London, Luton, Birmingham, Blackburn, Bradford, along with one they were targeting in Dewsbury. But as it turned out, this list was too narrow; not encompassing Wes Streeting's Ilford North nor Jonathan Ashworth's Leicester South.

Throughout the campaign, Ellie Reeves would take charge of a 'twinning' strategy through which Labour would ruthlessly target resources. The party had learned a tough lesson in the May local elections that year and so wanted to replicate the success of the 2023 'Exporting London' experiment, by once again diverting staff and funds out of seats they believed to be safe, and into target councils. In the West Midlands mayoral election, where Labour sent every member of HQ staff and activists from across the region and beyond into Birmingham, and also asked every MP and parliamentary candidate to call fifty undecided voters during the week of the election, the strategy worked brilliantly. Labour's Richard Parker narrowly defeated the Conservative Andy Street by a margin so tight that organisers claimed it was equivalent to one vote per box across polling stations. However, a similar plan to divert resources from London to Harlow stalled when a narrative bubbled up predicting incorrectly that London mayor Sadiq Khan might lose, making activists reluctant to travel. As a result, Labour fell short by 50 votes in one ward and 30 in another, and allowed the Tories to narrowly retain control of Harlow council, with 17 council seats to Labour's 16.

In the general election, all constituencies were twinned, with candidates in safe seats, or those where there was little chance of victory, asked to take all their activists into target seats two or three times a week. The plan caused a little unrest among MPs who felt nervous about losing their own majority and wanted to be seen out on the streets in their local communities. However, Reeves warned them in writing that there was 'too much activity in some of our held seats'. Regional directors, who were frustrated by candidates' and their team's reluctance to travel to targeted seats, could threaten to switch off the party's Contact Creator database, which provided all the canvassing data, and would do so if they failed to comply. One source complained about a candidate 'wasting huge amounts of resource' on voter contacts in a seat where Labour ultimately came fourth. They justified this strategy stating that MPs were only being asked to focus elsewhere for a short five-week campaign; after all, they would have five years to shore up support in their own constituencies.

As the ground war got underway, an air war was also playing out in the national media. The image of their dripping-wet leader was just the start of a bumpy few days for the Conservatives. Reflecting on what happened, some of his allies mused that so often in politics it feels as if the bad simply gets worse while the good gets better in a vicious or virtuous cycle. Take the next gaffe, when Sunak visited Belfast's Titanic Quarter only for a reporter to ask him, 'Are you captaining a sinking ship going into this election?'

One frustrated Tory strategist, who felt Sunak was also unfairly treated when he asked Welsh voters if they were looking forward to the Euros, cried, 'The area is 185 acres!' ('Rishi was sat next to an English fan and the others were brewers excited about the football,' he told me.)

Aides were convinced that journalists were simply searching for controversy in everything, including a photograph of the PM standing under an 'exit' sign on a plane, and his decision to show off his (less than perfect) football skills. Sunak's campaign team were pleased, however, when the PM announced a plan for mandatory national service, in the military or charity sector. Although the policy was ridiculed by some Tory MPs, who felt it was sprung on them and were also frustrated by the lack of detail attached to the proposition, aides felt it was eye-catching, it dominated the agenda, and contrasted to Labour's lack of ideas.

For Starmer's party, the good had initially got better, with a strong focus on the economy placing Rachel Reeves front and centre of election coverage. On Tuesday 28 May, she delivered a speech at a Rolls-Royce factory near Derby, pointing to a letter of endorsement for Labour signed by 120 senior business leaders. Although no FTSE 100 bosses had added their names, this show of business support, which had been put together by Katie Martin, Vidhya Alakeson and their teams, featured some impressive names. Reeves told me that the only way to fulfil what Starmer had asked of her – to win back economic trust – was by 'securing the backing of business, as they are the lifeblood of a successful economy.' This letter, she said, was a 'signal Labour had changed and that the work of the previous few years had paid off.'

A clear narrative had formed: Labour seemed more ready for this election than the Conservative Party, who had actually set the date. But then two huge stories broke in a single day.

I had been with ITV News colleagues, Iona and Dan, covering Rachel Reeves's Rolls-Royce speech, then we had jumped on a bus to Stevenage to pick up the trail of Keir Starmer's election tour, when the first story dropped; this one, concerning his shadow deputy prime minister, was positive for Labour.

As far as politicians go, Angela Rayner has a fairly unique background. She was brought up on a council estate in Stockport and left school at 16, pregnant and with the words ringing in her ears that she would never 'amount to anything'. As her grandma stepped in to help with the baby, Rayner began working at night in social care, a job that would eventually lead her to become a full-time union rep for Unison, and from there, in 2010, Labour MP for Ashton-under-Lyne.

Some months before the election was announced, I'd been listening to an interview with Rayner on Alastair Campbell and Rory Stewart's *The Rest is Politics*, one of the UK's most popular podcasts, when she said something that stopped me in my tracks. She was talking about her mum's illness with bipolar disorder and her decade-long diagnosis journey and describing just how much damage this had caused her family. My highly intelligent and wonderfully creative brother had also suffered with bipolar and sadly died at just 37. Wondering if an earlier diagnosis might have saved his life, I asked Rayner if she would speak to me about her own experiences. At her home in Ashton-under-Lyne, we talked about just how tough it had been for her to watch her mum suffer.

Soon after our interview, in April 2024, Rayner's personal and professional life was sent into a spin by the news that Greater Manchester Police were investigating claims from a Conservative MP that she had avoided Capital Gains Tax on the sale of a home. The accusations led journalists to the Stockport streets where she had grown up, knocking on doors in an effort to get friends and neighbours to talk. In the run-up to the election campaign, the alleged scandal had virtually silenced one of Labour's best media performers. Despite the allegations, Starmer – whose relationship with Rayner had much improved since the 2021 botched reshuffle – had stood firmly beside his deputy. But the Tories had pushed the story hard, judging that Rayner was a 'Marmite' figure and the negative press might encourage wavering Conservative voters to think twice before switching to Labour. (At least one Tory strategist questioned the thinking, arguing that in the eyes of voters Rayner had become unquestionably net positive for Labour.)

News of the police decision to drop the case and clear Rayner came while we were in Stevenage, and so we found ourselves madly running across a bridge outside the railway station looking for somewhere to set up a camera and do a 'live'. But ten minutes before I was due to go on air, another story flashed up – this one likely to cause Keir Starmer a major headache.

'Diane Abbott to be banned from standing for Labour,' read *The Times*'s headline, suggesting Starmer was ready to block the veteran left-wing MP, who in 1987 became the first Black woman to enter Parliament.[1] The story caused a minor explosion among some of Starmer's aides, with one telling me they were 'pissed off' that it had been leaked. An hour later, a source told me that Abbott had in fact been re-admitted to the party. So what on earth was going on?

Abbott was a close ally of Jeremy Corbyn with a huge following in her Hackney constituency where in 2019 she secured a majority of more than 33,000. I was surprised to see the story, as it was my understanding that the Labour Party was close to an agreement with Abbott over a scandal that had been rumbling on for some time. It had all begun in April 2023 after she wrote a letter to the *Observer* newspaper in which she suggested that Jewish people did not experience racism as Black people did. 'It is true that many types of white people with points of difference, such as redheads, can experience this prejudice. But they are not all their lives subject to racism,' she wrote.[2]

The letter caused outrage and resulted in a sanction from the Labour Party. Abbott was required to undertake an online training course on anti-Semitism, which she completed in February, and the complaint was closed in early March 2024. It is unclear why it then took so long for the party to restore her whip, but when Sunak announced the election in May, Abbott was still suspended from the parliamentary Labour Party. She therefore had not been formally selected to stand again in Hackney. *The Times* report by Patrick Maguire, a journalist known for his Labour-related scoops, seemed to suggest that Abbott was being positioned alongside Jeremy Corbyn as part of a narrative about purging the left. The problem for Starmer was that Abbott was held in different and high regard by women throughout the Labour movement and from all political persuasions, from left to right. Even those who fiercely disagreed with her politics recognised Abbott's role as a trailblazer to all women of colour. And she had also faced unacceptable levels of abuse. When I had previously posted stories about her on social media, I saw Abbott inundated with racist abuse and also faced a large number of racially abusive messages myself.

Behind the scenes, the Labour whips had been bombarded by pleas from women MPs to resolve Abbott's case by readmitting her to the party, or perhaps arranging a peerage for her to sit in the House of Lords. Sympathy for her was all the greater given it had been revealed in March that the Conservative Party's biggest donor Frank Hester had told colleagues that '[looking at Abbott makes you] want to hate all Black women', and suggesting she 'should be shot'.[3] (A controversy that led the prime minister to brand Hester racist – before accepting more money from him.)

Genuine concerns about Abbott's health had led some to ask if she might be able to retire with dignity, and at least some of her friends suggested that this might have suited her too. But if that were true, the leak to *The Times* pushed her in the opposite direction. That night a furious Abbott appeared on the steps of Hackney Town Hall surrounded by supporters chanting, 'We stand with Diane'. 'By any means possible, I will be the candidate for Hackney North and Stoke Newington!' she declared.

As far as I can tell, although there were members of Starmer's team who hoped and believed that Abbott would not stand, no one had actually ordered that she be 'banned' from doing so. But when the story began to dominate news headlines, instead of shutting it down, Starmer's response was to say that no decision had been made.

This uproar came as Labour's NEC were urgently trying to fill the final few candidate-places after a number of MPs announced they were stepping down. Sources told me that just under twenty openings were being 'carved out' between candidates chosen by Starmer and Reeves; the Labour to Win group, on the right of the party; trade unions such as Unison and GMB; and some military candidates. On 29 May, the tougher regime on social media posts and other alleged misdemeanours had also been used to make last-minute decisions to force out Faiza Shaheen in Chingford and former MP Lloyd Russell-Moyle in Brighton Kemptown (who was replaced by Starmer's old aide Chris Ward). These deselections had caused fury on the left.

The Diane Abbott furore was still top of the agenda when the next morning, on 30 May, I was offered the first television interview with Angela Rayner since the police had cleared her of any offences relating to the earlier allegations. We met at the Unison headquarters near Euston in central London and started by discussing how painful the investigation had been for her family. Then I asked about Abbott. 'Diane Abbott has given thirty-seven years of service to the Labour Party … For me she is iconic,' said Rayner. So should she be able to stand? I asked. 'I don't see any reason why Diane Abbott can't stand,' came her reply. And with that, Rayner had committed news, because she had gone further than Starmer who had refused to personally intervene. Rayner's team believed that the way she had responded to the Abbott question was consistent with Starmer's position; that while she had stated her view, there was still space for a final NEC decision if there was evidence relating to the case that Rayner was unaware of. But by speaking so frankly from the heart, she had gone further than Starmer's more cautious approach – and in a manner that those close to the leader admitted they found 'frustrating'. Labour HQ were not happy about the suggestion in the media that Starmer was being pushed around by his deputy, but they knew he needed to shut the story down and allow Abbott to stand.

And so the next day, that is exactly what Starmer did.

14

Rishi's Worst Week

Dressed in a white shirt with pink tie under a traditionally-styled British coat, Nigel Farage was grinning widely. Against the backdrop of the cliffs of Dover, hazy under the fog and rain, he hitched up his arm, gripping the handle of his transparent umbrella. It was a pose for the cameras, basically designed to troll Rishi Sunak. 'If you need an umbrella for the campaign, I've left you one behind in Dover @ rishisunak,' wrote Farage on X.

It turned out that the Conservative Party strategists had been right: Farage had been planning to announce his candidacy in Clacton later that week, ready for an autumn election, and by going to the polls early they had seemingly managed to wrong-foot him.

'The snap election caught me off-guard,' Farage admitted to my colleague Harry Horton, explaining his decision not to stand in a constituency, saying he could do 'more for the cause, more for the party' by touring the country to make his arguments on behalf of his Reform UK Party. He was grateful to its leader, Richard Tice, for keeping the party going after it had stepped aside in hundreds of seats in support of Boris Johnson in 2019, but he felt it was organisationally weak and not ready for a national election. This news was a welcome relief at CCHQ where the flood of bad headlines framing the start of their campaign was starting to take its toll. One senior

Conservative adviser confided glumly to a friend that the mood was terrible. 'But at least Nigel Farage isn't standing,' they said.

But then Farage changed his mind because of three telling moments; one in Skegness, one in Ashfield, and one in London. Farage visited Skegness on Friday 31 May and as he walked down the town's high street he was mobbed by supporters who crowded around him and shouted his name, while the town's Reform UK candidate, the party leader Richard Tice, went barely noticed. At one point, a group of people came up to ask for a photograph and handed the phone to Tice to ask if he would oblige. But that day, the media's questions to Farage were all about American politics.

The night before, at just before 9.40 p.m., I was on the phone to my editor to discuss the introduction to our piece on Diane Abbott when I heard someone in the background shout, 'The decision is in for Trump!' All eyes turned to New York, where a jury delivered thirty-four guilty verdicts, the first time a former US president had ever been convicted of felony crimes. In Skegness, Trump's friend Farage headed inside an ice cream parlour to give his response to the news. 'Are you still backing Donald Trump despite his convictions?' Harry Horton asked Farage. 'More than ever, more than ever,' he said, without missing a beat. 'The American judicial system stinks ... I think it guarantees [Donald Trump] victory.'

The next day, Farage travelled to Ashfield where former Tory MP Lee Anderson was standing as the Reform UK candidate and was delivering a speech from the top deck of an open-top bus. Below him, Farage was looking down at an adoring crowd gathered in a beer garden. During a helicopter ride back to London, Farage's aides, Dan Jukes and Gawain Towler, urged their boss to reconsider his decision not to stand. Back in the capital, they all headed to a pub near the river in Battersea, an area not known for its right-wing politics and where Farage wanted to avoid any abuse, so he found a quiet table down a side terrace. When half-time struck in a football game playing on the screens inside, around thirty young men came out of the side door, making Farage feel nervous. But then the group started asking for selfies. 'I thought, if young men in London are excited, then something is happening,' he later told me.

That Sunday Farage walked his dogs and went fishing, before suggesting to his team that they all jump on a Zoom meeting at 2 p.m. He'd made a decision. The next morning, Farage set newsrooms buzzing with his revelation that he was holding an 'emergency general election announcement' that afternoon.

It was the news that CCHQ had dreaded, with many watching events unfold in stony silence. The mood was 'subdued', said a source, as Farage began his press conference by saying that he felt 'a terrible sense of guilt.'

'I can't let down those millions of people. I've changed my mind!' he declared, promising to launch his campaign in Clacton-on-Sea at midday the following day. And there was more. Farage was making another move. 'I'm coming back as leader of Reform.'

For all that went wrong for Sunak in the 2024 General Election, many would argue that nothing was quite as bad as this; the return of Farage raised the likelihood of millions of disaffected Tory voters opting for his party. Aides said Sunak was deeply frustrated but also resigned to the reality of the Reform UK threat. And if he needed cheering up, then perhaps the next day helped.

The first television head-to-head debate between Sunak and Starmer was aired on ITV on 4 June, hosted in Salford by my colleague Julie Etchingham. There had been scrupulous negotiations to get both men through the door, with Sunak keen to have lots of debates as he searched for anything that might help shift the dial. In preparation, both sides had plenty of questions: Labour wanted to know the size of the lectern and if the two men would shake hands; the Tories, whether Sunak would be able to look audience members in the eye (a question thrown up by an American debate-expert working with the PM). Both men turned up in casual outfits carrying suits to change into, with Starmer relaxed, while Sunak seemed more tightly wound and his team a little downbeat. But he had a strategy in mind and planned to stick to it.

Almost from the very start of the debate, Sunak began hammering one accusation. 'He would put up everyone's taxes by £2,000 … £2,000 of higher taxes … You want to put everyone's taxes up by £2,000.' Sunak claimed the figures, widely considered to be misleading, were from costings worked up by impartial civil servants. And for some time, the Labour leader failed to push back, perhaps trying to take a more polite stance or perhaps blindsided by the early attack. In a break, Labour's director of communications Matthew Doyle came down to the podium for a quiet word with his leader, and afterwards Starmer responded: 'This £2,000 is absolute garbage.' But with the programme watched by almost 5 million people, the Tory attack had started to cut through. And worse for Labour, a bit like for the '£350m for the NHS' on the side of the Vote Leave bus, when the party subsequently tried to rebut the figure, more people heard it for the first time.

When the debate ended, Sunak walked into his green room, and his aides burst into applause. Starmer was quieter as he headed off, clearly mulling his performance. He got into a car with his aide Jill Cuthbertson to drive back to London. She tried to reassure Starmer, telling him to think of the bigger picture, but the Labour leader was kicking himself and spent much of the night sitting at his kitchen table rolling the debate over in his mind.

At Labour HQ, McSweeney and McFadden were in no doubt that this was the most effective Tory attack so far. And frustratingly, Starmer had a potential comeback no one knew about. Sitting in the email inbox of shadow chief secretary, Darren Jones, was a letter from the Treasury's most senior civil servant James Bowler stating that any figures quoted 'should not be presented as having been produced by the Civil Service.' But the Labour team knew there was no time to let past mistakes fester; the party had to move forward. Aware that they did not want to repeat the tax figure anymore, Labour decided to simply brand Rishi Sunak a liar. First Starmer, and then shadow cabinet figures Steve Reed and Emily Thornberry, went out to the media to do their best. Polling figures had shown that 28 per cent of people had noticed the tax claim, while 14 per cent were seeing the 'lie' – but soon that gap started to close.

It wasn't the first time that Starmer kicked himself during the campaign. Despite making relatively few mistakes, he felt them when they happened, including once tripping up over a policy in an interview with Nicky Campbell on BBC Radio 5 Live. Starmer didn't speak as he waited for a train with Matthew Doyle and Jill Cuthbertson, nor for half the journey back to London. When they asked if he was OK, he replied, 'I hate messing up.' After a few minutes of back and forth, Cuthbertson placed both hands on the table and told Starmer, 'You have to snap out of this!'

Snapping out of things was McSweeney's style, too, warning colleagues that while mistakes would inevitably be made by both sides, the party must avoid the instinct to focus on the past and get stuck. And, despite significant bad press over Diane Abbott and the tax claim, Labour managed to get past such controversies with considerable speed. Meanwhile, things were about to get worse for the Conservatives. After managing only around an hour's sleep, a car picked up an exhausted Starmer for the commemorations of D-Day.

To mark eighty years since the allied landings, when German forces were attacked on the beaches of northern France, there were three main events: the first in Portsmouth on the south coast, and then two in Normandy. Given how few living veterans are left, the youngest now 98, it was a particularly poignant moment.

Rishi Sunak's programme for that day had been arranged well in advance and was planned to mirror that of King Charles, spending time in Portsmouth, and then travelling the next morning to Normandy. Sunak and his wife, Akshata Murty, spent some time talking to wheelchair-bound veterans who had crossed by ferry in what could well be for many their final journey back across the Channel. If Sunak had understood the significance of missing a further event that evening with world leaders at Omaha beach, there was no sign of it as he travelled home to the UK. He had left five minutes after the King. In London, Sunak's team had arranged an interview with my colleague Paul Brand at around 4.45 p.m. in Conservative Party headquarters. It was due for broadcast the following week.

Meanwhile, Starmer had decided to stay for the evening event. Jill Cuthbertson had received a message to say that Ukraine's President Zelensky was keen to meet Starmer and was trying to work out how they could bring the two men together in a space that was not that easy to navigate. Officials eventually ushered Starmer to sit with the British delegation led by Defence Secretary Grant Shapps but also including Foreign Secretary Lord Cameron. When they met, Cuthbertson introduced herself to the former prime minister, reminding him that her husband had been one of his aides. Starmer was pictured meeting with Zelensky, telling him that if the UK government changed hands, its position on Ukraine would remain constant.

At the same time, sources tell me that Cameron received a message that President Macron wanted to see him, and he was ushered down to join other world leaders. As they chatted, Macron waved over the German Chancellor Olaf Scholz and US President Joe Biden. The four men, in sombre suits and dark ties, stood side by side for a press photograph with just one oddity: the British representative was no longer the main man. When Sunak finished with Paul Brand, he was perhaps unaware of the scale of the controversy about to engulf him. Although most of his ITV interview would air the following Wednesday, a clip about the tax-and-lies row with Starmer needed to go live that evening, alerting other journalists to Sunak's early exit from the D-Day event in Normandy. And in another faux pas, when pressed by Brand on what he had given up as a child, Sunak gave the example of Sky TV, a comment with such 'cut-through' that I heard it repeated back all over the country.

Sunak was incredibly upset about the D-Day gaffe, which was ultimately his decision, although in terms of the blame-game, campaign figures argued he was in the hands of the government machine. Conversely, government officials claimed they thought it was the election team who wanted him back in London as quickly as possible. In truth, there had been discussions among the team members about whether he should stay on for the evening function but the urgency of the domestic agenda won the day and his team felt that he would have met veterans during the day's commemorations and would see the world leaders a week afterwards at the G7 summit in Apulia, Italy. But they soon knew they'd got it wrong.

I have been told by three separate senior sources that there was written advice to Downing Street urging the prime minister to attend the international element of the commemorations. The guidance, which I've been told was issued to Number 10 by a team under Britain's national security adviser, Tim Barrow, described the two days and divided the activities into 'core' and 'discretionary' options. One source said that the Portsmouth event, the Normandy morning and the international gathering were all listed as 'core', making clear that this meant the PM ought to attend. Papers within the Foreign Office also suggest it had sent 'consistent' advice to attend both French events, with one email after the event suggesting the guidance had made 'it clear that in D-Day 60/65/70 [previous anniversary celebrations] the international event, French-led but by design, international, dominated the media coverage'.

Sunak was fast to apologise but he and his team had handed the Labour Party's campaigners a scandal, and they were not shy of leaning into it. The next day at a housing development in Brent, north west London, I watched Starmer rub it in. 'Those veterans had made the most incredible effort to be there. [It] was physically difficult to get there ... emotionally it was difficult ... You could see the effort they were putting in, to try to get out of their wheelchairs, to stand up for the King,' he said. 'Most of them did, even for a few minutes, a few seconds. I thought it was important for me to be there. Rishi Sunak will have to answer for his own actions; for me there was nowhere else I was going to be.'

I heard a mixed bag about the impact of D-Day on the doorsteps. Some Conservative activists claimed it had only come up once or twice in the subsequent days. But Alistair Thompson, a PR specialist who was knocking doors in the military town of Portsmouth alongside the Conservative leadership hopeful, Penny Mordaunt, admitted it was a problem. 'The optics were terrible and it is appalling no one realised that. This was a self-inflicted wound,' he said. Thompson said he had been involved in Conservative elections since 1995 and felt that good MPs including Mordaunt were lost because of what he called 'the worst centrally-run campaign in my lifetime.' 'We stumbled from blunder to blunder and never got on the front foot.'

When the subject turned to Labour and tax, Thompson felt buoyed. But soon that was torpedoed too.

While D-Day was unquestionably Sunak's lowest moment at that point in the campaign, astonishingly things were about to get worse. The next weekend, senior Conservative figures received an unexpected call from the Gambling Commission. On Friday 17 May, a routine check by an employee at Ladbrokes on a random sample of new accounts revealed that someone called Craig Williams created a new Ladbrokes account and then placed a bet on a summer election date. A little more digging had suggested that Williams was a Conservative MP in Montgomeryshire; and not just that – he was parliamentary private secretary to the prime minister. Four days later, on Tuesday 21 May, there was a slight shift in the odds for that bet. This was quite a niche market, and it only took a few hundred pounds to make a difference, but Ladbrokes's interest was piqued. And then, the very next day, Rishi Sunak called an election. Wondering if Williams had placed the bet with insider information, Ladbrokes flagged the case with the Gambling Commission, who in turn asked for the names of every person who had bet correctly on the coming election over the previous month.

As investigators scanned through the bets another name caught their eye: Jeremy Hunt. Suddenly, the betting company wondered if they had a major scandal on their hands. In fact, it was a case of mistaken identity. However, others would be identified, including a police officer who worked in personal protection for the prime minister.

It did not take long for the story to come out, with the *Guardian*'s Pippa Crerar breaking the news about Craig Williams's bet. Then, a few days later, BBC political editor Chris Mason had more. He discovered that a Tory candidate in Bristol, Laura Sanders, was also being investigated and, what's more, she was married to Tony Lee, the Conservative Party's director of campaigns. He, too, was being looked into.[1]

When Sunak received word about Williams, who had been a close and trusted aide, he is said to have been deeply disappointed and sad, rather than angry. 'He was resigned to it, he didn't have the energy to be angry anymore,' said one ally.

But as the scandal kept rolling on, with revelations about the Gambling Commission even investigating candidates who had bet on themselves to lose, the prime minister was accused of taking far too long to act. The scandal raised eyebrows in the betting industry where experts asked, how can an MP be accused of match-fixing? Nevertheless, when an allegation emerged about Labour candidate Kevin Craig betting against himself, Starmer did not hesitate to act, suspending him immediately.

With echoes of Partygate, for many Tory MPs this was the final nail in the coffin in the run-up to the election. On doorsteps voters asked them, 'Are you taking the mick?' Back was the sense of 'one rule for them, and one rule for us.' And the reality for Sunak was that this further scandal was simply pushing undecided voters further away from his Conservative Party. Many would turn to Reform UK.

On 4 June, I interviewed for ITV the leaders of the Liberal Democrats and the Green Party, the SNP's Westminster leader, and Reform UK's Richard Tice, now demoted from party leader to chair. In preparation, I spent a lot of time with my programme editor, Laura, digging deep into the parties' policies, preparing to hold each politician to account. Reform UK's agenda was certainly bold.

Alongside strict limits on immigration, the party was promising £88 billion of tax cuts, almost twice the amount that Liz Truss and Kwasi Kwarteng had set out in their mini-budget. Reform UK also claimed that it could save £30 billion by scrapping net zero goals, arguing that climate change has 'happened for millions of years, before human-made CO2 emissions.' When I put to Tice the view of 97 per cent of scientists that the opposite is true and that failure to cut emissions would cost rather than save money, he hit back: 'It is killing our jobs, it is killing our economy and it is killing old people who can't afford their heating.' His party also wanted a public inquiry into excess deaths and vaccine harms.

Had voters expected Reform UK to be a real contender for government, I suspect some of those policies would have faced more of a challenge. In fact, as soon as Farage took over as leader it was clear that he himself planned to add a layer of scrutiny to the content his party was pumping out. But for this election, no one expected Reform to win overall, and the party offered an alternative to millions of voters disillusioned with the Conservatives. Moreover, after Farage's entry into the race, Reform UK was creeping up in the polls. And then, one day, he achieved the thing that Tories had been dreading: crossover.

It was just one poll from YouGov, but the news on 13 June that Reform UK had hit 19 per cent, one point ahead of the Tories, was devastating to Sunak and music to Farage's ears. As it happens, that evening the Reform leader was in Salford for a second live ITV debate, this one featuring seven parties. Producer Michael Clarkson was in the Reform dressing room, explaining the debate rules to Farage, when his adviser Dan Jukes suddenly shouted that Reform UK had overtaken the Tories, but he couldn't get the internet on his phone. As Michael pulled up a tweet by *The Times*'s political editor Steven Swinford setting out the poll findings, the room crowded around him to take a look. Jukes, Farage and the party's deputy David Bull began jumping up and down and cheering, pumping their fists in the air. A grinning Farage said he would mention the poll in the debate, starting his pitch by telling the audience, 'Just before we came on air, we overtook the Conservatives in the national opinion polls. We are now the opposition to Labour.'

Farage's party would continue to poll well, but he knew he had other problems to sort out. The party had failed to vet candidates sufficiently and as the weeks went by, he faced a series of scandals. And then in an exclusive report, undercover reporting from Darshna Soni at Channel 4 News revealed disgusting, racist and homophobic language from a Reform UK canvasser, who spoke of 'kicking all the Muslims out of the mosques' and called Rishi Sunak a 'fucking P**i'.

It was up to the prime minister's communications director, Nissy Chesterfield, to tell him what had been said. Afterwards, he was silent for around twenty seconds. 'I just can't believe this is something I'm even having to think about in this day and age,' he said. Sunak pulled together a group of his closest advisers to discuss what to do. When asked about the comments by my ITV colleague Shehab Khan, Sunak replied, 'When my two daughters have to see and hear Reform people who campaign for Nigel Farage calling me a "effing P**i" it hurts and it makes me angry and I think he has some questions to answer,' adding, 'I don't repeat those words lightly. But this is too important not to call out clearly for what it is.'

Before this interview, the prime minister had had an intense conversation with his aides about whether he should repeat the offending word, and some were very nervous that he chose to do so. Soon the question of his language was being fiercely debated in our newsroom as the bosses tried to decide whether to play his comments in full or bleep them. My instinct was that if an Asian man had chosen to say the 'P' word to emphasise its pain, who were we to censor him? And some others agreed. But as the conversation ballooned, I realised that many colleagues also from ethnic minority backgrounds felt very differently. One said there was no justification to play the full clip with the offensive word, calling it a 'slippery slope'; others argued that it would still have the same impact if it was bleeped, which in the end was what we decided to go with.

The question of Sunak's race was something I often thought about at other junctures during this campaign. For example, I decided never to raise the widely-made insinuation that Sunak would race off to California as soon as he lost, and was hoping to get his girls into school there that September. It was a line of questioning that undoubtedly carried justification because of Sunak's California home, his 'tech-bro' status, and that Green Card he had held onto for too long. But although many colleagues, friends and even my husband disagreed, there was something that made me, perhaps as an Asian woman, feel uncomfortable about the claim. To me, the focus on California carried an implication that Sunak was somehow less rooted in Britain than others. And I did not feel that either Boris Johnson or Nigel Farage, each with their own US links, were questioned in quite the same way.

I've discussed the question of race with Rishi Sunak directly, speaking frankly about both of our childhoods. I'm extremely proud of my Indian heritage but as a young child who had already witnessed racism, I once rubbed talcum powder into my skin in a desperate bid to scrub away the difference. Was race as dominant for him? 'You are conscious of being different,' he told me, describing hearing racist insults hurled at his siblings in a fast-food restaurant when they were children. '[Racism] hurts in a way that other things don't', he admitted, describing how his mother sent him to drama lessons to avoid any hint of an accent that could prevent him fitting in.

And in government he did fit in. When things were going well for Sunak as the 'furlough chancellor', seen to save so many livelihoods, I don't think race mattered. Nor do I think it is an issue for the vast majority of people in this country. But racism exists, so does it affect elections? Well, yes. Oxford Professor Stephen Fisher found that in both the 2017 and 2019 General Elections it did matter, with Black and Asian candidates facing an 'ethnic penalty'.[2] In 2017, he calculated a penalty of 3.6 points for minority Tory candidates, then 3.3 in 2019. Where white candidates followed minorities, the votes went up by more than the average, while when minorities followed white candidates, their results were squeezed.

So what about when the overall party leader is not white? Fisher told me that it would be hard to provide a serious, numerical estimate of the impact, but said he 'wouldn't rule out the possibility that there was a substantial negative effect.' Nevertheless, when it comes to the Conservative Party in 2024, I do not believe that Rishi Sunak's race goes far towards explaining the overall election result. Much more significant factors were the catastrophic loss of trust in the Conservative Party as a result of Partygate; the disastrous mini-budget; and Tory in-fighting and disunity during his short-lived premiership.

As for Farage, with Reform UK gaining momentum, his aim now was to professionalise his party and in doing so was looking in an interesting direction. 'You can compare and contrast what Reform is today with the Lib Dems, who have branches, structure, campaigns and a sense of purpose on the ground. Reform doesn't have those things yet. But we do now have 72,000 members,' Farage told me this summer. He said he had admired how the former Lib Dem leader, Paddy Ashdown, had transformed his party in the 1990s into a 'well managed, disciplined machine'. He described how they had targeted council by-elections to put down roots in constituencies, before designating them as target seats in a general election. Farage spoke of his new party chairman, Zia Yusuf, and his desire to get funded and organised: 'There is a vast amount to do, but I am working on it every day.'

And he wasn't the only one thinking about what the Lib Dems had done thirty years ago to drive up their seat numbers from 18 in 1992 to 46 in 1997. The current Lib Dems were also looking back in time. When the slides of one of the party's strategy presentations were leaked to me in 2024, they had dubbed their efforts 'The Paddy Playbook' – and once again, it delivered extraordinary results.

15

Fragmentation

One of the most striking things about the 2024 Election is not the number of people who voted Labour but the sheer numbers who did not vote for either Labour or the Conservative Party. As Jane Green, polling guru and professor of political science and British politics at the University of Oxford, pointed out, this election delivered the lowest ever two-party share; a process of fragmentation through which support splintered out in an array of directions. Smaller parties did better than at any time in the past 100 years, which almost certainly inflated the size of Labour's overall win, and placed Keir Starmer at the top of a fragile majority. But we'll come to that. First, how did it happen?

Arguably the most impressive performance of the election came from Liberal Democrat leader, Ed Davey. The unedifying sight of the 58-year-old in a tight wetsuit and red life jacket kneeling down on a paddleboard is one few of us can forget. When Davey attempted a wobbly rise and then, almost cartoon-like, thrust his arms in the air and toppled backwards into the water, a relative of mine commented, 'Is he absolutely stupid!?' It was a question that perhaps crossed many people's minds, including my own. And yet, the more I delved into the Lib Dems' thinking, the more I came to see Davey's occasionally ludicrous stunts as his party playing a strategic blinder.

Bar one constituency in Sheffield and a handful in Scotland, all of the Lib Dem's target seats were Conservative-facing, and so the party had been riding on a wave of anti-Tory sentiment that had carried them into a series of stunning by-election wins. But by early 2024 Ed Davey was faced with a serious problem. It was encapsulated on the front page of the *Evening Standard* on 15 January with the head-line 'Sir Hypocrite'. Underneath was a picture of Davey with his hands held out.

The Post Office scandal is one of the most egregious examples of the miscarriage of justice in British history. In May 2021 when I interviewed one of its victims, Janet Skinner, I was reduced to tears as I listened to the nightmare she had endured – jailed for a computer error over which she had no control. But it was Gwyneth Hughes's excellent ITV drama, *Mr Bates vs The Post Office*, that helped bring about a fresh reckoning for the men and women who were accused of failing to act. The pressure was particularly intense on those in charge of the Post Office itself, but failures were highlighted across all main political parties and Davey was one who came under the spotlight. As the Post Office minister between 2010 and 2012, he had in fact met the former Llandudno subpostmaster Alan Bates but failed to take adequate action, eventually apologising for 'failing to see through the Post Office's lies.'

As the Lib Dems approached the 2024 Election, the campaign team wanted voters to know who Davey was and not to associate him solely with this scandal. They believed it was vital to focus on a single issue that resonated both with him and voters and put in place a ruthlessly targeted campaign. Alongside politicians, volunteers and activists, at the heart of the Lib Dem operation were a handful of key figures, including Davey's chief of staff Rhiannon Leamon and press secretary, Tim Wild; Baroness Olly Grender, director of communications (and once Paddy Ashdown's political coordinator) and her head of media Paul Haydon; and the chief executive Mike Dixon, once a Labour adviser and then charity boss. Dixon had been recruited just days before the disastrous 2019 Election performance alongside a new party president, Mark Pack, and Baroness Kath Pinnock who would chair the 2024 campaign. Where Labour had Morgan McSweeney, the Lib Dems would point to chief of staff Rhiannon Leamon and also their field director, Dave McCobb. McCobb's organisational skills were renowned in Westminster, with one MP (now a senior cabinet minister) forwarding an email to me outlining McCobb's strategy in North Shropshire because they had found it so impressive. When the Lib Dems, who normally find themselves up against Tories in suburban and rural seats, took control of Hull Council from Labour in 2022, some wondered if it was because McCobb had a special interest since he lived in the city.

But what were all the campaign stunts about? Davey didn't just stick to paddle-boarding; there were so many exploits that online news site *Politico* ranked 19 of them, including: flying down the Ultimate Slip 'n' Slide attraction near Frome, Somerset, in a rubber ring; slamming down drumsticks on a giant exercise ball in time (-ish) to Queen's 'We Will Rock You' with care home residents in Hampshire; being called 'sexy' by Australian actor Jason Donovan after an ITV *This Morning* makeover; wheelbarrow racing; swing dancing; aqua aerobics; doing an interview on a rollercoaster; and bungee-jumping from a crane.[1] My relative remained firm in his view that Davey looked 'stupid' but then he wasn't the type of Lib-Dem switcher they were trying to appeal to anyway.

With colleagues branding him a 'centrist dad', the aim was to win over soft Tories open to persuasion that Davey was cuddly, fun and didn't take himself too seriously. The stunts were also designed to highlight Lib Dem policies, for example when Davey backflipped into Lake Windermere, where earlier in the year there had been a massive sewage spill. The strategy also was to try to crowbar the Lib Dem leader into television news bulletins and with some success; as we would say in our newsroom, no one could deny it was 'great picture'. One senior figure argued that political commentators tend to 'massively overemphasise words and ideas and underplay images and emotion.' And when the *Evening Standard*'s headline shifted from 'Sir Hypocrite' to 'Help me tear down the Blue Wall' accompanied by a giant cartoon of a paddle-boarding Davey, they knew that their ploy had reaped rewards; but it was only the first part of an overall election strategy spearheaded by Leamon.

Davey's stunts were really designed to tease voters' interest before phase two landed. In an incredibly moving party political broadcast, designed by Grender to emphasise the issue the Lib Dem leader cared about most because of how profoundly it affected his own family, footage showed Davey, the father, in warm interaction with his severely disabled teenage son, John. In an interview for ITV *Tonight* with Rachel Younger, Davey described how he juggled work with his caring responsibilities for John, who can't walk and has limited speech, and a new challenge for the family: his wife Emily's illness with MS. He also spoke emotionally about how, as a teenager, he had nursed his mum, Nina, when she was dying of cancer. The aim was to persuade voters that they could trust Davey on health and social welfare issues, because this was who he was. 'It made him more credible and gave an emotional connection,' said a source.

Davey's campaign team had also been scrutinising polls and focus group feedback that showed a steep decline in trust in politicians and believed that his personal story would help to demonstrate that he cared. The Lib Dems have previously been accused of exploiting their position as a party of protest to say one thing to voters in the South of the country, and another in the North. But this time, they tried to be more consistent; again, with local messaging, but built around a much more limited set of national policies focused on the environment and tackling sewage, the cost-of-living crisis, but first and foremost, health and social care.

According to the aforementioned strategy document, this was a part of the 'Paddy Playbook'. In the 1990s Ashdown had focused on a single flagship policy: an additional £2 billion for education funded by an extra 1p in the pound on the basic rate of Income Tax. Davey's 2024 equivalent was a tax on banks to pay for the NHS. The strategy paper said Ashdown had gone for 'ruthless messaging' but also 'ruthless targeting', and that is where Leamon's work with Field Director Dave McCobb and chief exec Mike Dixon came in.

The Lib Dems already had some impressive by-election wins in the bag. In those campaigns, traditionally the party would send in an advance team to simply knock on 200 doors and listen to voters to understand their concerns. They then would build the campaign messaging around addressing these issues. In Amersham and Chesham, North Shropshire and Tiverton, canvassers heard frustration about missed GP appointments, the struggle to secure dentists, and fury about the environment. With this overlaid on a wave of anti-Tory sentiment flowing from the Partygate scandals to the mini-budget, they had been able to ride to massive victories. But still, as election year approached the party was fairly conservative in its expectations, initially hoping to treble the 11 seats it had won in 2019.

In the 2022 by-elections, the Lib Dems had identified 32 held and target seats, a group they called 'advance seats' which were given a huge amount of field support, to help build teams and create messages. Then, in September 2023, they decided to stretch their ambitions, with a new category of 'moving forward seats' adding 35 to the original 32. These were constituencies where the party was in second place and had made progress in council elections. They were offered support but less than the original 'advance seats'.

In January 2024, teams in these constituencies could purchase literature, delivery and artwork plans bought in bulk and provided by the central office, and many received match funding. As a result, from that spring the party was ready to swing into action in around 60 seats or more. The Lib Dems knew that the 'air war' playing out on national media was meaningless without an effective 'ground war' in target seats; after all, in 2010 the Lib Dems had hit 30 per cent in national polls thanks to their then leader's surging popularity – aka 'Cleggmania' – but had lost seats overall. A review of the 2019 results had led to a new strategic priority: under the UK's first-past-the-post system, the party must always prioritise seats over national vote-share.

In the run-up to the 2024 Election, the Lib Dems' financial plans had assumed winning around 28 seats. But they were soon revised to account for the possibility of 40 seats, then 55, and finally 70. They knew something big was happening. By May, their party election broadcast was ready to go. When Sunak announced the election later that month, they had 3 million printed leaflets they could start to pump out in their target seats before the spending restrictions came into play, claiming they did not see the same level of literature from their Tory opponents. Another challenge for the Conservatives was that with so many MPs standing down, they spent a lot more of their time struggling to fill candidacies than other parties, who had focused on little else than election prep.

But for all the successes of the Lib Dems' campaign plan, few could deny that they were benefiting hugely from the dramatic fall in Conservative support. One canvasser described knocking on 100 doors in the most Conservative ward in a Conservative-held seat, telling me, 'I only met one Conservative, and then I met lots of people who were undecided. But the one thing they were sure about was that they wouldn't vote Conservative.' A similar sentiment to that expressed by one of Sunak's closest advisers.

The canvas also posed a problem for the Lib Dems, however. If the Labour vote was surging, would these 'don't knows' opt for Starmer's party and prevent them getting over the line in Conservative/Lib Dem marginals? So, in the final two weeks the campaign team put in place the other element in their 'Paddy Playbook'. According to their strategy document, the party had identified '125,000 voters across our target seats who have not yet decided between us and the Labour Party.' They had to encourage mass tactical voting by people who wanted the Conservatives out of power.

One of the reasons the Lib Dems have long called for electoral reform is because, time and again, the party would achieve a national vote-share much higher than the percentage of seats secured in the House of Commons. In 2024, for the first time, those two figures were almost aligned, suggesting that their targeting strategy had worked. Moreover, overtaking the SNP to become the third party in Parliament with seventy-two new MPs – making it the largest third party in Parliament for a century – brought significant financial benefits and a much higher profile for Ed Davey in Commons' debates, including the weekly PMQs. The issue of health and care was embedded throughout the Lib Dem campaign and at the heart of its manifesto and is likely to be the top priority for the party for at least the first half of this Parliament.

The Lib Dem surge hugely helped Labour. By reducing the number of Conservative MPs in other seats, it brought down the electoral mountain facing Keir Starmer. The Reform UK upswing similarly helped, by eating into Tory votes in those seats the party had gained in 2019 and helping Labour to come through the middle.

But in other areas fragmentation of the vote hurt Keir Starmer's party. As with the Liberal Democrats, the Green Party had also made dramatic changes in its election planning. Jointly led by Carla Denyer and Adrian Ramsay, the Greens' ambition was to have more than a single MP, so there would be a sense that the party had at last arrived in Parliament. Its single representative, historically Caroline Lucas, had a huge profile but it was primarily a personal one; and, in terms of representing an entire party in parliamentary debates, was spread thin: 'Just one Green in such a big room cannot be heard as well,' said a party source.

In 2020, the Greens decided that they would aim to target 4 seats, while also trying to achieve a record vote-share across the country. They decided to stand candidates in 574 of the 575 constituencies in England and Wales, but also introduced a new process through which they would identify the handful of constituencies which would get significant additional resources.

There was never any question about trying to defend Brighton Pavilion, where Siân Berry stepped in after Lucas decided to step down before the election. Bristol Central was another obvious choice. Although this meant a gruelling battle with a Labour shadow cabinet member, Thangam Debbonaire, the constituency's demographics suggested there was a good chance of persuading residents to switch to the Green Party: a younger, highly-educated, and traditionally quite volatile set of voters who were likely to think that Labour needed to be bolder. According to an analysis by More In Common, many of these voters did not approve of Starmer's decision to oust Jeremy Corbyn and feared that the Labour leader would offer more of the same. The think-tank pointed to a group of voters it called 'progressive activists' as particularly attracted to the Greens; people who were politically engaged, environmentally conscious and wanted to tackle marginalisation on the basis of race, gender, sexuality or poverty.

But the Green Party had another advantage this time; a drive to win council seats had resulted in much more local representation. With Brighton and Bristol decided, the Greens turned to two more-rural, and previously Conservative, constituencies, where they had a growing number of councillors – Waveney Valley and North Herefordshire. 'There are fewer rungs to climb on the ladder, if you are already halfway there,' said the party's head of elections, Chris Williams. 'The Green Party has gone through a big transformation in recent years, completely professionalising its election operation.' Part of Waveney Valley, for example, fell under Mid Suffolk Council, which was run by the Greens, and stretched into East Suffolk, where the party is in coalition.

The Green Party did not force activists to travel to their 4 target seats, but they did encourage it. As election day drew near, they flooded the seats with around 1,000 party members and activist residents, knocking on every door in each constituency more than once in the final few weeks. Of course, the logistical challenges were quite different in Bristol Central, which was 3 miles wide and involved a ferocious fight with Labour, than in the more rural target constituencies, but they found smart ways to overcome this obstacle. In North Herefordshire, for example, which took an hour to cross by car, the campaign team managed to persuade 1,000 out of 40,000 homes to place a Green Party placard at the end of their drive, garden or land, while the candidate Ellie Chowns carried out thirty-one US-style village hall meetings.

As to the Green Party's election pledges, I noticed when I was preparing to interview their co-leader Adrian Ramsay, that over the years they had put forward some eye-catching and controversial policies, from reducing medical interventions in childbirth, to having stringent sound-limits on fireworks, and drug liberalisation. These ideas had emerged from the party's policy development strategy which was extremely inclusive of members. However, these propositions did not make it into the 2024 manifesto, which instead focused heavily on big tax, and big spend. With eye-watering figures not dissimilar to those in Reform UK's manifesto, the Green Party also wanted to ramp up public spending (by £160 billion a year), but this was to fund giveaways such as free personal care. And rather than tax cuts, instead the party said it would raise £170 billion with tax increases. The Institute for Fiscal Studies was a little sceptical, agreeing that increasing National Insurance and restricting pension tax-relief could raise a considerable sum, but remaining unconvinced that the party could really conjure up £90 billion with a Carbon Tax. And the party also contrasted with Labour through its position on foreign policy.

In the most left-wing manifesto from any party, help for Gaza was front and centre. Think-tank More in Common found that 23 per cent of people cited the party's support for Palestinians in the top three reasons for their voting Green. The same number said they could not stand behind Keir Starmer's Labour Party.

Whether it was the Green Party's unequivocal policy on Gaza, or perhaps their strategic push for more representation on councils – which resulted in the Greens having at least one council cabinet-member in 10 per cent of local authorities and some 800 councillors overall – in 2024 they succeeded in securing a record national vote-share of 7 per cent and four MPs.

The Greens proved a headache for Starmer in Bristol Central, where he lost his high-profile shadow cabinet member Thangam Debbonaire. But they were not the only opposition piling pressure onto Labour over the issue of Gaza. It is easy to think that Labour's problem with Muslim voters began on 7 October 2023, but that simply isn't true. For at least a year before the Hamas attack and Israel's response, the party had been concerned about a loss of trust among this demographic. In fact, Director of External Affairs Vidhya Alakeson had begun to set up a number of community engagement programmes to better understand what was going on.

Labour's difficulty in winning the trust of ethnic-minority voters was not limited to Muslims, either. In fact, in 2022, the party had also started outreach programmes for Black voters and those of Indian heritage too. On the latter, I had seen previously how determined the Conservatives were to reach out to Hindu and Sikh voters. While travelling around the country with David Cameron in 2015 it was a clear part of their strategy, not least because their research suggested that many of these minority voters had instinctively small-c conservative values. And yet, in 2010 just 16 per cent of Black and minority ethnic voters had backed the Tories, while 68 per cent turned to Labour.

The reason for this huge divide can be found by reaching back into history. When minority communities arrived in the UK, Labour was the party that seemed to stand up for them against discrimination, while the Conservatives' twentieth-century narrative was littered with race-related controversies. From the 1964 by-election in Smethwick, where the Conservative candidate told voters: 'If you want a n****r for a neighbour vote Labour'; to Enoch Powell's ill-famed Rivers of Blood speech, delivered in Birmingham four years later; to the 'cricket test', set by Norman Tebbit in 1991, about which national team immigrants would choose to support. The Tory grandee's suggestion that an Asian person's loyalty should be judged by which side they cheer for in a cricket match (Pakistan, India or England, say), was still causing the Tory Party problems with Hindu and Sikh men nearly twenty-five years later.[2]

But in 2024, Cameron's push to win over Indian voters combined with Sunak's status as Britain's first ever prime minister of Indian heritage was causing Labour a headache. Moreover, in the very week that Starmer revealed plans for a Race Equality Bill (later included in the King's speech) to extend equal pay to ethnic-minority workers, the party faced scepticism about how serious its intentions really were, as illustrated by the headline of Britain's leading Black newspaper, the *Voice* – 'Keir Starmer doesn't care about Black people.'[3] And in the meantime, there was an increasingly worrying loss of support among Muslim voters who for decades had been overwhelmingly likely to back Labour.

Vidhya Alakeson warned colleagues that they must urgently respond to this sense among minority communities that Labour had become disconnected from their lives. In a presentation, she identified 47 seats with significant minority populations where candidates would be offered additional support, including Bolton West, Dudley, Uxbridge and South Ruislip, and Finchley and Golders Green, with its large Jewish population. She warned that these mixed communities demanded a 'bridging and not divisive' narrative.

The teams were told that British Indians had disliked Labour wading into controversial debates over Kashmir; saw a lack of representation within the party; and saw the opposition party as focused on Muslims first and foremost. One policy said to go down badly among Indian voters, for whom education was a leading issue (with some from lower-income households stretching to get their children into the independent sector), was VAT on private schools. For Muslim voters, family, religion and the cost-of-living crisis were identified as key concerns, and there was a sense that an historic connection with Labour had weakened. Black voters also felt that Labour had moved away from its roots and wanted the party to call out social injustices related to race and class. Although these voters liked the idea of Starmer's 'missions' they were seen as lacking substance and credibility.

The plan would be to engage much more heavily with these ethnic-minority voters, by marking festivals and community events, ensuring more diverse images of Labour and also building non-religious connections. So, for example in Muslim communities, shadow cabinet members held roundtables with entrepreneurs, visited nurseries and health projects and focused on hate crime against women. Starmer also met with Indian business leaders.

The response to 7 October and Keir Starmer's LBC interview unquestionably led to a gear-shift in anger among Muslims in Britain, but there was already negative sentiment rumbling. During the election campaign, to get a better sense of what was happening on the ground, my producer Elisa and I visited Jess Phillips in her Birmingham Yardley constituency where boundary changes meant the number of Muslim voters had risen from 25 to 40 per cent. Phillips was passionately defensive of her community, arguing that, like most people, Muslim residents cared about the NHS, safe streets and the cost of living. She refused to allow a negative depiction to be 'exploited' by others. And as we travelled around the city to various constituencies, I could see exactly what she meant. The Muslim voters I spoke to were as likely to raise Starmer's refusal to lift the two-child benefit cap as his response to the war in Gaza.

These were working-class people, in urban areas, who had been some of the worst-hit by austerity. Their politics tended to be on the left, and despite years of voting for Labour nationally and locally, their lives did not feel like they were improving. Once again, council failures loomed large and I couldn't help but think that what I was seeing here was another crumbling 'Red Wall' that could well collapse for the party, although with less impact in the 2024 election because of likely gains everywhere else.

A second Red Wall, or perhaps even a fourth; like the traditional Labour voters tempted by the BNP in east London in 2006; the Scottish voters who abandoned the party in 2015; or the white working class who had turned to Boris Johnson in 2019. Contending that 'canaries in the mine' had been missed in the past, Phillips said that if Labour were to win the election they must 'rule with consensus and make sure that in heartland places like this one, we don't ignore what has happened.'

Labour candidate Heather Iqbal, who was defeated in Dewsbury, said: 'Labour has heard that there is a problem, now we need to listen to why Muslim people feel disenfranchised. We have to show we are serious about foreign policy.' Her loss and others were signs of how Gaza had caused Labour woes in this election. But there were also claimed of aggressive and threatening. Iqbal described a 'relentless' battle in which she was followed by a man in a van screaming insults at her. She told me she felt 'exposed' and facing 'so much hatred I couldn't even process it. It was so personal.' Meanwhile, Rushanara Ali spoke of death threats in Tower Hamlets and the need for police protection; in Birmingham Ladywood, Shabana Mahmood said masked men disrupted a community meeting 'terrifying' those who attended; and Jess Phillips herself said that a female party activist had been filmed and shouted at by people in the street and her car tyres had been slashed.

During the campaign, Starmer gave the example of Bangladeshi asylum seekers arriving by boat in the UK as those who could be returned to their home country. Given that Bangladeshis make up a small proportion of those arriving illegally, the comment itself drew huge anger. Starmer had highlighted the south Asian country because of a recent returns agreement, but many Bangladeshis felt insulted that the Labour leader had singled out their community in what felt like a deeply derogatory way. The councillor Sabina Akhtar who was the deputy leader of the Labour group on Tower Hamlets Ccouncil resigned and Rushanara Ali admitted there had been 'considerable concern and upset'.

Then disinformation worsened the problem. When I was in Birmingham, a woman pulled out her phone and showed me a video. Starmer's comments had been heavily edited to give the impression he was ready to deport any British Bangladeshi; the recording was highly misleading but it had already gone viral. Meanwhile, a recording of Wes Streeting was circulated in which he was asked, 'Don't you care about Palestinian children being killed?' to which, apparently, he replied, 'No I fucking don't.' But the recording was entirely fictional – a deepfake.

Predictably, perhaps, on an otherwise joyous election night for Labour, the impact of this loss in Muslim support was stark. In Bethnal Green and Bow, Rushanara Ali's majority was cut from over 37,000 to under 2,000; in Birmingham Ladywood, Shabana Mahmood was just 3,421 ahead compared to over 28,000 in 2019; Jess Phillips hung on in Birmingham Yardley although with a majority of less than 700, when it had been higher than 10,000; but in Dewsbury, Heather Iqbal lost. Those were seats that Labour had been anxious about, but they didn't see Wes Streeting's close call in Ilford North coming. The MP slated to become Labour health secretary won by just over 500 votes. And worse was to come. In late 2022 I had spent time in Leicester South with Jonathan Ashworth who in the 2019 Election had secured a majority of over 22,000. As we walked around his constituency, I had witnessed what looked like strong relationships with the local Muslim community. But now, with this dramatic shift in attitude away from Labour and a dizzying anger, in just two years the shadow cabinet secretary, who had been a key figure in the national campaign, was out.

After the election, Sunder Katwala of the think-tank British Future pointed to polling by Ipsos which placed Labour on 46 per cent with ethnic-minority voters, and the Tories on 17 per cent – a greatly changed picture since 2010 – and an 18 per cent decline in support for Labour among Asian voters. With Alakeson now in the heart of Downing Street, it is likely that the party will be thinking hard about this profound electoral challenge.

Overall, however, Starmer's campaign was moving in a positive direction, with a number of Conservative and SNP opponents telling me how impressed they were by Labour's digital campaign.

Digital Director Tom Lillywhite was one of Starmer's longest serving members of staff. By the time of the election campaign, his digital operation had been moved out of the communications department, with Lillywhite and his deputy Caitlin Roper overseeing a team of 110. They pumped out early content featuring voters who had decided to switch, and also tried to push the boundaries with funny videos including one featuring a raccoon having a go at Sunak. Others did not pass taste checks, but Lillywhite's team were well aware that positive content got less shares than attacks. Before the election, some in the party had reacted with fury to a Labour advert featuring a picture of a smiling Rishi Sunak next to the words: 'Do you think adults convicted of sexually assaulting children should go to prison?' The *Guardian* quoted frontbenchers describing the advert as 'spectacularly misjudged', but there were plenty inside Labour who revelled in the controversy, seeing the message shared much more widely than other digital content.[4] At the start of the campaign, Lillywhite reserved advertising space in polling week with major newspapers, so that when readers browsed online, news and feature articles were wrapped in Labour banners with huge pictures of Keir Starmer (or, in one case where Labour cancelled their pre-booked slot, Nigel Farage). Why didn't the Conservatives do the same?

The response from one senior Tory source? 'Why do you think?' The simple answer was money, he said. The Conservatives had raised plenty of funds in advance, including millions from businessmen such as Frank Hester and Mohamed Mansour and property developers like Graham Edwards, and had previously outdone Labour on the campaign chest. But as the election neared, and polling continued to suggest a change in government, Starmer attracted increasing donations including from the Labour peer Waheed Ali but also hedge-fund figures like Sir Victor Blank, Martin Taylor and Sir Trevor Chinn (the pair who bankrolled Labour Together), and the Sainsbury dynasty. During the campaign Labour declared a total of £9.5 million which amounted to more donations than all other parties combined (and included a single £2.5 million from Lord

David Sainsbury), while the Tories brought in just £1.9 million (a tenth of the amount raised in 2019).[5] Lillywhite therefore could afford to spend up to £10 million, and did so, mainly on Facebook but also YouTube, while Conservative sources admitted that with less money they had to decide against options like 'takeover ads', which looked great when circulated on social media, but weren't the most efficient way to drive voting numbers in key seats with limited resources.

Labour's digital team worked alongside Paul Ovenden's attack unit – mischief-makers who placed dozens of stories in national outlets, and also spent hours researching Starmer's time as a human rights barrister and then director of public prosecutions. The idea was to provide solid rebuttal to the Conservative dossier on Starmer's legal past, including accusations that he 'invoiced' the Islamist group Hizb ut-Tahrir. Meanwhile, as Matthew Doyle and Steph Driver trailed the Labour leader around the country, they made sure that he kept rolling out that all-important four-part message – the Tories had failed, Britain wants change, Labour has changed, and this is our plan …

While the Conservatives sprayed out financial giveaways – with promises to cut National Insurance, extend child benefit and remove Stamp Duty from more homes, all while clamping down on welfare spending – Labour's manifesto was deliberately surprise-free. They stuck to their pledge to focus on wealth creation – to bring in sweeping planning reforms to help build 1.5 million new homes; introduce a national wealth fund; abolish the non-dom tax status; and to raise tax on private schools to pay for those 'first steps' in delivering extra NHS appointments and teaching staff. And, wrapping itself in the Union flag, and unveiling fourteen ex-military candidates including Calvin Bailey, a former RAF wing commander, and the former Royal Marines Colonel, Al Carns, the party stuck to that pledge of a 2.5 per cent defence spend (when affordable). The party pledged not to raise Income Tax, VAT or NICs and claimed there would be no need for rises in other taxes either. Instead, there would be a relentless focus on achieving growth, with spending severely restrained until it had been realised. It was an argument that led the Institute for Fiscal Studies to claim there was a 'conspiracy of silence' from the two biggest parties, who were failing to be honest about the financial black hole that already existed. Behind the scenes, a Labour strategist would argue that the party must stand firm; how could it talk about distributing the economic 'cake' more fairly when 'the Tories had eaten the cake and burnt down the kitchen'?

As Tories watched the polls remain stubbornly wide, a source suggested I search online for a digital advert the party had been pumping out via Facebook ads. Surprised by what I saw, I talked about it that night on the *News at Ten*. In a move that initially looked bizarre to me, the Conservatives were playing out MRP polling which suggested Labour would win 422 seats to their 140. The video advert, aimed at those dithering about backing Reform UK, then warned that voting for Starmer could result in the Tories being pushed into third place behind the Lib Dems, with just fifty-seven MPs remaining. I was wrong to find the advert bizarre. This warning of a Starmer 'supermajority' was a deliberate tactic to pull voters back to the Tories, and it probably worked to a degree.

Nevertheless, something big was unfolding on the ground. In Labour HQ, as polling day drew near, the party narrowed its 'core battleground', taking the tough decision to divert resources even from those constituencies where they had to overturn significant Conservative majorities to flood harder-and-harder-to-win seats with activists and digital targeting. Some of the most impressive wins would come in the South East where Regional Director Teddy Ryan focused on this strategy. First Aylesbury, with a Tory majority of more than 17,000 in 2019, came into play; then Chatham and Aylesford with over 18,000; Bracknell with almost 20,000; and even Folkestone and Hythe with a majority of 21,000 (staunchly Tory since its creation in 1950 and once the seat of former party leader Michael Howard). There was also additional effort in Portsmouth North where Labour was keen to oust a prominent Tory leadership-hopeful – Penny Mordaunt. Labour won them all, with the number of seats in the South East rising from 8 in 2019 to 36 – 14 more than Labour had won in this region in Tony Blair's landslide victory of 1997.

Things were also feeling good for Labour in Scotland. When Imogen Walker had first moved back north in 2020, she lived in the Lanark and Hamilton East seat, which predated boundary changes and felt unwinnable for Labour. In 2019, the SNP had a majority of more than 5,000 and the Conservatives were in second place.

But the SNP had suffered a number of bumpy years, with senior figures including Nicola Sturgeon embroiled in a police investigation; a vicious leadership campaign in her political wake that led to headlines of a party at war with itself; and then the ultimate demise of its victor Humza Yousaf, who was forced out after the collapse of a power-sharing agreement with the Scottish Greens. Sturgeon had once claimed that the 2024 General Election would act as a de-facto referendum on independence. In the face of declining party support, a new leader, John Swinney did not want to take on that level of political risk but still kept the stakes high, telling the Scottish independence supporters that an SNP win would unlock future negotiations.

However, the problem for the SNP was that north of the border, Labour support had surged with an enticing message in a nation with plenty of anti-Tory sentiment: Vote Starmer to Get Sunak Out. SNP politicians would argue that in order to win power in Westminster Labour has never needed Scotland, but their pleas were failing to win over SNP waverers and, in the new seat of Hamilton and Clyde Valley, Walker could feel it. The popularity of Labour's leader in Scotland, Anas Sarwar, she posited, had helped drive a new positivity. Candidates in other parts of the country sometimes spoke to me of a semi-enthusiastic response to Labour (alongside sheer fury at the Conservatives), but north of the border the mood felt different.

'People started to shake my hand when I knocked on the door,' said Walker. 'It suddenly became emotional for people; as if they did not just want us to win, they needed us to.' She described the throngs of 'star-struck' voters queuing up to meet Rachel Reeves when the shadow chancellor turned up in the constituency on her battle bus. With so many target seats spread across Scotland's central belt, the notion of 'twinning' seats and bussing in activists was much less achievable in Scotland, but perhaps it was not needed.

Imogen Walker was on the doorsteps until late on 4 July before she jumped in the car. She wanted to get home to change before heading out to her count, but she got stuck behind a lorry and was delayed. Walker wondered if it was a good idea to be driving when the exit poll landed at 10 p.m.

More than 400 miles away, two contrasting scenes unfolded at that moment, almost perfectly mirroring the election night reactions almost five years earlier.

In Labour's Southwark headquarters, a silent crowd stared at one big screen, poised, before a screech rang out across the room. As they exploded with excitement, jumping in the air, screaming, pumping their arms in the air, one woman let out a long 'Fuuuuuckkkk!' At the same time, across the River Thames in Conservative headquarters, there was almost 'pin-drop' silence as the team took in the news; a mix of devastation and some relief that the party had not been entirely wiped out.

Sitting in her car, Walker listened to the radio presenter announce that the Tories and SNP were set to be crushed, with the Lib Dems surging, and Labour likely to win over 400 seats. It was then that she knew that she was about to become the new MP for Hamilton and Clyde. When she got home, she messaged her husband, Morgan McSweeney, and told him she was really proud of him.

At a flat in central London, there were tears among some of the aides who were watching the result with Keir Starmer, including Sue Gray, Jill Cuthbertson, Matthew Doyle, Steph Driver, Paul Ovenden and Ben Nunn. They had first reacted with a momentary silence, in shock almost, before the in-coming prime minister wrapped his wife and children in a hug, and his team cheered. When Rishi Sunak absorbed the news that he knew was all too likely, he was at home with his family in Yorkshire. The out-going PM picked up the phone to aides, including Isaac Levido, and made it quite clear that the election loss was his responsibility. Over the next few days, Sunak would call each and every Conservative MP who had lost their seat that night.

How had the political pendulum swung so hard in just four years? Much of the societal tumult that shook Britain between 2019 and 2024 came from outside politics; the worst health crisis in more than a century that demanded eye-watering borrowing levels, beginning an inflation crisis which was then magnified by Russia's invasion of Ukraine. As wages stagnated, prices spiked in the supermarket, at the petrol station and with energy bills, before a Conservative mini-budget seen as wreckless appeared to add mortgages to this list of gloom. Next came ballooning NHS waiting lists and rolling doctors' strikes, and the heightening sense that nothing was working in broken Britain. Into that grimness came Starmer, determined to take advantage of the Tory torment.

Was there ever a chance of Rishi Sunak winning? One of his closest aides argued that it was impossible: 'It would have required Rishi to not be Rishi. He was up against a wave of fourteen years of emotion and you can only match that with something equally emotive and big. But Rishi was much more of a stabiliser and realist and although he was good, and will get credit in the long run, it was never going to be election-winning. We were fighting the promise of change from Labour with five priorities. It was a good thing to have, but not enough to turn the tide of emotion.'

Another put it more crudely to me: 'Rishi is the most capable, hard-working, decent leader I've ever worked with. But to be successful in politics, sometimes you need to be a bit of a c**t and he doesn't have that. He was new to politics, he lacked political instinct, and he wasn't a brutal political animal.'

Is Keir Starmer a brutal political animal? I've certainly learnt that he is prepared to be politically ruthless. It is no accident that he chose as a chief strategist someone who, as one source told me, has an 'almost pathological desire to win', adding, 'If something does not contribute to us winning, it is noise to Morgan [McSweeney], his brain is incapable of taking it in.'

According to Labour's communications chief Matthew Doyle, Starmer always knew he would 'either go down in history as the man who won the election, or blew a 20-point lead', telling me that the Labour leader felt liberated by the victory. Jill Cuthbertson agreed, arguing that being out of power had deeply frustrated Starmer; that while he appreciated the role that his party had played in holding the government to account, he knew that his hunger to deliver real change would never be satiated from the outside. She said that opposition had been a bit like a fly buzzing around Starmer's face that he was desperate to get rid of. So, now that he has swatted it away, how will he govern?

PART V

Governing

16

A New Prime Minister

Keir Starmer's premiership began with the same typically British challenge that Rishi Sunak's term had come to an end: it was wet. That morning, Friday 5 July, no doubt Jill Cuthbertson, director of the leader's office, was mildly panicking about the 92 per cent chance of rain flashing up on her weather app. Having been told that the number of supporters gathered in Downing Street should be capped at twenty, Starmer's aide had already had her first run-in with civil servants. 'As if!' she responded, demanding 200 spaces instead. She knew it was inevitable that the arrival of the first Labour prime minister in fourteen years would be compared to Tony Blair's 1997 win, and she wanted the same buzz and excitement.

When, after some back and forth, Cuthbertson got her way on the numbers, she turned to her concerns about the weather. She promptly sourced dozens of Union Jack umbrellas, bringing two benefits: they would keep the gathered Labour supporters dry, and add an eye-catching splash of colour for the cameras. But she still didn't want her boss to get drenched. On the phone, she explained to Starmer the steps he would go through when he arrived at Downing Street, starting with her placing his first speech on the lectern. 'When?' he asked her. Cuthbertson's eyes flicked to the sky, which had suddenly cleared to blue. 'Now!' she shouted, and they were off.

Two black ministerial cars drove in convoy through the imposing black iron gates, then the new PM stepped out with his wife, Vic, to the sound of cheers from the Labour staff lining the pavements. These were the people who had helped him secure the victory. At the end of the first line, he was hugged by a grinning Jess Leigh, the party's campaign head of broadcast, as she furiously waved a Union Jack, with her husband Stuart Ingham, Starmer's longest serving aide, smiling behind her. Starmer crossed the road to hug some more activists, some in tears, before he turned to the lectern. Britain's seventh ever Labour prime minister declared that the country had voted 'decisively for change, for national renewal and a return of politics to public service'. He argued that the lack of trust felt by a wounded nation could only be healed 'by actions not words.' Starmer promised that his government would put 'country first, party second', respect every voter, and 'tread more lightly on your lives.' And then, as instructed, he turned around and entered his new office and family home.

Inside Downing Street, Starmer met the cabinet secretary, Simon Case, received a series of briefings, wrote letters to the commanders of the four nuclear submarines, and then got on with appointing his first cabinet. Most of his frontbench in opposition had arrived in Westminster from electoral counts across the country, bleary-eyed on barely any sleep, waiting nervously to see if they got the call. Shadow health secretary Wes Streeting's phone rang when he was in his Westminster office, where he admitted to aides he felt 'emotionally battered' by the close call in his Ilford North constituency, which he'd held by just over 500 votes. Shadow transport secretary Louise Haigh had travelled from Sheffield to her London flat where patchy reception meant her phone cut out just after she heard an operator say, 'This is the Downing Street switchboard.' While her flatmate Lisa Johnson quickly ironed a pair of trousers for her friend, Haigh hurriedly rang the number back. As Rachel Reeves and

Angela Rayner strode up Downing Street to become two of Britain's most powerful women, calls rang through to Steve Reed, Liz Kendall, Jonathan Reynolds, Lisa Nandy, Peter Kyle, Lucy Powell, and more. Advisers Jess Leigh and Stuart Ingham had left Downing Street and crossed over to a café with colleagues to treat themselves to a bottle of Champagne. There they saw the party's campaign coordinator Pat McFadden, who was about to become one of Starmer's key fixers in the Cabinet Office, sat with his family waiting for his phone to ring.

But in nearby Islington, shadow attorney general Emily Thornberry began to have a sinking feeling. She told friends that she had started to get 'freaked out' after her access-talks with civil servants suddenly stopped and some Labour aides seemed to be avoiding eye contact at an election party the night before. Thornberry was right to be nervous. After serving in Labour's shadow cabinet for eight continuous years, Thornberry would be forced to watch her demotion live on television, as Richard Hermer KC entered through that famous door to be appointed attorney general. There would be no role for Thornberry, who remained loyal to Starmer throughout, but confided to friends that missing out on a job felt a little like grief. This was perhaps the first sign of Starmer's political ruthlessness moving with him from opposition to government.

Inside Downing Street, members of his new team were meant to be gathering in two separate rooms: one for those already appointed, the other for those still waiting their turn. But after hearing her colleagues cackling on the other side of the divide, Rayner had thrown it open. Just appointed secretary of state for business and trade, Jonathan Reynolds was already receiving teasing messages from friends who, having loved watching him walk up Downing Street with such a huge grin on his face, had clipped it up and overlaid music. The line 'who do you think you are?' from Jean Knight's 'Mr Big Stuff', played over the image of him reaching Number 10.

As one by one they went into the Cabinet Room, many noted that Starmer, flanked by Sue Gray, looked entirely at home. Some wrapped him in a hug, all were told that he expected them to 'deliver'. When Wes Streeting emerged, ready for a security briefing, a momentary look of panic crossed the face of Bridget Phillipson as an official accidentally announced him as the new 'education secretary'. Looking over to his colleague, Streeting smiled as he quickly corrected them. 'I'm the health and social care secretary!' he said.

Most of the roles were as expected: Chancellor of the Exchequer Rachel Reeves; Deputy Prime Minister Angela Rayner, now also secretary of state for levelling-up (although she had to return to the King for a new seal after immediately changing the department name back to Housing, Communities and Local Government); Foreign Secretary David Lammy; Home Secretary Yvette Cooper; John Healey in defence; Shabana Mahmood the secretary of state for justice, and so on. The new environment secretary Steve Reed walked out to a waiting car to take him immediately to his department to set out priorities including cleaning up water, clamping down on waste, ensuring food security, and encouraging nature recovery. He later told me that Starmer's Downing Street speech was 'pretty much the most Keir speech I'd ever heard – service, delivery, treading lightly on people's lives, unburdened by doctrine.'

Many were overwhelmed by the receptions they received inside their new departments. Reynolds had experienced five general elections as an MP and was used to accepting his victory in Stalybridge and Hyde in Greater Manchester overnight, then waking up the next morning to Labour's national defeat. This time he was being clapped-in to office by hundreds of officials lining a corridor and then, as he turned a corner expecting it to end, hundreds more crammed along the next one.

No doubt football-mad Starmer had hoped that his first Downing Street reception would be to welcome a victorious England team fresh from the Euros, but ultimately it wasn't to be. So, instead he threw open the doors to business leaders. While FTSE 100 bosses may have been reluctant to endorse Labour during the election campaign, now they were only too happy to descend on Downing

Street, delighted to be the first invited to do so. 'I think people underestimate the resolve this cabinet has to get the economy going,' said Reynolds. Speaking about policies designed to drive growth, he said the motivation of his colleagues was to ensure others received the same chances they had enjoyed. 'This is the most working-class cabinet in history. We fundamentally understand where the country has gone wrong, because we did well from our backgrounds in a way that feels out of reach for many others like us, now.'

New work and pensions secretary Liz Kendall agreed on this shared priority, declaring: 'Your background should not determine your future.' She had been a special adviser in 1997 when Harriet Harman was secretary of state for social security but almost three decades on, she argued, the challenge was hugely different. 'Now, 70 per cent of children in poverty are in a household where someone works. Back then it was about getting people into work, but now that is not enough. We need to help people get on [with pay and promotion] in work.' Within days, she and her employment minister, Alison McGovern, had visited the department's second headquarters in Leeds and held a phone call with 22,000 workers, including in the country's job centres.

In the Department for Energy, Security and Net Zero, aides described Ed Miliband (who was returning to the role he had held before the 2010 election) simply getting stuck back in it, as if he had never left. By Monday 8 July, the new energy secretary had lifted restrictions to the development of onshore wind farms. Meanwhile, Wes Streeting's first call as health secretary was to a patients' organisation (National Voices), and his second to Vivek Trivedi, co-chair of the British Medical Association's committee of junior doctors, to say he wanted to quickly start up talks to try to end the rolling strikes that had inflicted so much damage to the NHS. This five-minute phone call spawned positive headlines and even made the news bulletins that day, with Streeting joking to officials, 'It will get harder than this.' But in fact, it was only a matter of weeks before a pay rise of just over 22 per cent across two years was offered, and recommended by the BMA to its members (at the time of writing, the vote was outstanding).

As they had planned, Starmer's operation tried to frame his government's first acts around his five campaign goals. They quickly established 'Mission Boards' to deal with growth, the NHS, clean energy, safer streets and opportunity, which the PM would chair himself whenever possible. During the first session on economic growth, Rayner talked about planning-reforms while Reynolds brought up trade policy, and plans for an investment summit in autumn 2024, to include asset managers and those running sovereign wealth funds, was agreed.

But before any of that, on 5 July when Starmer entered Downing Street, there was the daunting reality of the global conflict which almost immediately propelled him onto the world stage.

Just five days after the election result, I was standing between the roaring engines of two planes on the tarmac of a London airport when I first came face to face with our new prime minister. As he prepared to travel to Washington, DC for the 75th-anniversary NATO summit, out-going military chief General Sir Patrick Sanders had warned in *The Times* that this was the most dangerous moment for the world since 1945 and declared Britain's army depleted and too weak to efficiently serve.[1] As Starmer stepped in front of the gathered media, I leaned forward, lifted my microphone and raised my voice over the din, to question him about a Russian strike just days earlier on a Ukrainian children's hospital. 'On the eve of this summit, what is your message to Vladimir Putin?' I asked.

'My message is very clear: that this NATO summit is an opportunity for allies to stand together to strengthen their resolve, particularly in light of that appalling attack, against Russian aggression.' His country's support for NATO was 'unshakeable', he said, before walking with his wife Vic to board the plane.

If the transition from opposition leader to prime minister is mind-blowing in its speed, surely no part of the transition is as surreal as the international visits. Soon Starmer would find himself bang in the middle of the journalists' mid-air huddle, responding to a barrage of quick-fire questions about every possible domestic and international policy. On arrival in DC, he stepped out onto a red carpet and into a convoy to race through the American capital with a police escort. And then he would line up for the 'family photo' as a world leader before meeting President Biden in the Oval Office. This was a different level of media spotlight.

Late at the summit meeting, I was watching on a big screen as Biden made a horrendous gaffe, accidentally introducing Ukraine's President Zelensky, as 'President Putin'. There were gasps in the media room, with one American journalist muttering, 'He's toast'. My eyes quickly flicked to Starmer standing in the row behind, his expression impassive as he took care not to react. But from there Starmer had to race to a press conference with British journalists. How would he respond?

'Would you urge [Biden's] critics to hold back?' I asked. The new prime minister said his American counterpart deserved 'credit' for leading efforts that week to support Ukraine – an eminently diplomatic response that had been speedily formulated with the help of his communications director, Matthew Doyle. Starmer was proving quick on his feet, and some of the Number 10 officials whom we had dealt with during the Conservative years were impressed by his first international engagement, one saying he had taken to the new role 'like a duck to water'.

Perhaps Starmer had hoped to enjoy a drawn-out honeymoon, boosted by the much hoped-for victory of Gareth Southgate's England team at the Euros in Germany. On the international trip, the prime minister had joked that England had never lost under a Labour government. Luckily for him, however, his government's fortunes do not rest on the success of England's football team, which suffered an agonising defeat to Spain in the Euros final on 14 July. But as the nation's short-lived boost of optimism died, for the new prime minister the reality of the challenges began to hit home.

As I have set out in some detail, Starmer took control of Labour's levers of power in opposition, with Matt Pound delivering a secure majority on the National Executive Committee while Matt Faulding oversaw selections that steered the parliamentary Labour Party towards a supportive back bench. But that will not silence unrest for long, not least given the sheer number of new MPs itching to make their mark.

Some tried to do so early on. On 17 July 2024 Starmer unveiled his first King's Speech, promising to 'fix the foundations' in accordance with rigid fiscal rules; confirming a National Wealth Fund and advancing planning reform as well as moves to nationalise the railways. Other moves would include massive devolution and an employment rights' bill, which would ban exploitative (but not all) zero-hour contracts and, in most cases, put an end to fire and rehire practises. But when seven of Labour's most left-wing MPs chose that moment to vote with the SNP in favour of lifting the two-child benefit cap, Starmer's ruthless streak flared once more. All of them, including former shadow chancellor John McDonnell, were suspended from Labour for six months, no doubt with the intention of scaring others into staying in line. But this tiny rebellion masks much wider unease about this particular policy, which has driven up poverty among some children. Many activists, MPs and affiliated unions are crying out for reform and those calls will grow louder if changes aren't made in an autumn budget.

For his part, Starmer has insisted that ending child poverty will be at the heart of this Labour government's philosophy. Bridget Phillipson and Liz Kendall, respectively education and welfare secretaries, will jointly chair a dedicated taskforce to look at factors of poverty across the board, including income-related inequality. Sources have argued that while lifting the cap would have an immediate impact on those children in larger families, there are other measures that could benefit a much wider group.

Speaking to sources in government, I fully expect the Labour Party to raise the cap in time (with a suggested time-frame of around eighteen months or so of the July election), but for now Starmer seems almost determined not to act because the policy has become a symbol of Labour's fiscal discipline. His stance has upset some critics, who say it was a political choice to push this policy down his priority list.

Sharon Graham, general secretary of the Unite union, which is affiliated to Labour but has had a rocky relationship with Starmer, took only two days to set down her challenge to the new government. On the Sunday following the election, she told the BBC that she could either be a 'critical friend or a pain in the proverbial'. Graham called for investment, claiming Starmer's promised growth would not come quickly enough. 'Workers and communities cannot wait for growth, nor can they be told to pay for another crisis not of their making. People are struggling,' she said.

Perhaps the leadership will not mind a little tension with Unite, more associated with Jeremy Corbyn's left-wing leadership. But even those in the union movement who have been supportive of Starmer's project will hold his feet to the fire. Take the Unison general secretary, Christina McAnea, who told me: 'For me as a union leader my priority will always be to push the party towards policies that will support public sector workers, and that we believe will be good for the country. Everyone is ecstatic about the election result after fourteen years of not just Conservatives, but the worst Conservatives you could ever imagine. They lost all sense of decency, or vision. [...] We have to have faith that things can change, and we understand that Labour has inherited a mess.'

But in representing her members, McAnea will be pressing Labour hard to deliver decent pay deals for workers in the health and care sectors; to maintain its promises on workers' rights; and to remove the two-child benefit cap that she thinks is a 'disaster'.

Labour figures point out that there is plenty that is radical in their programme including the creation of GB Energy – a public company to drive up investment in green energy – and the plans for railways and buses that Louise Haigh described as 'one of the best ways to show we are prepared to take action when the private sector has failed'. She has given the department a new mantra: 'To move fast and fix things.'

It has been a similarly dizzying start for Chancellor Rachel Reeves. On entering the Treasury, she had been blown away by the reaction to her first speech to civil servants, who cheered wildly when she told them that it was a privilege to be the first female chancellor. Over her first weekend in Number 11, Reeves and her political team gathered in the bathroom attached to the her private office to gawp at the urinal, a symbol of a job done for 800 years only by men which now has been rapidly separated off by a Perspex screen. A rare moment of light relief for a team barely rested since the relentless election campaign, who were swiftly ushered into a series of sombre meetings. In a 'jaw-dropping' moment, Reeves and her chief of staff Katie Martin were briefed about an additional in-year overspend of £22 billion, driven by a variety of factors including the Tory's massive overspend on the asylum system.

On 29 July, the chancellor expressed her fury at these 'undisclosed' sums, in the first of a number of concerted attempts by the new government to blame their travails on the 'inheritance' from the previous government. This fiscal black hole, she said, necessitated spending cuts, including restricting universal pensioner benefits such as winter fuel payments, to those who qualify for means-tested pension credits.

On the same day as Reeves set out the economic challenges, any remaining glow in Starmer's honeymoon period faded with the horrifying news that a 17-year-old boy had entered a Taylor Swift-themed dance class in Southport on a knife-wielding rampage which left three girls dead: six-year-old Bebe King, seven-year-old Elsie Dot Stancombe, and nine-year-old Alice de Silva Aguiar.

Having served in the last Labour government, Yvette Cooper's walk up Downing Street had felt more familiar. And as she emerged into the hallway as the new home secretary a familiar Henry Moore sculpture sitting in an alcove, just as it had in 2010, triggered a muscle memory. Like her new cabinet colleagues, Cooper was greeted by cheering civil servants, who welcomed her into the Home Office, before she embarked on a series of meetings about Labour's mission on crime: to tackle serious violence, including against women and girls; and to restore public faith in the police, in the first instance by increasing the number of neighbourhood police officers.

Barely an hour before Cooper was due to face Home Office questions in Parliament, aides gave her the news about what had happened in Southport. That evening, she drove north with her new media adviser, Jess Leigh, to lay flowers at the scene of the atrocity. When Cooper met the distraught police officers and paramedics who had been first to the scene, she hugged them all, tears filling her eyes.

Then came disinformation in the form of social media posts claiming wrongly that the killer was a Muslim asylum-seeker, triggering riots by far-right activists that spread from Southport across the country. Cooper was furious that the same officers who had been faced with the tragedy of three murdered children, and the horrific injuries of many more, were now being attacked, bricks hurled at them. Sources described a 'steely' response from the home secretary. For Cooper, the riots underlined a breakdown in respect for law and order and policing. She told me that from the start, she was 'determined to do things differently'; not attacking the police, as had sometimes happened in the past, but working in partnership. 'We needed to restore respect for law and order, respect for communities, and respect for our criminal justice system,' she said.

Behind the scenes, aides were clear that Starmer would not conflate legitimate concerns about legal and illegal migration with the totally unacceptable scenes of far-right protesters attacking police officers, breaking into buildings which housed asylum seekers, and marching outside mosques.

'Anyone trying to make wider arguments about the riots are just enabling them,' said one source. 'There are acceptable concerns about immigration, its level and management. But if you are a racist hooligan, marching on a place of worship, then this is a law-and-order issue, and you will be arrested and pushed through the system as fast as possible.' Morgan McSweeney, meanwhile, stuck to his line from long before the election that the Labour government must never respond by punching down at immigrants.

Starmer had been director of public prosecutions during the 2011 riots across the UK, and Cooper shadow home secretary, which proved to be useful experience. Justice secretary, Shabana Mahmood warned that whatever the cause, 'If you turn up in a mask, with a weapon, intent on causing disorder, you will face the full force of the law.' And soon enough those responsible shed tears from the dock as they received prison sentences of two years or longer.

At the same time, the new science and technology secretary, Peter Kyle, had begun conversations with global social media giants to try to combat the disinformation that had spread almost unchallenged. We are likely to see the Labour government take tougher action to police the spread of disinformation on sites including Facebook, TikTok and X, perhaps in the form of new legislation.

But one thing the riots did underline is the sheer scale of public distrust in politics, a factor that likely contributed to the low turnout and fragmented result of the 2024 General Election. While Reform UK leader and new MP for Clacton, Nigel Farage, condemned the 'truly disgusting and appalling' action of far-right thugs, he said they alone were not to blame, pointing to 'mobs of young Muslims'. And when a video emerged of a counter-protester calling on people to 'cut all their throats and get rid of them' to cheers, he parroted the owner of X, Elon Musk, in accusing Starmer of 'two-tier' policing. In fact, the man in question had been promptly arrested and charged.

In responding to Musk, Farage did seek to conflate the riots with policy, suggesting that the British media were complicit: 'Open borders are fantastic, come in everybody, we don't care if you speak our language or share our values. We don't care about the population explosion, meaning our kids can't get houses.' It is the type of argument that almost certainly helped elevate Reform UK to its election success in 2024 – and a sentiment that could help build on that success five years from now.

An anti-politics mood has increasingly gripped parts of the nation in recent years as populists have capitalised on the shock of Covid and the cost-of-living crisis that followed it. It is a mood that has spawned conspiracy theories which have then been amplified through social media, in a manner that simply did not exist decades ago. This shift hasn't turned decent hard-working people into far-right activists. But it may make some of those who are economically insecure and disillusioned, more susceptible to their arguments.

When people argue that Keir Starmer isn't nearly as loved, or even liked, as Tony Blair, some respond that 2024 isn't like 1997; and on the trust point that is certainly true. Late in 2023, an Ipsos survey found that only 9 per cent of people trusted politicians to tell the truth, the lowest figure ever to a question that had been asked repeatedly for forty years. (The number was never high, but did reach 23 per cent in 1999.) In terms of trustworthiness, politicians were now at the bottom of Ipsos's long list, with nurses, pilots, librarians and doctors leading the way (but journalists languishing just three places above MPs).

When I asked a leading political scientist, Professor Will Jennings at the University of Southampton, about this, he spoke of several bumps along the way that had shaken people's faith in politics – from the Iraq War to the MPs' expenses scandal; Brexit (initiating a steep decline in trust among Remain voters); government handling of and behaviour during the pandemic; and then more recent scandals. Jennings was a little sceptical about the notion of a lost golden era, arguing that trust has diminished equally in the past. In fact, he highlighted Mass-Observation diaries from 1945 and 1950 in which there were descriptions of politics as 'a dirty business', 'a game' and 'guttersnipe', citing 'petty squabbles' and 'mud-slinging'. Sound familiar?

It is also worth remembering that, however we look upon Winston Churchill's tenure now, his Conservative Party was badly punished in the 1945 Election, losing 189 seats, while Clement Attlee's Labour Party gained 239 to win a significant majority, under a promise of change that ushered in the creation of the National Health Service.

If people are hoping for that level of transformation today, their government maintains its hands are tied by fiscal rules. Speaking to the former Labour leader Lord Kinnock about this, he argued that Starmer must be straight with voters. 'He has to be as candid as possible about the dilemmas he faces. Not everyone will like it, but it is what treating the electorate like adults means.' But Kinnock acknowledged the scale of the task. He contended that everyone in Labour wants to lift the two-child benefit cap, but only if done permanently and as part of a wider assault on family poverty. He said it was better not to pretend there was a 'secret drawer' filled with cash but to focus on the longer-term, pointing out that it was three years after the 1945 Election before Nye Bevan heralded the birth of the NHS (in the face of deep opposition from the right-wing media and British Medical Association).

So how can Starmer build trust? He has to deliver, and not only deliver, but do so in a way that people actually feel the impact.

Inside Downing Street, just below the prime minister but with immense power, are two characters who are described by those around them as deeply impressive, and extremely different. Even the way that Sue Gray greets people (colleagues describe her as a 'hugger') contrasts to the more reserved approach of Morgan McSweeney. By appointing one to be his chief of staff – focused on the mechanics of government – and the other his chief adviser – focused on the politics – Keir Starmer has created two power bases in the heart of government. It is a move that has already spawned stories of a Downing Street struggle, forcing a spokesman to tell the *Sun* newspaper that the reports were 'bollocks', while a column in the *New Statesman* proclaimed, 'the power tussle is real'.[2] Could this be the new fault-line, like the one that divided the Blairites and the Brownites through the New Labour years?

'It is common for there to be a tension between the political and campaigning objectives of a party that is thinking of electoral success and the difficult and often unpopular decisions that need to be taken in government,' said Alex Thomas, programme director at the Institute for Government.

Insiders have admitted to me that Gray and McSweeney do not always instinctively agree on every issue, and neither is shy of saying so in meetings, even with the prime minister present. But they are also said to get on well and respect each other's points of view. In fact, when I asked one long-standing, senior civil servant (who has seen a few of these administrations come and go) about the suggestion of a feud, they snorted with laughter. 'There is nothing there,' they said, arguing that instead it felt in sharp contrast to the 'dripping poison' that characterised some of the recent Conservative years. Alex Thomas added that disagreeing in front of the PM was a positive sign, arguing 'Keir Starmer needs to hear different points of view'.

One senior minister confessed there had been times when they had wondered if the relationship would become tense, but if there were any hostilities there was now a 'ceasefire', and a suggestion that if it holds the Gray/McSweeney duo could in theory be Starmer's 'super-power'. After all, on one side of his team is a seasoned civil servant who perhaps understands the structures of government better than almost anyone else; on the other a brilliant political strategist who helped take Labour from a crushing defeat to a landslide victory. And this is how the roles have been divided.

From the moment she arrived, Sue Gray has led on the transition into government, building a close relationship with Starmer from the very start when he offered her considerable loyalty in the face of furious Conservative attacks. She immediately put in place structures that mirrored the Downing Street operation, with a smaller set of ministers turning up to an 8.30 a.m. daily meeting (nowadays the 'quad' of Starmer, Rayner, Reeves and McFadden) – a more formal cabinet session without phones – and inter-ministerial groups around specific issues. While in opposition, after 7 October 2023, Gray had brought in a daily meeting on the Middle East crisis, in government she introduced one after events in Southport, with the home and justice secretaries present and the Liverpool mayor Steve Rotherham also dialled in.

When Gray first arrived in Starmer's team, the deputy chief of staff was Helene Reardon-Bond, who had already engaged external consultants and held roundtables with former permanent secretaries to help shadow ministers prepare for office. The work had resulted in reams of information on the policy priorities across government and on the risks down the line. Reardon-Bond also helped to coordinate access talks with Gray. Much of this work was kept under the radar because of an almost 'superstitious' desire by Starmer to avoid looking like he was measuring up the curtains.

Once in Downing Street, the new chief of staff developed a mission unit that would work with the cabinet to implement a 'relentless focus on delivery'. One source pointed out that in previous Whitehall roles, Gray was heavily involved in a scheme that was designed to support the rehabilitation of prisoners by employing them in the Civil Service, for which she spoke to the shoe- and watch-repair, key-cutting and dry-cleaning company Timpsons, making it likely that she was the driving force behind the eye-catching appointment of its CEO James Timpson as minister of state for prisons, probation and reducing reoffending.

The transition into government has not been seamless, however. There have been plenty of complaints from Labour folk, inside and out. Some who'd worked closely with Starmer for years in opposition described being dropped unceremoniously, without so much as a text message explanation, while within government I've heard complaints about delayed contracts and a cull to the number of political adviser roles. Those details were being overseen by the Civil Service, not political teams, but one source admitted that sometimes the chief of staff could become a 'lightning rod' for all frustrations within an administration.

Morgan McSweeney heads up a politically focused team, with two branches – one led by Vidhya Alakeson (now Starmer's political director) and the other by Paul Ovenden (director of political strategy). Alakeson's team know that delivery alone is not enough if voters do not feel that their lives have changed, and so with their eyes already firmly on the 2029 election, they are also thinking about 'connection' and 'accountability'. The team knows that since the financial crisis, voters have seen scandal after scandal without anyone being held to account. This is why the first King's Speech included the Hillsborough Law, to tackle a 'culture of denial', and Martyn's Law, relating to safety at public venues. Meanwhile, Steve Reed immediately called water bosses in to make clear what is expected of them. Alakeson's job will be to build ties to MPs and beyond; and, with McSweeney and Ovenden, to spread a layer of politics across government, with weekly meetings between the team and special advisers to impress on them the need to ensure political messaging – blaming the Tories for the dire inheritance, for instance – alongside the policy. Sources say that one possible tension between the focus of the Gray and McSweeney camps could be on how much ministers are focused on pure delivery, and how much the efforts will focus on the political messaging that is all about connecting with voters. When it comes to taking on the threat of Reform UK, McSweeney and David Evans will no doubt be drawing from their experience in Barking and Dagenham in 2010, where fixing local issues that had been causing anxiety and frustration was seen as key. Where there were eyesore gardens in 2010, there maybe a plan to fix potholes in 2024 (with other priorities including hospital waiting times).

Meanwhile, Ovenden's job will be to think relentlessly about voters. In the early weeks, he delivered a briefing to cabinet ministers in which he argued that the working-class voters in marginal seats who switched to Labour from the Tories, had delivered Keir Starmer's majority, but it was the 20 per cent of 2019 Conservatives who switched to Reform UK who had turned the win into a landslide. He also explained that Labour had slumped 3 points (from the 37% predicted by Labour's own pollsters) to a 34 per cent vote-share in the final days of the campaign because of those who opted to vote 'tactically' for the Lib Dems where they could beat Tories, but also others deciding to go with their 'hearts', voting for the Greens or Independents, certain that Starmer would be prime minister either way.

The result is that Labour's voter coalition is far more fragile than the overall numbers suggest. Academic Rob Ford described Labour's 2024 strategy as a 'masterpiece of electoral Jenga' in which Labour withdrew the blocks from its safer seats close to the base, to throw everything at the marginal constituencies to build up the height of the tower. However, Ford warned that: 'It will not take much to bring this teetering tower tumbling down.'

Labour understands only too well how stretched its majority is, and how quickly the political mood can change – the question now is whether, and how, these factors might affect the way in which the party governs.

Ovenden has told ministers that they must put Labour's majority out of their mind and imagine that they are 'nil-nil' in the next political race. Jonathan Ashworth, who lost in Leicester and now leads Labour Together, agreed, warning of a massive shift in how much voters change their minds. 'I am the talking, breathing proof that there is no such thing as a safe seat. We have gone from the Red Wall collapse in 2019 to a landslide victory in parliamentary seats – there is huge volatility these days and we cannot assume we will win the next general election,' he said.

And that is why Keir Starmer's first speech to the Labour Party conference as prime minister is about urging 'no complacency'; arguing that, however big their 2024 win, there is no guarantee of a decade in power.

If Labour fails to repair and rebuild trust, then when it comes to 2029, they could well lose.

Notes

Chapter 2: Sir Keir

1. https://www.theguardian.com/politics/2016/jun/25/hilary-benn-jeremy-corbyn-labour-leadership-eu-referendum-brexit
2. https://www.gq-magazine.co.uk/article/labour-keir-starmer-brexit

Chapter 3: The Morganiser

1. https://unherd.com/2024/05/the-mcsweeney-project/

Chapter 4: Labour Together

1. https://www.newstatesman.com/politics/labour/2023/11/what-is-labour-together
2. ibid.

Chapter 5: Leaning Left

1. https://pressgazette.co.uk/news/labour-blames-press-for-echoing-tory-message-on-brexit-after-huge-election-defeat/
2. https://www.mirror.co.uk/news/politics/who-next-labour-leader-runners-21087938

Chapter 6: Covid

1. https://www.theguardian.com/politics/2021/mar/16/hartlepool-labour-mp-mike-hill-resigns-with-immediate-effect

2. https://www.theguardian.com/politics/2021/may/07/election-results-expose-the-deep-problems-for-starmers-labour

Chapter 7: Ruthless

1. https://www.theguardian.com/politics/2020/apr/12/hostility-to-corbyn-curbed-labour-efforts-to-tackle-antisemitism-says-leaked-report
2. https://www.theguardian.com/commentisfree/2020/jun/29/responsibility-actions-antisemitism-rebecca-long-bailey
3. https://www.parentkind.org.uk/about-us/news-and-blogs/news/parentkind-supports-the-national-education-unions-five-tests-for-government-before-schools-can-re-open
4. https://www.theguardian.com/education/2020/apr/29/schools-must-only-reopen-when-safe-says-rebecca-long-bailey
5. https://www.channel4.com/news/factcheck/factcheck-corbyns-claim-that-labour-antisemitism-numbers-are-exaggerated
6. Livingstone later responded to say he was 'deeply hurt' and to 'fully reject' the claims, arguing he was a 'life-long anti-racist'
7. https://www.theguardian.com/commentisfree/2021/sep/28/keir-starmer-leadership-labour-leader-left

Chapter 8: The Reset

1. https://www.thetimes.com/uk/politics/article/fired-up-rachel-reeves-takes-her-axe-to-corbyns-magic-money-tree-60bsph7mn
2. https://labourlist.org/2021/09/watch-we-are-in-favour-of-common-ownership-absolutely-says-ed-miliband/
3. https://inews.co.uk/opinion/starmers-ruthless-reshuffle-confirms-blairites-back-2591919
4. https://www.tatler.com/article/who-are-the-super-rich-labour-donors-bankrolling-sir-keir-starmer

Chapter 9: Boris

1. https://www.bbc.co.uk/news/uk-politics-53172995
2. https://attoday.co.uk/58-percent-of-people-agree-with-health-and-social-care-levy-new-survey-finds/
3. https://www.mirror.co.uk/news/politics/boris-johnson-broke-covid-lockdown-25585238
4. https://www.independent.co.uk/news/uk/politics/rishi-sunak-akshata-murthy-non-dom-wife-tax-b2052251.html
5. https://www.bbc.co.uk/news/uk-england-stoke-staffordshire-61342948

Chapter 10: Liz

1. https://www.bbc.co.uk/news/uk-62890879
2. https://www.schroders.com/en-us/us/intermediary/insights/what-does-the-rise-in-bond-yields-mean-for-the-economy-/
3. https://www.efginternational.com/uk/insights/2022/uk-mini-budget-sparks-gilt-market-mayhem.html

Chapter 11: Rishi

1. https://www.theguardian.com/politics/2022/oct/21/boris-johnson-gaining-ground-on-rishi-sunak-in-tory-leadership-race
2. https://www.telegraph.co.uk/politics/2022/10/23/rishi-sunak-candidate-fits-bill-prime-minister/
3. https://www.itv.com/news/2022-11-15/rishi-sunak-condemns-russias-barbaric-war-in-ukraine-at-g20
4. https://twitter.com/joepike/status/1631559338601873408
5. https://www.theguardian.com/politics/2023/jul/03/sue-gray-breached-civil-service-code-over-keir-starmer-job-inquiry-finds
6. https://www.theguardian.com/politics/2023/jun/12/boris-johnson-formally-steps-down-as-mp
7. https://www.thetimes.com/uk/law/article/pro-palestine-protest-london-met-police-cbqnxbtv3

Chapter 12: The Fourth of July

1. https://www.bbc.co.uk/news/uk-politics-66231718

Chapter 13: The Campaign

1. https://www.thetimes.com/uk/politics/article/diane-abbott-mp-labour-general-election-2024-fvgnbprdm
2. https://www.theguardian.com/theobserver/commentisfree/2023/apr/23/success-for-women-not-same-as-for-men-letters
3. https://www.theguardian.com/politics/2024/mar/11/biggest-tory-donor-looking-diane-abbott-hate-all-black-women

Chapter 14: Rishi's Worst Week

1. https://www.bbc.co.uk/news/articles/c722014r42xo
2. https://www.theguardian.com/uk-news/2018/dec/04/minority-candidates-face-ethnic-penalty-in-elections-study-shows

Chapter 15: Fragmentation

1. https://www.politico.eu/article/19-crazy-ed-davey-campaign-stunts-and-1-serious-moment/
2. https://www.theguardian.com/commentisfree/2014/aug/17/david-cameron-tories-ethnic-minority-appeal
3. https://www.voice-online.co.uk/news/uk-news/2024/02/01/keir-starmer-doesnt-care-about-black-people/
4. https://www.theguardian.com/politics/2023/apr/07/labour-defends-ad-claiming-sunak-doesnt-think-child-sex-abusers-should-be-jailed
5. https://www.bbc.co.uk/news/articles/cg3j131327yo#:~:text=Labour%20declared%20more%20donations%20than,%C2%A39.5m%20in%20total

Chapter 16: A New Prime Minister

1. https://www.thetimes.com/uk/politics/article/re-arm-now-or-face-threat-of-global-conflict-ex-army-chief-warns-58tfn2sdd
2. https://www.newstatesman.com/politics/commons-confidential/2024/07/the-power-tussle-sue-gray-vs-morgan-mcsweeney

Acknowledgements

They say 'it takes a village' and sometimes it felt like that with this book. Or a small town. I'm not saying it was quite as full on as raising a child, but coming straight after a general election, this was hard and so many people helped me get over the line.

First, a huge thanks to all of those inside and out of political parties who spoke to me for this book. In total, I had in-depth conversations with more than 100 different sources, many of them hours-long and repeated over many months. Thank you for being so generous with your time.

As for turning it all into print, I was lucky to have two wonderful editors. Thank you to the exceptional Rosemary Davidson, who worked magic with the copy and worked late into nights to get me to the deadline. You are a wonder, Rose! And to the brilliant Jonathan de Peyer for taking this idea from inception, guiding it through development and turning it into reality. I'm so grateful to Jon and his colleagues at HarperNorth.

I would also like to thank Alex Fleming-Brown, who worked as a researcher on this book, spending hours trawling back through the annals of Keir Starmer's rise to power.

At ITV and ITV News, thank you to Michael Jermey and Andrew Dagnell for supporting me in this project and backing me in so many others. I'm very grateful to many more ITN colleagues but a special shout-out to the Westminster team led by Rachel Bradley, Belinda Adair and Catherine Janes with sensational producers Jack, Elisa, Maya, Denny and Iona, with whom I have LOVED chasing politicians around the country and the world (from Bali to the US), with brilliant Dan too. There are too many others to mention, including a fantastic team of correspondents, but a special thanks to Harry Horton for his help on this book, and our stand-out political editor, Robert Peston.

Speaking of Peston, I could not do any of this without the entire ITV *Peston* team and especially Vicky Flind, Kishan Koria, and our shining star, Lili Donlon-Mansbridge.

So often during this book I thought of the wonderful Jo Cox who was such a lovely friend and a brilliant MP. I know she is so badly missed across Parliament.

There are too many friends and family to name, so I hope you know I love you all. But for their support on this book, a huge thanks to Clara Nelson and Rowan Yapp for their advice, Tammy Holmes and Carolyn Roberts for reading so much and feeding back, Amber de Botton for letting me bounce ideas off her and the ever-generous Grundys, Shona and Carla, for giving me the perfect hide-out to write, and for feeding and watering me throughout. I couldn't have done it without you.

Finally, my family. Thank you to my incredible parents, Jagdish and Aruna Asthana, who are always there with emotional and practical (childcare/cooking/ironing) support. And most of all, my wonderful husband Toby, whose backing was endless and without whose sometimes single-parenting to our boys, Ethan, Rory and Leo, and dog Rosie, I would never have got this done.

Now I can finally say to them – Mum's back!

Harper
North

Book Credits

HarperNorth would like to thank the following staff
and contributors for their involvement in
making this book a reality:

Fionnuala Barrett

Peter Borcsok

Lauren Braggs

Ciara Briggs

Katie Buckley

Sarah Burke

Fiona Cooper

Alan Cracknell

Rosemary Davidson

Jonathan de Peyer

Tom Dunstan

Kate Elton

Sarah Emsley

Simon Gerratt

Lydia Grainge

Monica Green

Natassa Hadjinicolaou

Grace Howarth

Jo Ireson

Megan Jones

Jean-Marie Kelly

Taslima Khatun

Petra Moll

Alice Murphy-Pyle

Adam Murray

Genevieve Pegg

Amanda Percival

Natasha Photiou

Florence Shepherd

Eleanor Slater

Emma Sullivan

Katrina Troy

Tom Whiting

For more unmissable reads,
sign up to the HarperNorth newsletter at
www.harpernorth.co.uk

or find us on Twitter at
@HarperNorthUK

**Harper
North**